Pidgin and Creole Languages

Pidgin
and Creole
Languages

by ROBERT A. HALL, JR.

CORNELL UNIVERSITY PRESS

ITHACA, NEW YORK

CORNELL UNIVERSITY PRESS

First published 1966

Library of Congress Catalog Card Number: 65-24702

Printed in the United States of America
By The Maple Press Company

TO MORTIMER GRAVES

Preface

IT IS MY aim, in this book, to present an over-all survey of the languages known as pidgins and creoles. These languages are widely used in such areas as the Caribbean, Africa, and the South Pacific, and are coming to have more and more importance in the life of these regions. It therefore behooves us to have an accurate knowledge of their characteristics, function, and importance. To meet this need, I have provided a general discussion of their nature, origins, and present distribution; of their structure, both in itself and in relation to the languages out of which they have arisen; and of their significance in linguistic, social, and political matters. Much of the material contained in this presentation has been adapted from my earlier publications on pidgin and creolized languages, especially from Hall, 1955a (see Bibliography); I have tried, however, to fuse this material into an integrated and unified discussion. Many of the examples have been drawn from Neo-Melanesian (Melanesian Pidgin English) and Haitian Creole, chiefly because they are the two that I know best, and because they are the ones on which the most extensive linguistic analysis has been carried out.[1]

In this treatment, I have aimed at presenting only a general, preliminary picture. This book is not—and, in the present state of our knowledge, cannot be—an exhaustive treatment of all the

[1] Throughout this book, I use the term "Melanesian Pidgin English" to refer to this language in its earlier stages, or in its historical development; and "Neo-Melanesian" (the name by which it is coming to be called in order to avoid the misleading implications of the term "Pidgin English") to refer to it in its present state.

pidginized and creolized languages of the world.[2] As of now, only a few pidgins and creoles have been studied with any approach to accuracy or completeness; an extensive comparison on a structural basis will (I trust) eventually be made, but it will have to wait until a great amount of further data has been gathered on many more languages. It is to be hoped that this book may succeed in arousing further interest in the field, so that future workers in linguistics will devote more time and attention to these customarily neglected languages.

Thanks are due to Thomas W. W. Haines, Frances A. Hall, and Charles F. Hockett, who have kindly given criticisms and suggestions for improvement of the book in earlier drafts. This book is dedicated to Mortimer Graves, who first realized the importance of a knowledge of pidgins and creoles for our national "stock-pile of strategic language competence," and who was instrumental in directing my attention to this field in 1942.

Robert A. Hall, Jr.

Ithaca, New York
May 1965

---

[2] A full bibliography and an extensive discussion of the social nature and function of pidgins and creoles are given in Reinecke, 1937 (see Bibliography); but, given the nature of most of the data on which Reinecke worked, he could of course not have made a structural analysis of any of these languages at that time. I am especially indebted to Dr. Reinecke for permission to utilize material from his bibliography in the preparation of this book and in many of my earlier studies on pidgins and creoles.

Contents

Introduction

IN THE modern world, many hitherto neglected phenomena have assumed new importance. In the field of language, there has been a tremendous upsurge in the last fifty years, bringing with it a wholly new concept of linguistics as the scientific analysis of language. This new approach has broadened our field of interest to include hundreds, even thousands, of languages previously considered of little value and unworthy of serious study: the dialects of our own language, the tongues of "primitive" tribes, and even a number of linguistic structures that have, until recently, not even been thought of as "true" languages. Under this last heading come those reduced languages called "pidgins," and their outgrowths known as "creoles." Pidgins and creoles are of major importance, despite their humble social status, because of both their interest for linguistic and anthropological theory and their practical value. In many newly developed regions—such as New Guinea, West Africa, and the Caribbean—pidgin and creole languages are vitally important for effective communication. By now, it has become obvious that pidgins and creoles can no longer be neglected, but must be given their rightful standing as the equals of other languages. We can therefore no longer afford to go without a clear idea of the nature, structure, and function of these languages.

To understand the problem of pidgins and similar languages, we must of course start with clear definitions of the terms "pidgin" and "creole," as well as of the expression "lingua franca," which is often used in this connection. In scientific linguistics, all three of these terms are used with quite clearly delimited reference:

1. The most general of the three is "lingua franca," which denotes any language (no matter what its structural characteristics or social standing) that is used as a medium of communication among people who have no other language in common. Thus, when a Telugu-speaking Indian and a Hindi-speaking Indian converse together in a train or make speeches to each other in the Indian parliament, using highly literary and formal English with an Oxford accent, English is serving as a lingua franca; but it is also a lingua franca when used by a group of students in a youth hostel, some or all of whom are native speakers of other languages and have a rather less than perfect command of English.

2. On the other hand, it often happens that, to communicate with each other, two or more people use a language in a variety whose grammar and vocabulary are very much reduced in extent and which is native to neither side. Such a language is a "pidgin." For hundreds of years, Italian guides, or ciceroni, showing foreigners around churches and museums have been in the habit of using a simplified Italian to describe the beauties of their cultural heritage —for example, *Questo èssere molto bello pittura Michelàngelo* "This be very beautiful picture [by] Michelangelo"—and their charges speak to them in the same kind of Italian. If only one side were to speak this way, and the other were to use normal Italian, then we could not call the reduced language a pidgin; it would simply be "broken Italian." For a language to be a true pidgin, two conditions must be met: its grammatical structure and its vocabulary must be sharply reduced (for instance, in the Italian example cited, grammatical gender is lost, the infinitive is used instead of an inflected form of the verb, and the preposition *di* "by, of" is not used before *Michelàngelo*), and also the resultant language must be native to none of those who use it. Thus, the Italian cicerone does not normally substitute the infinitive for inflected verb-forms, eliminate grammatical gender, or leave out prepositions in his every-day speech with other Italians; the pidgin Italian in which he and foreigners converse is not native to him. Pidgin languages can be found at all social levels and in all kinds of situations, but they have arisen most frequently in short contacts between persons desiring to trade or do other things in which detailed exchange of information or minute co-ordination of activity is not required.

3. A creole language arises when a pidgin becomes the native language of a speech-community. When Negroes were imported

from Africa to the Caribbean area, their new masters deliberately separated slaves who came from the same African tribe, so as to lessen the danger of conspiracy and revolt among those speaking a common language. The only language the plantation slaves had in common was a pidginized variety of their masters' tongue: English, French, Spanish, or Portuguese, as the case might be. As time passed, the slaves married and raised families; the children of such unions perforce learned, as their first language, the pidgin that their parents and the other slaves spoke together in default of any other common tongue. As successive generations grew up using the new language from earliest childhood, they re-expanded its grammatical and lexical resources to meet all the needs of their way of living. In the French West Indies and Louisiana, the slaves' language was called *créole*, using the French word for "indigenous" (from Spanish *criollo* "native"); this term has come to be applied to any language that has undergone a similar development, growing out of a pidgin to become the first language of a speech-community.

Not all creolization takes place under conditions of slavery or economic oppression. It can develop whenever multilingual groups come together of their own free will, as has happened in a number of villages in present-day New Guinea: at such places as Dagua (on the north coast of New Guinea) or the coast of the island of Manus, groups that were previously separate and spoke different languages have formed new settlements, where the lingua franca is perforce Melanesian Pidgin English (also known as Neo-Melanesian). The children of these communities are growing up with Neo-Melanesian as their mother tongue, and so it too is becoming creolized.

Creolization is simply one manifestation of a broader process which, for want of a better term, we can call "nativization." A language is nativized when it is taken over by a group of speakers who have previously used some other language, so that the new language becomes the native language of the group. This process of language-replacement has taken place many times in history, as when the tribes of Italy, Gaul, and Iberia gradually gave up their earlier languages and went over to Latin, which then developed into the various Romance tongues, being handed down from one generation to another by a tradition of first-language learning. It is happening at present, wherever English, Spanish, or French comes to be the first language of larger or smaller groups in such regions as India, the Philippines, Latin America, or Central Africa. Not all nativization implies creolization, by any means, any more than all use of a lingua franca involves pidginization: although, say, Indian or Philippine English is different from both British and American English, and involves carry-over of features from native Indian or Philippine languages, there has nevertheless been no violent reduction or restructuring of English in the process. On the other hand, all creolization implies, by our definition, the nativization of a pidgin.

Pidgin and creole languages are usually treated together, because they have a number of features in common. When a language is pidginized, it is reduced drastically in structure, as we shall see in detail in chapters 3 through 7. A short time is sufficient for such a reduction: only a few hours' trading is necessary for the establishment of a rudimentary pidgin, and a few months or years suffice for the pidgin to assume settled form. Once reduced, the pidgin is markedly different in structure from the language out of which it has grown, and the new orientation of its structure is carried over into any creole that may later arise from the pidgin.

Certain other terms, which are often used in meanings close to those of "pidgin," should be clarified before we go any further. "Argot" and "jargon" are often used nearly interchangeably with "pidgin"; linguistic analysts prefer to restrict them to special types of vocabulary, without reference to the grammatical structure with which they occur. Both "argot" and "jargon" have slightly pejorative overtones, especially the former, which is used widely to refer to thieves' special terms or peculiar uses of ordinary words: for example, *gat* for "gun", *moll* for "woman", etc. However, "jargon" is also used for any type of specialized vocabulary, including the terms peculiar to a given trade (for instance, printers' *pi* for used type that has been jumbled prior to being melted down) or a given group, such as teen-agers (compare the usage of J. D. Salinger's characters in his *Catcher in the Rye*). In England, "slang" and "cant" are widely used in much the same sense as "argot" and "jargon," respectively (*gypsy slang; tinkers' cant*). Such slangs or cants often serve to set off a particular group from the rest of society. An interesting feature of British public school life is that each school has its own slang, which newcomers are required to learn as part of their initiation; Winchester is said to have gone farthest in this direction. In the United States and England alike, however, "slang" is often used in a much more general sense, to refer to any kind of current fashion in language, particularly one that involves exaggeration, violent shifts of meaning, or inane repetition, and that is not liked by the person labeling it slang. Many people confuse general, normal, every-day colloquial speech—"shirt-sleeves language," as someone has called it—with slang. A "lingo" is simply any peculiar way of talking ("I don't get your lingo"); workers in linguistics have not found this term of great use.

When studied in and for themselves, pidgins and creoles prove to be very interesting and rewarding. There is, in analyzing and using a pidgin, something of the same pleasure that one gets in looking at or using a skillfully made miniature object. From the scientific point of view, a great deal of interesting light is cast on language history by the origins of pidgin and creole languages, and the study of their structure is of great value for the general theory of language. Furthermore, there are several respects in which they are of major importance in practical matters, both social and political, in the areas where they are spoken. In the rest of this book, therefore, we shall take up the origin and present distribution of pidgins and creoles, their linguistic structures and relationships, and their significance from the linguistic, social, and political points of view.

REFERENCES

The references given at the end of each chapter are to titles in the Selected Bibliography (Appendix B), cited by the name of the author and the year, with an identifying initial if more than one title is listed for the same author for a given year, and (if necessary) with chapter, section, or page numbers. The references follow the order of topics within each chapter; for each topic, references are arranged chronologically.

General definitions and discussions of pidgins and creoles: Schuchardt, 1884; Grünbaum, 1885; Jespersen, 1922 (chap. xii, "Pidgin and Congeners"); Tagliavini, 1931; Bloomfield, 1933 (pp. 472–475); Hesseling, 1934; Hall, 1955a, 1961a.

Nature and History

Pidgins

PIDGINS and creoles are probably not recent innovations in the history of human language. It is quite likely that even Egyptian, Sumerian, and Chinese soldiers and traders may have spoken some kind of pidgin with the "barbarians" whom they encountered on the borders of their empires, but we have no direct record of those varieties of speech. In Greek drama, foreigners are represented as speaking "broken" Greek, and it is perhaps not too much to suppose that the Greeks themselves may have, on occasion, spoken back to the "barbarians" in the same fashion, thus creating a true Pidgin Greek. Undoubtedly the Romans must have done likewise; in fact, given the extent of the Roman Empire and the variety of peoples along its borders, it would be surprising if some Pidgin Latin had not been spoken. However, the Romance languages (the modern continuators of Latin) show no clear traces of such pidginization or of subsequent creolization; all the changes from Latin structure which they manifest can be shown to be the result of gradual change over the twenty centuries that separate us from Roman times, and the most important changes did not take place until after the Roman Empire had broken up.

The earliest pidgin of which we have any direct record was that used during the Middle Ages by European crusaders and traders in the eastern end of the Mediterranean. It was known as the "Lingua Franca," after the West Europeans (called *Franci* from the fact that the French were so numerous and dominant among the Crusaders) who used it in their dealings with the Levantines. From this original use, the term "lingua franca" has been gradually extended to cover any language used as a means of communication among people of different language backgrounds. Linguistic scholars normally make a sharp distinction between the Lingua Franca (a proper name, referring to the mediaeval Levantine pidgin, used with the definite article and written with capital initials) and a lingua franca (a technical term, spelled with small initials). The proper name *the Lingua Franca* has no plural, whereas the technical term, being a borrowing from Italian, has the Italian plural *lingue franche*. The Lingua Franca was a pidginized variety of Romance speech, based on the language of the Riviera between Marseilles and Genoa, whence came a large number of the ships and sailors that traded with the Near East in mediaeval times. We have references in historical documents to the existence and use of the Lingua Franca, but very few attestations have survived. It served as a vehicle for the borrowing of words, particularly sea terms, from the Romance languages into Greek, Turkish, and Arabic, and vice versa: for example, Spanish *ferreruelo* and Italian *ferraiuolo* "a kind of cloak" from Arabic *fergûl*, ultimately from Latin *palliolum* "a little cloak". One interesting survival of the Lingua Franca in our every-day use is the term "lingo." This word (from Latin *lingua* "tongue, language") betrays its South French origin by its final vowel, since Latin *-a* had normally become *-o* in southern France by the time in question.

Outside of Europe, there have undoubtedly been many pidgin languages wherever groups of people have come in contact. Even before the white man came to America, Indians in the Northwest were using a pidginized variety of Chinook for their trading, and in South America a similar situation prevailed with Pidgin Tupí-Guaraní, which the Portuguese settlers of Brazil named the Lingua Gêral, or "general language." It has been suggested that pidginization and creolization are "endemic," as it were, in the South Pacific: the Melanesian languages are clearly related, but, although they show Malayo-Polynesian structural pattern and grammatical elements, they have only a minority of Malayo-Polynesian words. This fact, some analysts consider, may point to transference of language structure from the brown Malayo-Polynesians to the Negroid Melanesians through a series of pidginizations and resultant creolizations. This theory has been correlated with migrational contacts between Malay traders and the aboriginal tribes of Melanesia, particularly along the coasts of New Guinea.

From the fifteenth century onwards, attestations of pidginized languages begin to multiply. Everywhere the West European went he seems to have adopted the same linguistic behavior towards the natives of the territories he discovered. The European was normally too sure of the superiority of his own culture to deign to take any interest in indigenous languages; so the native had to do his best to make himself understood to the newcomer in what he could pick up of the latter's tongue. Naturally, his first attempts at talking Portuguese, Spanish, French, or English would be halting. At this point, the European (whether explorer, sea-captain, trader, or sailor) would assume that the native's incomplete efforts at speaking the European's language were due, not to insufficient practice, but to inherent mental inferiority. So the European would conclude that it was useless to use "good language" to the native, and would reply to him in a replica of the latter's incomplete speech, adding also some of the patterns of baby-talk commonly used by mothers and nurses in his own country. The aboriginal, not knowing any better, would assume that this was the white man's real language, and would delight in using it. (In New Guinea, Neo-Melanesian is normally known among the natives as *tok waitman,* "the European's language.") He would also carry over into the new pidgin various habits of his own native tongue, not only in pronunciation, but also in grammatical forms and syntax, and of course in vocabulary. (Our schoolboys do this whenever they have not caught onto the underlying pattern of the foreign language they are studying; one student of mine once formed the French compound *paille-chapeau* on the model of English *straw hat,* and another translated "my mother's house" as *ma mère's maison!*) The pidgin thus becomes institutionalized, with its grammatical structure crystallized at this initial stage of language-learning.

The Portuguese began the process of pidginization early in their contacts with non-European peoples, and it was under Portuguese auspices that the unholy association of pidgin speech with slavery began. From the earliest years of the African slave-trade, Negroes who had picked up a smattering of Pidgin Portuguese or Pidgin Spanish were known as Ladinos and commanded a higher price than the others. In the course of their imperial expansion, the Portuguese spread pidginized versions of their language far and wide; Reinecke reports that there has been a Pidgin Portuguese in virtually every Portuguese colony. Even in what is now Dutch Guiana and in Canton, where the Portuguese were formerly located, a Pidgin Portuguese existed, and left many traces in the pidgin or creole English that took its place. The word *savvy* for "know", which is perhaps the most widespread of all words in the different kinds of Pidgin English, and is almost the hallmark of Pidgin, entered our language through Chinese Pidgin English, as a borrowing from Cantonese Pidgin Portuguese (Portuguese *saber* "to know", third person singular *sabe*). Similarly, Chinese Pidgin English *joss* "god" and *mandarin* are survivals of seventeenth-century Pidgin Portuguese (Portuguese *dios* "god" and *mandarim* "commander, ruler", respectively). The word *piccaninny* is first attested in Chinese Pidgin English (*yu kari pikanini hola* "do you want a small whore?"), used as an adjective and meaning simply "small", from Portuguese *pequenino* "little".

Pidgin Spanish seems to have been less widespread—partly, perhaps, because the natives were exterminated more rapidly in the areas colonized by Spain, and partly because Spanish priests (who were deeply and sincerely interested in the well-being of the Indians) educated those who were left, using standard Spanish. In Mexico, Guatemala, Venezuela, and perhaps other parts of South America, there are various simplified varieties of Spanish (probably recent formations, not continuations of a colonial Pidgin Spanish) that serve as contact languages for trading between speakers of Spanish and members of Indian tribes. From North Africa, we have some sixteenth- and seventeenth-century material in what was still called the Lingua Franca; from its scanty attestations, this would seem to have been a kind of Pidgin Spanish, rather than a direct continuation of the mediaeval Lingua Franca.

Pidgin French, likewise, arose in parts of the world where France established colonies. In some French tropical colonies where African slaves were imported in the eighteenth century to work the plantations—Louisiana, the West Indies (especially Haiti, then known as Saint-Domingue), Réunion, and Mauritius—the Pidgin French that was established served as the basis for later creoles (see Chapter 3). Along the northern coast of Africa, the French-based pidgin was known as *sabir* (again from the ubiquitous Romance word for "to know", this time in a specifically South French form, as shown by the vowel *i* corresponding to the close *e* of other Romance languages in this word) or as *petit-nègre*. The epilogue to Molière's *Le Bourgeois Gentilhomme* includes an imitation of this Pidgin French. In some parts of North Africa, *sabir* or *petit-nègre* still survives; the most recent information indicates, however, that it is on its way out in North Africa, and is used little or not at all in central Africa.

The English came onto the scene late in founding colonies, but pidgin varieties of their language apparently arose immediately in their contacts with natives. One of the first, abortive English attempts at colonization was Leigh's colony at the mouth of the Oyapock River (today the boundary between Brazil and British Guiana) in 1605 and 1606. We have no documentation of a reduced variety of English from this colony, but we do have in its records the attestation of the term *Pidian*, referring to the local Indians and probably taken from an indigenous word meaning "people". In the popular English pronunciation of the time, *Pidian* would have become *Pidgin*, just as *Indian* became *Injun*, *soldier* became *soljer*, etc. If this etymology is valid, the term "pidgin" would have originated in one of the very first English colonies, with some such meaning as "native who is willing to trade", and "pidgin English" would have been "the English used by and in contacts with the Pidians or Pidgins". This term, brought back from South America, may well have been known to sailors centered on the lower reaches of the Thames or in other English seaports, who would then have carried it to the East Indies and to China. This derivation is far more likely than that usually suggested, namely that *pidgin* was a variant form of the English word *business*, created by the non-English speakers of Chinese Pidgin English. At a later time, /pígın/ did come to be used in China, in the meaning of "business", as in /ðǽt blɔ́ŋ jú pígın/ "that's your affair", and passed thence (usually with the spelling *pigeon*) into British English, usually with a mildly humorous connotation ("That's none of our business; it's your pigeon, old chap"); but it now seems likely that this was a later, secondary development of the term "pidgin."

The first Pidgin English of which we have record is attested from North America. Here, the first documentation is from 1641, in which an Indian is reported as saying "They say, *Englishman* much foole! Lazie *squaes!*", that is, the Englishmen were fools because they did not require their women to work, as the Indians required theirs to do. (The spelling *squaes* probably stands for the pronunciation /skwa·z/, with long /a/.)[1] About 1673 a warrant

---

[1] We enclose phonemic transcriptions in slant lines, phonetic transcriptions in square brackets. For a list of symbols and their values, see Appendix C.

was issued to an Indian in these terms: "You, you big constable, quick you catch um Jeremiah Offscow, strong you hold um, safe you bring um afore me, Waban, Justice Peace." These sentences already show certain of the main characteristics of all pidginized English: the equational clause, without use of the verb *be;* the juxtaposition of two nouns without the preposition *of* or any possessive suffix *(Justice Peace)*; the use of nouns without definite or indefinite article; and the element *-um* /-əm/ (from unstressed *him* or *them*) suffixed to a verb that has a direct object *(catch um Jeremiah Offscow* probably stands for /kǽčəm ğèrəmájə ɔ́fskàw/).

On the other side of the world, the English established their first "factory" or trading post at Canton in 1664, and immediately a variety of Pidgin English grew up there. Here, the social situation was especially interesting. The English regarded the language of the "heathen Chinee" as beyond any possibility of learning, and began to pidginize their own language for the benefit of the Chinese. The latter held the English, like all "foreign devils," in extremely low esteem, and would not stoop to learning the foreigners' language in its full form. They were willing, though, to learn what they perfectly well knew to be an "imperfect" variety of English or of some other Western tongue, and considered that this was abasing themselves less than learning "real" English. In other words, the English wanted to hold the Chinese at arm's length, and the Chinese wanted to do likewise to the English; Pidgin served the purpose admirably for both sides. However, we must not think that the Chinese variety of Pidgin English was a direct outgrowth of the American Indian kind. Rather, the various types of Pidgin English arose in various regions, as a result of the same basic stimulus: English seamen and traders (many of whom may have voyaged to more than one region) were moved to simplify their language when they were dealing with indigenous peoples—an example of the process termed "stimulus diffusion."

Chinese Pidgin English got its start in Canton and was used principally there until 1843, when the so-called Treaty Ports were established along the south-eastern coast of China and in the Yang-Tze valley. From then until the end of the nineteenth century might be called the "classical" period of Chinese Pidgin, when it was in widespread use in English "factories," clubs, shops, and homes, primarily between Chinese tradesmen, merchants, and servants on the one side, and English businessmen and house-wives on the other. With the gradual westernization of China, the younger generation around the turn of the century, especially the intellectuals, came to realize that the English-speaking community held Pidgin in low esteem and often ridiculed it. Consequently, the Western-educated Chinese began to reject Pidgin and to insist on learning standard English, leaving the use of Pidgin to the lower classes. In 1944, when I was working on Chinese Pidgin, I asked two outstanding Chinese linguists if they would serve as informants for me; they answered that, unlike most Chinese intellectuals, they would have been glad to do so, but they knew no Pidgin, having refused to learn it in their youth at the beginning of the century. Since the decline of Western influence in China in the middle of the twentieth century, Pidgin has gradually passed out of use, and just before the Second World War, Hong Kong was the only place where it still survived to any extent. Even there the former clearly-structured, traditional Pidgin has been replaced by a more or less improvised simplification of English on the part of house-wives, maids, etc., which has little or no connection by direct oral transmission with the earlier Pidgin.

Elsewhere in eastern Asia—for example, in Japan and in Borneo —there were English-based pidgins in the nineteenth century, but these have died out. From nineteenth-century India, we have reports of a language called Babu English, the name being derived from *babu* "a low-ranking Indian civil servant"; but it is not clear whether this was a true pidgin or simply the "broken English" used by the Indians in speaking to the English. From Anglo-Indian usage, however, some terms were carried by the English into Chinese Pidgin: for example, *shroff* "merchant's agent" and *maskee* /máski/ "never mind". During the Korean war of 1950–1951 and after, there sprang up between American soldiers and Koreans a pidgin nicknamed Bamboo English, but this did not survive the nineteen-fifties.

In connection with the slave-trade in the late seventeenth and eighteenth centuries, there grew up another kind of pidginized English on both sides of the Central Atlantic—in West Africa on the east, and in the Caribbean area and what is now the south-eastern part of the United States. This speech, which we might term Central Atlantic Pidgin English, has left creole survivors all around the Caribbean (see Chapter 2), and has continued as a pidgin down to the present in West Africa. In this latter area, it is now gradually being assimilated to somewhat substandard English in the large towns such as Lagos, but still survives in country regions as a lingua franca among different African tribes.

From the beginning of settlement in Australia, a similar Pidgin English was spoken between the first settlers and the aborigines. Early nineteenth-century documents attest aboriginal pronunciations of *Mr. Flinders* with the spelling *Midgah Plindah* (probably /míǧa plínda/) and of *coffee* with *caw-be* (probably /kɔ́bi/). The Europeans and their aboriginal followers helped to spread, through this medium, such words as *kangaroo, boomerang,* and *gin* "aboriginal woman" from one tribe to another. New Zealand also had a variety of Pidgin in the mid-nineteenth century. In recent years, however, Pidgin has wholly died out in New Zealand, and is becoming more and more restricted in Australia. Nowadays it is found only in the tropical regions of the continent, and even there, with the spread of schooling in English, Australian Pidgin is being replaced by a substandard variety of English.

In the South Sea islands to the north and north-east of Australia, English-speaking sailors, traders, whalers, and recruiters of indentured labor ("blackbirders") were pursuing their activities and teaching a pidginized English to the natives, from the New Hebrides to the Carolines. This South Seas Pidgin came to be known as Beach-la-Mar, from the name of a kind of sea-slug, *bêche-de-mer*, which was an object of extensive trade (the sailors used to obtain it and sell it in China, where it was a favorite ingredient of soup). This early nineteenth-century South Seas Pidgin left many traces in the native languages of the whole region, such as *pig* throughout all of the Carolines, *lam(p), ring, marit* "marriage", and a number of other words. However, in some parts of the South Seas, missionaries and administrators tried to uproot Pidgin; they were successful in some places where the populations were small enough or Pidgin had not gained a firm hold. Thus, when the German imperial government took over Micronesia and part of Melanesia (Northeast New Guinea, the Bismarcks, and the northern Solomons) in the eighteen-eighties, an order went out that the governors were to discourage the use of Pidgin English, and Baron von Hesse-Wartegg declared that it would be a source of lasting disgrace for the "world standing" of Germany if Pidgin were not rooted out. They succeeded in the Carolines, but not in Melanesia. Similarly, in Papua under British rule, the first governor,

Sir Hubert Murray, who is said to have been trained as a classical scholar, had a violent antipathy to Pidgin. He therefore did his best to wipe it out; but the drive to pidginize was so strong that in its place Sir Hubert encouraged the use, not of standard English, but of a pidginized variety of a native language of the region, Motu. Pidgin has been reintroduced into Port Moresby (capital of Papua) since the end of the Second World War, by the influx of migrant labor from the Territory of New Guinea, and especially by the native police and army force.

In Melanesia, however, it proved quite impossible to eradicate Pidgin, since it was far too firmly implanted and too useful as a lingua franca. Therefore, the German administration followed the philosophy expressed in the old proverb "If you can't lick 'em, jine 'em": finding that they could not do away with Pidgin, they made its use official. German administrators and missionaries took Pidgin seriously, analyzed its sound-system and its grammar by treating it as a language in its own right, and devised a sound orthography for it. They took as their standard the usage of Rabaul, then the capital of the German colonies in Melanesia. Hence the presence in Neo-Melanesian of a number of German words, such as *mark* "shilling"; *tais* "pond" (from German *Teich*); *raus* "get out" and *rausim* "throw out" (from the German *heraus* "get out!"); and *didiman* "botanical garden; Department of Agriculture" (from a Dr. Bredemann, the German head of the Botanical Garden in Rabaul until 1914). Rabaul, too, has left its mark on Melanesian Pidgin English, through the presence of a number of loan-words from Kuanua, the native language of the Rabaul region: for example, *kiau* "egg" and *malolo* "rest".

When the Australians ousted the Germans in 1914, the situation with regard to Pidgin English continued as before. Of the missions in the area, the Protestant groups in general tried to work through the native languages, whereas the Roman Catholics usually made use of Pidgin to a much greater extent. The Catholic missionaries developed great skill at preaching in Pidgin, and their presses at Alexishafen and at Vunapope (near Rabaul) put out a considerable amount of material in Pidgin, including a *Liklik Katolik Baibel*, a *Katekismo Katolik*, and various hagiographical items and periodicals. Apparently the Australians, in the early nineteen-twenties, mooted some kind of plan for replacing Pidgin by using several native languages as lingue franche in the various parts of the Territory; but Pidgin was too firmly entrenched, and the Australians had to continue using it. In the Second World War, during the Japanese advance, considerable use was made of leaflets written in Pidgin and dropped from aeroplanes to instruct the natives as to what the Allies wished them to do. After the war, with the return of European administrators, educators, and traders, extensive use was made of Pidgin in radio broadcasts and in education, particularly in the preparation of technical manuals for such subjects as medicine and store-keeping, and the publication of mimeographed or printed newspapers at such centers as Lae, Madang, Wewak, and Rabaul.

In the British Solomon Islands, Pidgin was never given official status as it was in German (later Australian) New Guinea; nevertheless it is widely used in every-day contacts. It has come to differ somewhat from the pidgin of the mandated territory, especially in vocabulary. British Solomon Islands Pidgin never underwent the influence of German or of Kuanua, and on the other hand it has taken over many more words from standard English. Thus, we find in the British islands such features as the use of /kæliko/ instead of /læplæp/ for "loin-cloth"; /mɪdelde/ instead of /bɛlo kajkaj/ "noon"; or /wɪdɪm/ "with" instead of /lɔŋ/. In the British Solomon Islands, Pidgin has been used relatively little for education or instruction, and to date no standard orthography has been devised, as was done in the German territories.

Little or no Pidgin German seems to have developed in the colonies that Germany took over at the end of the nineteenth century, but some varieties of pidginized Dutch have existed—in the Virgin Islands, for instance. On a basis of Russian and Norwegian, there grew up a pidgin known as Russonorsk, which was used for about a hundred years before the First World War, between Russian and Norwegian fishermen along the Arctic coast of Norway. Apparently this pidgin grew up around the chance identity of the preposition /pɔ/, with the approximate meaning "on, in", in both Russian and Norwegian. Each side was firmly convinced it was speaking the other's language, and so the "slogan" sentence of Russonorsk was /mója pɔ tvója/ "I [will speak] in your [language]". Many of its lexical items had two variants, one Russian and one Norwegian, as in /njét/ or /íkke/ "not", /drogój/ or /ánner/ "another, next", and /snái/ or /véit/ "know". Certain lexical and grammatical elements of Russonorsk were of Dutch or English origin (for example, /slí·p/ "sleep", /váter/ "water", /ju·/ "you",

/je·s/ "yes") and perhaps entered Russonorsk from an earlier
Muscovite Pidgin English which may have been used between
English traders and Russians in Elizabethan times.
Outside of the Indo-European family, we have already mentioned the formation of Chinook Jargon and the Lingua Gêral of
Brazil. In Africa, various native languages have served as bases for
pidginized lingue franche. One of these, Swahili, is widely used
across a large belt of central Africa; and another variety of pidginized Bantu has sprung up and become widespread in South Africa
under the name of Fanaga-Lò or Kitchen Kaffir. In fact, such ex-
travagant claims have been made for the universal applicability of
Fanaga-Lò throughout Africa that it has been necessary for respon-
sible linguists to deflate them. One non-Indo-European pidgin de-
serves especial mention, because its development casts light on the
possibilities of development of pidgin languages. In the Dutch East
Indies, a pidginized variety of Malay, known as Bazaar Malay or
Pasá Malay, was the established lingua franca between the Dutch
and their colonial peoples. The Dutch insisted on this use of Bazaar
Malay and in general refused to allow Indonesians to learn Dutch,
as a means of enforcing caste separation; but their efforts boomer-
anged when Bazaar Malay came to be a vehicle for Indonesian
nationalism, serving as the starting-point for the development of
the present-day Indonesian language (see Chapter 2).

REFERENCES

Full bibliography of all pidgins and creoles up to ca.1936:
Reinecke, 1937. From 1952 on: sections entitled "Langues mixtes"
(later "Langues créoles") at the end of each year's CIPL bibliog-
raphy of linguistics (CIPL, 1949 ff.).
The Lingua Franca in the Mediterranean: Schuchardt, 1909;
Tagliavini, 1932. Words borrowed from Italian and Greek into
Turkish through the Lingua Franca: Kahane, Kahane, and Tietze,
1958.
Spanish *ferreruelo* and Italian *ferraiuolo:* Corominas, 1948.
Chinook Jargon: Jacobs, 1932; Grant, 1944, 1945.
Lingua Gêral: Hartt, 1872; Nimuendajú, 1914; bibliography in
Tenório d'Albuquerque, 1929, and in Medina, 1930.
"Endemic" pidginization in South Pacific: Ray, 1926; Kroeber,
1941.

"Ladinos" in Central Atlantic slave-trade: Donnan, 1930 (1.72).

Portuguese-based pidgins and creoles: Coelho, 1881–86; Schuchardt, 1881, 1882a–b, 1883a, 1883d, 1888a–d, 1889a–c, 1890; Leite de Vasconcelos, 1897–99; Lopes da Silva, 1957; Valkhoff, 1960; Batalha, 1961; Thompson, 1961a–b.

Pikinini in Chinese Pidgin English: attestation quoted in Hall, 1944a (p. 109).

Spanish-based contact vernaculars in the Philippines: Schuchardt, 1883b; McKaughan, 1954, 1958; Whinnom, 1956. In the Americas: Wagner, 1920. In Venezuela: Riley, 1952.

Pidginized and creolized varieties of French: Adam, 1886; Schuchardt, 1888e; Göbl-Gáldi, 1934.

English-based pidgins: Schuchardt, 1888f; Kloss, 1952.

Origin of English word *pidgin:* Kleinecke, 1959.

American Indian Pidgin English: Hall (with Leechman), 1955d.

Chinese Pidgin English: Hall, 1944a.

Indian Babu English: Yule and Burnell, 1886.

Korean Bamboo English: Algeo, 1960; Webster, 1960.

New Zealand Pidgin English: Baker, n.d.

Australian Pidgin English: Hall, 1943c; Baker, 1945.

Beach-la-Mar: Churchill, 1911.

Micronesian Pidgin English, loan-words surviving from in native languages: Hall, 1945b.

Melanesian Pidgin English (Neo-Melanesian): Schuchardt, 1883c, 1889d; Friederici, 1911; Landtman, 1918; Nevermann, 1929; Mead, 1931, 1959; Schebesta and Meiser, n.d.; Hall, 1942a–b, 1943a, 1943d, 1944b–c, 1954a–e, 1955a, 1955c, 1956a–c, 1957b, 1959b, 1959d; Murphy, 1943; Reed, 1943 ("Appendix I: The language adjustment: Melanesian Pidgin"); Sayer, 1943; Höltker, 1945; French, 1953, 1955; Mihalic, 1957.

British Solomon Islands Pidgin English (Neo-Solomonic): Hall, 1945a, 1955e.

Dutch-based pidgins: Pontoppidan, 1881; Hesseling, 1905, 1933b; Schuchardt, 1914a; De Josselin de Jong, 1924.

Russonorsk: Broch, 1927.

African lingue franche: Kitubu and Bulu: Nida, 1955. Sango: Samarin, 1955, 1962; Taber, 1964.

Swahili: Broomfield, 1930.

Fanaga-Lò: Cole, 1953.

Bazaar Malay and Indonesian: Kahin, 1952 (p. 39).

Creoles

AT present, a number of creolized languages are serving throughout the world as the native speech of large and growing populations, and some have become, or are on the way to becoming, standard languages.

In the southeastern part of the United States, the original English of the Negro slaves seems to have been a creolized variety, going back to a pidgin of which we have no record. This American Negro Creole English began quite early to take over more and more features of standard speech—and hence to disappear through assimilation. However, even the nineteenth-century stage of Negro speech, recorded in stylized form in such sources as the "Uncle Remus" stories of Joel Chandler Harris, shows a good many structural features characteristic of creoles, such as relics of a simplified vowel structure in words like *laig* /lég/ for "leg" or *haid* /héd/ for "head", or the use of simple uninflected verb-forms in all persons, together with such aspectival and tense prefixes as *gwine* /gwájn/ (from "going to"). By now, most American Negro speech has lost virtually all of these characteristics, which have come to be regarded as badges of inferiority; but markedly aberrant Negro creoles are still spoken in the coastal region around Charleston and Savannah, especially on the Sea Islands off Georgia, in the language known as Gullah.[1]

Around the Gulf of Mexico and the Caribbean, on the other

---

[1]The term "Gullah" is often applied rather loosely to any variety of Negro speech in the Charleston and Savannah area, but, strictly speaking, it refers only to the very aberrant varieties spoken by the Sea Islanders and other isolated groups, not to the speech of the city or ordinary country Negroes of the region.

hand, there are a number of creolized varieties of French, Spanish, and English. In Louisiana, three varieties of French are in use, all quite different from each other, although outsiders frequently confuse them. There is the local provincial variety of standard French, which is the language of the old established upper classes in New Orleans and the surrounding country; this is a full-sized "normal" language, with all the resources of literary French, though with a few archaic features (as is usual in provincial standard languages). The descendants of the Acadian refugees of the seventeen-sixties (about whom Longfellow wrote *Evangeline*) live up-country from New Orleans, in the backwoods regions of Louisiana; these people, of predominantly white stock, are known as Cajuns (the normal development of the word *Acadians*) and speak a dialect of French, likewise called Cajun. This, too, is a full-sized language, though not standard; it is a French dialect which, like the other North American French dialects, has developed out of French country speech of the seventeenth century. Then there is Louisiana Creole, which is radically different from both the provincial standard French and Cajun. It is spoken by the descendants of plantation slaves, and linguistically it is closely related to the other French-based creoles of the Caribbean area, showing the same drastic structural changes: for example, phonological simplification; loss of categories of gender, number, and person; use of aspectival and tense prefixes.

In the Antilles, there are a number of creoles close enough to Louisiana Creole to be mutually intelligible with it. The best-known of these is Haitian Creole, which is spoken as a mother tongue by the entire population of the Republic of Haiti, on the western end of the island of Hispaniola. Other French-based creoles are spoken in the Lesser Antilles on a number of islands, not all of which are still under French rule: Dominica, Martinique, etc., down to Trinidad and French Guiana. In the islands under French rule, there is of course a local variety of standard French, and the situation is somewhat comparable to that in Haiti; in those under English rule, the creole has only the standing of a local patois, and its speakers are normally illiterate, at least in the creole.

There are also numerous English-based creoles in the Caribbean area: in the Bahamas, on Jamaica, and on such islands of the Lesser Antilles as the Virgin Islands, Barbados, and Trinidad, as well as in British Guiana and Dutch Guiana (Suriname). In this latter colony,

there are two creoles: the speech of the city-dwellers of Para-
màribo, known as Taki-Taki, Nengre-Tongo ("Negro Language"),
or Sranan-Tongo ("Suriname Language," often abbreviated to
"Sranan"); and the language of the Saramaccá or Bush-Negroes.
Before the English took Guiana from the Portuguese, the plantations were owned by Portuguese Jews; from this fact came an
earlier name for Taki-Taki, "Jew-Tongo." The Saramaccá are
descendants of seventeenth-century Negroes who ran away from
the plantations into the bush, taking with them the English-based
pidgin they had learned as slaves, and then intermarried with
Indians. The language of the Saramaccá is especially interesting in
that it conserves numerous features of African speech that have
not survived in Taki-Taki, such as significant tone on individual
syllables. Both Taki-Taki and Saramaccá preserve many words such
as *grandi* "large" and *pasá* "pass" from the Guianese Pidgin
Portuguese spoken there in early colonial times. Taki-Taki has, in
addition, numerous borrowings (primarily in vocabulary) from
Dutch: this part of Guiana has been under Dutch rule since 1667.

Jamaican Creole has come by now to be, not so much
a markedly different language from English, as a spectrum of
varieties ranging all the way from the very aberrant "bongo talk"
of isolated groups in the mountains, to the provincial standard
English of town-dwellers, in, say, Kingston. An offshoot of Jamaican
Creole is found in Africa: a group of Negroes were repatriated in
the nineteenth century from Jamaica to Sierra Leone; in Freetown
their creolized language, under the name of Krio, is spoken by
twenty thousand or more of their descendants. In the mid-twentieth
century, Krio came to be one of the symbols of nationalist feeling
among those in the region who are violently opposed to the continuation of British influence and wish to make Krio as unlike English as possible, even in its orthography (see Chapter 4).

Along the south shore of the Caribbean, to the west and off the
coast of Venezuela, are the islands of Curaçao, Aruba, and Bonaire,
where an old-established creole named Papiamentu[2] is spoken. It
is often stated that Papiamentu is an outgrowth of an earlier Pidgin Portuguese, but all of its regular phonetic and morphological
correspondences point rather to a Spanish origin. It may well rep-

[2]This language is often referred to as "Papiamento," with the final -*o* of Spanish
nouns; however, in the language itself all such nouns end in -*u*, and the name of the
language follows this pattern, its speakers calling it "Papiamentu."

resent a fusion of two earlier pidgins or creoles—one based on Spanish (which constitutes the dominant element in present-day Papiamentu), and one based on Portuguese. Another type of mixed language, consisting of Spanish and Italian elements, and known as *cocoliche* or *lunfardo,* is found in Buenos Aires among Argentinians of Italian origin, and there has been a similar mixture of Italian and Portuguese in southern Brazil; but these are not true creoles, since they have not gone through a stage of drastic reduction and pidginization. The suggestion that Brazilian Portuguese dialects are the result of creolization has not met with general acceptance.

In the South Seas, Pidgin English is coming to be the native language of the youngest generation in some places, and hence is in a stage of incipient creolization. Another creolized variety of English in the South Seas is the somewhat misnamed Hawaiian Pidgin English; it is usually regarded as another outgrowth of the old South Seas Pidgin, and is by now the native speech of a large number of those who are born or brought up in the islands (no matter of what racial origin, Hawaiian or otherwise). It is widespread as a means of communication, though it is spoken in its earlier form only on outlying islands; in Honolulu and other populated areas, Hawaiian Pidgin covers, like Jamaican Creole, a whole spectrum from a strongly differentiated type of speech all the way to semi-standard English. Although it has little social and no official standing, this "Pidgin" is, for many Hawaiians, the language they speak for fun and relaxation.

In Southeast Asia, Bazaar Malay, which is still widely used as a contact and trade language, has served as the basis for a new national language, which has been rebaptized *Bahasa Indonesia* ("Indonesian language") and is now the official language of the Indonesian Republic. Here we have an example of a pidgin being deliberately creolized and made into the vehicle of a national culture, in which latter function it is highly respected thoughout the world. It is not known whether creolization has taken place or not in the case of other non-Indo-European-based pidgins such as the Lingua Gêral of Brazil. Other alleged instances of creolization, although not improbable, have not been definitely proven; it has been suggested that Afrikaans (an outgrowth of Dutch spoken by the Boers in South Africa), which shows considerable simplification in grammatical structure as contrasted with Dutch, may be the outgrowth of an earlier South African Pidgin Dutch, used by Negro house-servants in the seventeenth century and then learned by white children from their black nurses and cooks.

We naturally have no way of knowing how many times pidginization and creolization may have taken place in earlier linguistic history. One instance of possible pidginization in pre-historic times, however, is of interest to us as speakers of English. As is well known, English, Dutch, Frisian, German, and the Scandinavian languages have developed out of a common source, Proto-Germanic, of which we have no written records, but which we can reconstruct on the basis of its later outcome in the various Germanic languages. It must have been spoken in the first millennium B.C., probably in southern Scandinavia and nearby parts of northern Germany. In its turn, Proto-Germanic was one of the Indo-European languages, related to Latin, Greek, Sanskrit, Proto-Celtic, and Proto-Balto-Slavic. Now in Proto-Germanic, as contrasted with Proto-Indo-European, we find certain striking developments: particularly the great shift in the consonant pattern known under the names of Grimm's and Verner's laws; and the use of alternation in vowels (as in *sing, sang, sung* or *drive, drove, driven*), which had in Proto-Indo-European been automatic and meaningless, as a means for indicating changes in the tense of verbs. These developments seem to show the same kind of brusque restructuring that we find in pidgin and creole languages. Furthermore, Germanic has lost many of the words characteristic of Indo-European, using in their stead a number of words of unknown, but presumably non-Indo-European, origin, such as *wife, hand, leg*. On the basis of these phenomena, it has been suggested that Proto-Germanic may well have originated as a pidginized variety of Indo-European, which arose along the amber trade route from the Mediterranean to the Baltic in the first millennium B.C., and which then became creolized, replacing the native languages of the tribes around the lower Baltic.

In this survey, we have left Europe to the last, because at present—aside from the simplified varieties of language used by guides in speaking with groups of tourists, etc.—there are no established pidgins and hence no clearly identifiable creoles in modern Europe. This situation is due, of course, to the fact that the type of brief, casual contact that normally gives rise to the use of a pidgin is no longer to be found in Europe or in North America, where civilization is more complicated, and where even short contacts are likely to be more intensely weighted with cultural and social implications than in simpler cultures. However, whenever the more casual contact situation arises, the need for communication is still met by the development of a pidginized language. Apparently the readiness to form pidgin varieties of one's speech is strongly ingrained in the ordinary nonpuristic European or North American, and this readiness manifests itself whenever called for, as in the renewed pidginization of English in present-day Hong Kong.

REFERENCES

American Negro speech: McDavid and McDavid, 1951.
Gullah: L. D. Turner, 1949; Hall, 1950c; Blok, 1959.
Cajun: Read, 1931; Ditchy, 1932.
Creoles in Caribbean: Loftman, 1953; Stewart, 1962.
Antillean French-based creoles: Poyen-Bellisle, 1894; Cassidy, 1959; Taylor, 1960, 1961b, 1963; Stewart, 1962; Goodman, 1964.
Louisiana Creole: Mercier, 1880; Harrison, 1882; Fortier, 1884–85, 1891; Read, 1931; Lane, 1935; Broussard, 1942; Morgan, 1959, 1960.
Haitian Creole: Sylvain, 1936; Faine, 1937, 1939; Pressoir, 1947; Hall, 1949a–d, 1950d–f, 1952a, 1953; Taylor, 1953; Zumthor, 1953; Efron, 1954; Pompilus, 1961.
Dominican Creole: Taylor, 1945, 1947, 1951, 1952, 1955a, 1961a.
Trinidad (French-based) Creole: Thomas, 1869.
French Guiana Creole: Saint-Quentin, 1872; Horth, 1949.
Seychelles Creole: S. Jones, 1952.
Creoles in Réunion, Bourbon, and Mauritius: Bos, 1880, 1881; Baissac, 1880; Schuchardt, 1882c; Focard, 1885; Dietrich, 1891; Urruty, 1951; Valkhoff, 1964.
Martinique Creole: Turialt, 1874; Funk, 1950, 1953; Jourdain, 1956a–b; Hall, 1957d; Taylor, 1957.
English-based Creoles in Caribbean: Cassidy, 1959.
Sranan (Taki-Taki): Herskovits, 1936; Simons, 1941; Hall, 1948a; Rens, 1953; Donicie, 1954, 1956; Pée, Hellinga, and Donicie, 1953a–b; Voorhoeve, 1953a–b, 1957a–b, 1961a–b, 1962; Silva Neto, 1960; Echteld, 1961.

Saramaccá: Schuchardt, 1914; Herskovits and Herskovits, 1936; Voorhoeve, 1959, 1961d; Donicie and Voorhoeve, 1962.

Jamaican Creole: LePage and DeCamp, 1960; Cassidy, 1961; Cassidy and LePage, 1961; DeCamp, 1961.

Creoles in Africa: Schneider, 1960.

Krio: E. D. Jones, 1957, 1959; Berry, 1959a–b, 1960; L. D. Turner, 1964.

Papiamentu: Lenz, 1928; Hesseling, 1933a–b; Harris, 1952; Silva-Fuenzalida, 1952; Wattman, 1953; Navarro, 1953; van Wijk, 1958.

Portuguese "creoles" in Brazil: Mendonça, 1935; Silva Neto, 1960; Révah, 1963. In Macao: Batalha, 1961.

Cocoliche in Buenos Aires: Donghi de Halperín, 1925; Meo-Zilio, 1955a–c, 1956a–b.

Portuguese-Italian mixed language in Brazil: Nardo Cibele, 1900.

Afrikaans: Kloeke, 1950; Valkhoff, 1960.

Proto-Germanic: Feist, 1932.

Structure and Relationships

PART II

Phonology

From a structural point of view, the essential characteristic of a pidgin language is that it is sharply reduced in its pronunciation and grammar and in its vocabulary. In general, this reduction is in the direction of whatever features are common to the languages of all those using the pidgin, for mutual ease in use and comprehensibility, thus arriving at a kind of greatest common denominator. Usually, at least in modern times, the languages in contact have been a European tongue and some variety or varieties of speech indigenous to the area where the pidgin has been formed. Often there have been not merely one native language but several, or even a large number. Thus, colonial Pidgin French was formed through contact of speakers of French with speakers of many different African languages who had deliberately been mixed together on slave-ships, in the slave-markets, or on the plantations in the Caribbean and Louisiana. Similarly, speakers of a great number of different Melanesian and Papuan languages have used Melanesian Pidgin English and made it their own. We therefore must not think of a pidgin as representing a simple bilateral fusion; it is, rather, a development of a single language (usually a European language, in modern times) with strong influences from one or more others, sometimes a great many, and usually non-European.

In the development of a creole language out of a pidgin, on the other hand, the main change is in the direction of re-expansion of both structure and vocabulary. The source of the new material for re-expansion is, in some part, the inner structural resources of the erstwhile pidgin itself; in considerably greater part, however, the enrichment of the creole comes from outside sources, usually one

25

or more languages with greater cultural prestige. For the most part, creole languages develop in areas now or until recently under colonial rule, where some European tongue is in official use in government administration, courts, schools, religious services, and in the families of the governing or ruling classes. A language used in this way we shall call an "official language." Often enough, the European language thus used is the same one that was at the base of the pidgin out of which the creole developed. This has been the case in such regions as Haiti (with French as the official language) or New Guinea (with English). It can happen, though, that the European official language has not been involved in the formation of the pidgin. Thus, Dutch has been for centuries the official language in both Suriname (Dutch Guiana) and Curaçao, and as a result there have been numerous borrowings (mostly of vocabulary) from Dutch into both Sranan and Papiamentu. Nevertheless, the two creoles remain, despite their common borrowings from Dutch, of different origin and of markedly different structure.

In the sound-system, or phonology, of any given language we normally distinguish between its phonemic and its phonetic patterns: the former are the pattern of distinctive contrasts in sound, and the latter are the actual sounds themselves as made by speakers of the language. When passing, in our analysis, from the sounds to the phonemes (significant units of sound which make a difference in the meaning of words), we speak of one or more sounds being subsumed under a given phoneme or being allophones of that phoneme. When going in the opposite direction, we say that a phoneme is realized by a given sound, or that that sound is the realization of the phoneme, under particular conditions. Thus, in English, there is a marked difference between the way we pronounce t in star and the way we pronounce it in tar: in the former word, and anywhere it occurs after s before a stressed vowel, the t is not followed by a puff of breath (it is unaspirated), whereas elsewhere, and especially before a stressed vowel (as in tar), the t is often followed by a puff of breath (it is aspirated). We therefore say that the t sound in star is an unaspirated allophone of the phoneme /t/, and we transcribe it phonetically as [t];[1] and we say that the t sound in tar is an aspirated allophone of /t/,[2] transcrib-

---

[1] As is customary in linguistics, we enclose phonetic transcriptions, in which each letter or other symbol corresponds to a specific speech-sound, in square brackets [ ].

[2] Phonemic transcriptions, in which each symbol represents, not a single sound, but a single phoneme, are enclosed in slant lines / /.

ing it phonetically as [tʻ]. Sometimes it is more convenient to state the relationship between allophone and phoneme the other way around, and to say that the phoneme /t/ is realized as [t] after [s], and as [tʻ] in various other positions (but never after [s]). The phonemic systems of pidgin languages seem, in general, to be reduced in the number of contrasts they employ. So far as is known, all languages have two fundamentally different types of phoneme: vowels and consonants. The former are produced by breath which comes out of the organs of speech and is modified in various ways, but with the vocal organs being used only to produce resonance; whereas the production of consonants involves interruption of resonance by some type of noise. (Here, and throughout our discussion, when we speak of vowels, we most emphatically do not mean "a, e, i, o, u, and sometimes w and y," and when we speak of consonants, we do not mean "all the other letters of the alphabet." We are always—unless we clearly specify otherwise—speaking of sounds, not of letters, and our description of sounds will be in terms of their production and function in speech.) Every pidgin language that has thus far been studied shows the distinction between vowel and consonant phonemes. The vowel phonemes of pidgin languages are normally reduced toward the "cardinal vowels" of the well-known "vowel triangle."[3] It is relatively rare to find a pidgin language with other types of vowels, such as the front-rounded series (like French /y/ and /œ/). The front-rounded

---

[3] The "vowel triangle" is a schematic representation of the vowel sounds of human speech; it is arrived at by abstracting the positions that the top (not the tip!) of the tongue assumes in pronouncing them, and by placing the corresponding phonetic symbols in a similar position on paper. The "cardinal vowels" include the following:

Phonetic Symbol	Position of Top of Tongue in Articulation	Descriptive Term
i	Raised high in front of mouth, lips unrounded	high-front-unrounded
e	Raised to a rather high mid-position in front part of mouth, lips unrounded	high-mid-front-unrounded
ɛ	Raised to a lower mid-position in front part of mouth, lips unrounded	low-mid-front-unrounded
a	Lying flat in bottom of mouth, in central position, lips unrounded	low-central-unrounded
ɔ	Raised to a lower mid-position in back part of mouth, lips slightly rounded	low-mid-back-rounded
o	Raised to a rather high mid-position in back part of mouth, lips rounded	high-mid-back-rounded
u	Raised high in back of mouth, lips very much rounded	high-back-rounded

vowels are normally simplified in one of two directions: either the lip-rounding is lost and the fronting kept, so that /y/ (the vowel phoneme written *u* in French and *ü* in German) becomes /i/, and /œ/ (which is written *eu* in French and *ö* in German) becomes /e/; or the front articulation is changed to back, so that the resultant phonemes are back-rounded vowels, with /y/ being replaced by /u/ and /œ/ by /o/.

Both of these replacements just mentioned occurred in Haitian Creole at two different stages of its history. Words adopted from French at an earlier time show the latter change: for example, French /bryle/ *brûler* "to burn" > Haitian Creole /bule/;[4] French /syse/ *sucer* "to suck" > Haitian Creole /suse/; French /tye/ *tuer* "to kill" > Haitian Creole /tuje/; French /adjœ/ *adieu* "good-bye" > Haitian Creole /agjo/; dialectal French /jœ/ "they" > Haitian Creole /jo/; and French /gardœr/ *gardeur* "keeper" > Haitian Creole /gadò/ "baby-tender". But words taken over from French at a later stage (and such words are by now greatly in the majority) show the former change, replacement of front-rounded by front-unrounded vowels: for example, French /myr/ *mûr* "ripe" > Haitian Creole /mi/; French /kutym/ *coutûme* "custom" > Haitian Creole /kutim/; French /lary/ *la rue* "the street" > Haitian Creole /lari/ "street"; French /dyfœ/ *du feu* "some fire" > Haitian Creole /dife/ "fire"; French /(le)zjœ/ *les yeux* "the eyes" > Haitian Creole /že/ "eye(s)"; or French /lœr/ *l'heure* "the hour" > Haitian Creole /lè/ "hour, time". In this way, it is possible to separate two strata of words in the French-based lexicon of Haitian Creole: those that show Haitian Creole /u/ < French /y/

If these seven symbols are placed on paper in positions corresponding to those assumed by the top of the tongue in their pronunciation, they form a triangle:

		Front(-unrounded)		Back(-rounded)
High		i		u
	High	e		o
Mid				
	Low		ε	ɔ
Low			a	

In some transcriptions, the symbol ε is replaced by è, and ɔ by ò, chiefly for typographical convenience.

[4] The symbol > means "goes to, becomes, becoming"; and < means "comes from, coming from".

and Haitian Creole /o/ < French /œ/ belong to an earlier stratum than do those in which French /y/ > Haitian Creole /i/ and French /œ/ > Haitian Creole /e/. Thus, a word like Haitian Creole /djol/ "throat, mouth" < French /gœl/ *gueule* belongs clearly to the older stratum, and Haitian Creole /imid/ "damp, wet" < French /ymid/ *humide* is obviously a later borrowing. Similarly, in the earlier stages of English-based pidgins, the distinction between tense and lax vowels often disappeared, and there was no longer a contrast between the /i/ vowel of English *beat* and the /ɪ/ of *bit;* between /u/ in *fluke* and /ʊ/ in *book;* between /e/ in *bait* and /ɛ/ in *bet;* or between /o/ as in *coat* and /ɔ/ as in *caught.* Thus, in Neo-Melanesian, an earlier stratum of English words shows developments like English /gít əp/ *git up* (standard English /gét əp/ *get up*) > Neo-Melanesian /kirəp/ "arise"; English /lég/ *leg* > Neo-Melanesian /leg/ (compare the spelling *laig* in such sources as Joel Chandler Harris' "Uncle Remus" stories, evidencing a similar replacement in earlier American Negro English); English /púsi/ "pussy" > Neo-Melanesian /pusi/ "cat"; English /fɔrgív/ *forgive* > Neo-Melanesian /pogip/. Likewise, the retroflexed sound of English /ər/ (as in *burn, work*) was replaced, in an earlier group of English words in Neo-Melanesian, by /o/: thus, English /wə́rk/ *work* > Neo-Melanesian /wok(ɪm)/ "make", and English /bə́rn/ *burn* > Neo-Melanesian /bon(ɪm)/. In the same way, the distinction between the English low-front-unrounded vowel /æ/ and the mid-front vowel /ɛ/ was lost at the first stage of pidginization, as was that between the English mid-central vowel /ə/ ("uh") and the low-central vowel /a/: for example, English /kǽn/ *can,* "be able" > Neo-Melanesian /kə́t/ *cut* > Neo-Melanesian /kat(ɪm)/.

On the other hand, if a given phonemic feature is common to both sides in the formation of a pidgin, it can be preserved even if it is not an essential feature of the most widespread contrasts in human language. Thus, nasalization (symbolized by /~/ in phonetic and phonemic transcription) is not normally found in Neo-Melanesian or in most other pidgins or creoles based on English; but it is present in French-based pidgin and creole languages, especially those in which the native substratum languages were African. In many African languages nasalization is a common feature of pronunciation, and is often "contagious"; that is, it extends from a vowel to adjacent consonant phonemes or from a nasal consonant to the vowel of an adjacent syllable, as in Yoruba /ɔna/ [ɔnã] "road".[5] Thus, in Haitian Creole, we find nasalization as a phonemically significant feature, as it is in both French and West African languages. Interestingly enough, nasalization was, in the seventeenth-century and later French out of which Haitian and other French-based creoles developed, restricted to mid and low vowels; but, in Haitian Creole, it is found also with the high vowel phonemes /i/ and /u/, especially in words of African origin: for example, /būda/ "buttocks"; /vodū/ "vaudoun, voodoo"; /ūgã/ "vaudoun priest"; /ūfò/ "precincts of a vaudoun temple"; /pīga/ "look out!", "don't . . .".

Contrasts lost by this type of simplification are frequently restored at a later stage, when a pidgin has either been extended widely in its use or become creolized. In this way, some speakers of Haitian Creole, especially in urban centers like Port-au-Prince and in the north of Haiti, use the front-rounded vowels /y/ and /œ/, which they have learned from standard French, in such words as /žezy/ "Jesus", /œrœz/ "happy", /favœ̀/ "favor", instead of what would normally be /žezi/, /erèz/, /favè/, respectively. In Neo-Melanesian, likewise, many speakers now make the contrast between tense and lax vowels and use the vowel phonemes /æ/ and /ə/ and the combination /ər/, as in /kil/ "keel" versus /kɪlɪm/ "beat, kill"; /fæšɪn/ "fashion" versus /paspas/ "armlet" versus /fərstajm/ "at first". Naturally, there can occur various types of over-correction, when speakers extend a phonemic analogy beyond the point where it is justified; I have heard Haitians use /ly/ for /li/ "he" and /vlœ/ for /vle/ "wish"; and in New Guinea such forms as /banɪs/ < /bænɪs/ < /bɛnɪs/ "fence" are not infrequent.

Similarly, in the consonant-system, phonemic contrasts that are not in the stock common to both sides in the formation of a pidgin are likely to be lost. This is especially true of the dental fricatives of English, /θ/ and /ð/ (both spelled with *th* in our conventional spelling, as in /θɪŋ/ *thing* and /ðɪs/ *this*), which are exceedingly rare sound-types in the world's languages and are usually replaced by /t/ and /d/ respectively: for example, Neo-Melanesian /tɪŋktɪŋk/ "think"; Neo-Melanesian /dɪsfɛlə/, British Solomon Islands Pidgin English /dɪswən/, Sranan /disi/, Gullah /dɪs/, etc., "this". In many varieties of Pidgin English, /f/ and /v/—also

---

[5] Cf. Ward, 1952, p. 13.

quite rare in the world as a whole—were likewise replaced, in the initial stages, by /p/ and /b/, respectively: for example, Neo-Melanesian /pɪŋɡə(r)/ "finger" and /bɪlibɪm/ "believe"; or Chinese Pidgin English /béli/ "very". Likewise, in Neo-Melanesian /č/, /ǧ/, and /š/ were all replaced by /s/: for example, Neo-Melanesian /senɪs/ "change", /siki/ "cheeky, insolent". In Neo-Melanesian, /h/ was at first lost, as in /ambak/ < English *humbug*, /ariap/ < English *hurry up*.

More recently, however, many New Guinea natives have learned to make some or all of these contrasts, but they often apply them in some words and not in others. Furthermore, not all speakers have reintroduced them, so that an over-all description of the language has to take all these possible variations into account: thus, for "change" one may hear such variant pronunciations as /senɪs/, /šenɪs/, /čenɪs/, /šenis/, /čenš/, /čenč/, and /čenǧ/. From such extensive alternations there arises for the analyst a problem in phonemic transcription: whether to use a diaphonic transcription[6] so as to cover all the possible variations—for example, writing /č/ whenever there is an alternation between /č/, /š/, and /s/; or to represent only the simplest form of each word, in this instance writing only /s/. In a diaphonic transcription each letter comes to be a "cover symbol," often representing an extensive series of alternations. For some types of analysis this is a compact and useful type of representation, but in practical applications it presents difficulties (see Chapter 4).

Often consonant-combinations may prove unfamiliar to one side or the other; specifically, many of the clusters found in European languages are not present in most African, Melanesian, Micronesian, or Polynesian tongues, and were simplified in the earliest stages of adaptation. On occasion, this simplification took

[6] A "diaphonic" transcription is one that provides representation, not only for the phonemes of a single dialect, but for the over-all pattern of correspondences between two or more dialects; the term "diaphone" (given currency by the phonetician Daniel Jones) refers to an alternation between two or more phonemes in the same position in the same word, in its manifestation in two or more related dialects. Thus, in Neo-Melanesian, some words have only /p/ in all varieties of the language—for example, /putɪm/ "to put", /pen/ "pain"; but in other words we find an alternation between /p/ and /f/, with also an intermediate variety of sound [Φ], as in [fʊt] ∼ [Φʊt] ∼ [pʊt] "foot". For the former type of word, we will utilize the diaphonic symbol /p/, but for the latter type, a diaphonic transcription /fʊt/, with the symbol /f/ standing, not just for the sound [f], but for the alternation [p] ∼ [Φ] ∼ [f]. Cf. Hall, 1943, §1.32. pp. 13–14.

place by omission of one or more of the consonants in the cluster: for example, Haitian Creole /zòt/ "you others, you [plural]" < 17th-century French /(vu)zòtr/ *vous autres* "you others"; or Haitian Creole /ezekite/ "carry out, execute [an order]" < French /egzekyte/ *exécuter;* or Sranan /masra/ "master" < English /mástər/. At least equally frequent is the breaking-up of a consonant cluster by the insertion of a vowel sound. In Micronesian languages, there are a number of English words that entered in the nineteenth century through the Pidgin English then spoken in that region, and show this phenomenon: for example, Marshallese *inik* < English *ink,* or Trukese *Sepetember* < English *September.*

Clusters involving *s* + CONSONANT, or CONSONANT + *s*, seem to have caused special trouble to natives of many regions, so that we find such pronunciations as Neo-Melanesian [si'piə] for "spear", [si'ton] for "stone", or ['sɔsipɛn] for "sauce-pan". As long as the intercalated vowel is only lightly pronounced, whispered, or otherwise not fully syllabic, the phonemic status of the cluster is not changed, and one is justified in transcribing the words just given and similar words as containing clusters of /s/ + CONSONANT, or of CONSONANT + /s/: /spir/, /ston/, /sɔspɛn/. On occasion, however, the vowel comes to be fully pronounced, and the stress gets shifted to it, since in Neo-Melanesian the stress falls automatically on the initial syllable of each word. When the phonetically first syllable receives the stress, as in ['sipiə] or ['siton] for the first two words cited above, then the intercalated vowel acquires full phonemic status, and we must now transcribe these words phonemically as /sipir/ and /siton/, respectively. In other regions, such as Jamaica, the initial *s-* is lost altogether: for example, Jamaican Creole /plít/ "split", /kwíiz/ "squeeze", or /káj/ "sky".

Inevitably, with alternations of these different types existing in pidgin languages (as they exist in all other languages of the world, though not necessarily to the same extent), there arise over-corrections. Speakers who know that, say, an initial /h-/ is often pronounced in some such word as /ambak/ "humbug" or /ariap/ "hurry up" where they do not normally pronounce it, are very likely to insert an initial /h-/ not only in such words but also in other words where it does not belong, and thus to produce, say, /hæšɪs/ instead of /æšɪs/ "ashes" or /haj/ instead of /aj/ "eye". Sometimes, these forms that vary from the standard language, either by simplification or by over-correction, are useful for missionaries and

others who are embarrassed by certain words that have taboo connotations in the language from which the words originated. Thus, English *arse* "hind quarters, buttocks" became /a(r)s/ in Melanesian
Pidgin, but had its meaning greatly extended, so that it could be
used in such transferred senses /as bılɔŋ trəbəl/ "the cause of the
trouble", or /as bılɔŋ ɔlgɛdər səmtıŋ/ "the source of everything"
(said of the Deity). In the early part of this century, the German
missionaries who approached Melanesian Pidgin as a true foreign
language were not worried by the meaning of the term /a(r)s/ in
English, and used it without any qualms. Other missionaries, native speakers of English, were more aware of the taboo origins of
this word and took to using the over-corrected form /has/ as their
standard in the meaning "cause, source". Similarly, the Neo-
Melanesian word /šıt/ does not mean "excrement", as its English
counterpart does, but has come to have primarily such transferred
meanings as "remainder, anything left behind", as in /šıt bılɔŋ
fajr/ "what is left behind from the fire, ashes". Squeamish speakers
of English often use the form /sıt bılɔŋ fajr/, or even the over-
corrected form /čıt bılɔŋ fajr/, to avoid what for them are the
taboo connotations of the variant beginning with /š/. These taboo
connotations exist only for the speaker of English; the Melanesian
speaker has no such associations with the word /šıt/, since the
normal term for "excrement" in Neo-Melanesian is /pɛkpɛk/.

A dialectal divergence in the source language is often reflected
by the existence of alternate forms in a derived pidgin or creole.
Thus English /r/ is reflected in several ways in Neo-Melanesian
and Neo-Solomonic: (1) by a tongue-tip flap or trill against the
inner side of the upper front teeth or against the gum-ridge, even
when the /r/ follows a vowel; (2) after certain vowels (/i e o u/),
by a semi-vowel [a̯] or [ə̯]; (3) after /a/, simply by greater length
of the vowel sound; and (4) in the combination /ər/, unstressed,
by loss of the /r/. Type 1 represents an earlier stage of English,
whereas types 2, 3, and 4 reflect the pronunciation of British
Commonwealth (including Australian) English. Diaphonically,
these various realizations of /r/ can still be represented perfectly
well by using the letter /r/ in our transcription; and this analysis
is borne out by the fact that, in many of these words, the /r/
phoneme reappears as the sound [r] when it comes before a vowel
in related forms: for instance, alongside of [si'piə̯] "spear" (noun)
we find [si'pirım] "to spear" (verb). However, some speakers are

now replacing the nonsyllabic vowel [ə] or [ạ], in words like [sⁱ'piə], by a fully syllabic vowel, so that for them such a word is no longer phonemically /spir/, but /spia/ or /spiə/. This substitution is of course greatly favored by the presence and influence of a number of Australian government officials, planters, traders, and missionaries in New Guinea, and of speakers of British English in similar rôles in the British Solomon Islands; their Commonwealth English pronunciation of the /r/ phoneme serves to give prestige to types 2, 3, and 4 of realization described at the beginning of this paragraph.

As far as can be told from such studies as have been carried out to date, the intonation and stress systems of pidgins and creoles reflect, at least in large part, those of the languages from which they are derived. Thus, in Haitian and other French-based creoles, stress automatically falls on the end of each word, as it does in French: for example, Haitian Creole /buke/ [bu'ke] "tired", /vodũ/ [vo'dũ] "vaudoun", /kõtribisjõ/ [kõtribi'sjõ] "contribution, tax"; since stress is automatic, it is not phonemically significant, as is the case also in French. The intonation of phrases and sentences in Haitian Creole involves relative direction of the pitch on successive syllables (gradual-rising for non-final phrases, rising-falling for final declarative phrases, sharp-rising for final interrogative phrases calling for a yes-or-no answer, etc.); this is the same type of intonation-structure that is found in French and the other Romance languages. In Neo-Melanesian, Neo-Solomonic, Chinese Pidgin English, Sranan, and other English-based pidgins and creoles, the intonation-pattern involves four relative levels of pitch, and combinations thereof on phrases and sentences, such as is found in English. (For instance, a declarative utterance passes from a middle level of pitch to a higher one and then to a lower one.)

Stress in English is not predictable: it can occur on the last syllable, or the next to the last, or the third from the last, or even earlier in the word; compare *contrást* (verb) with *cóntrast* (noun), and many similar pairs. Since it is not predictable, stress is phonemically significant in English. This is the situation in most English-based pidgins and creoles also: compare Chinese Pidgin English /píǧɪn/ "business" but /bɪlɔŋ/ "to be"; Jamaican Creole /tidíe/ "today" but /líedi/ "lady". Yet in many English-based pidgins and creoles, such as Neo-Melanesian and Neo-Solomonic, and in the Jamaican-derived Krio of Sierra Leone, the position of stress in the word is automatic, as all words are stressed on the first syllable except for recent loan-words from English: for example, Neo-Melanesian /kajkaj/ ['kai̯kai̯] "food, to eat"; /bɪlɔŋ/ ['bɪlɔŋ] "of, for"; /karapɛlə/ ['karapɛlə] "propeller". It is still open to question whether this loss of phonemic status for stress, through its being always placed on the first syllable, is due to the influence of one or more native languages acting as substrata, or is simply a continuation and generalization of a widespread habit of speakers of English and Germanic languages in general to put the stress as near the beginning of the word as possible, as in vulgar American English *cígarette, víolin, éclipse, séegar* or lower-class British English *gárridge* for *garage.*

A special problem with pidgins and creoles in whose formation African languages were involved is that of pitch-variation in individual syllables. As is well known, in a great many African languages, especially in West Africa (whence came most of the slaves imported into the Americas), the level of pitch on individual syllables is just as important as are the vowel and consonant phonemes in making a difference in the meanings of words. Thus, in Yòruba, a West African language, *ba* with a high tone means "meet, overtake"; *ba* with a middle tone, "hide"; *ba* with a low tone, "perch, roost". It used to be thought that tonemic features had not been carried over into the pidgins and creoles that have an African substratum, since African-type variations in tone are not found in any of the French-based creoles, in Papiamentu, or in Jamaican Creole, Gullah, Sranan, etc.[7] It has been shown, however, that in the speech of the Saramaccá Bush Negroes, tonemic features are highly important in morphological and syntactic combinations. Thus, for instance, the word *deési* "medicine" can show

[7]Voorhoeve (1961a, p. 3) mentions the existence of only one word in town Sranan in which the vowel with a gliding accent carries difference in meaning: /pôti/ "poor" versus /poti/ "to place". Is it possible that in the first of the two we have, rather, an occurrence of emphatic stress (involving automatic pitch-gliding), associated with the emotional connotations of the word, as opposed to normal stress in the second word? There is a similar phenomenon in Haitian Creole—e.g. in /ˈmãmã/ "enormous" vs. /mãmã̄/ "mother" (cf. Hall, 1953, §1.72, pp. 24–25); and in Jamaican Creole—e.g. in the positive /it kjaaŋ híit/ "it can eat" vs. the negative /it kjáaŋ hiit/ "it can't eat", with the highest pitch on the last syllable of the positive sentence but with high pitch on the next-to-the-last syllable and low pitch on the last syllable in the negative sentence (cf. Cassidy, 1961, pp. 29–30). In any case the presence of an African substratum in these phenomena seems obvious.

the following pitch variations, depending on what elements precede or follow it in the sentence (the acute accent here indicates high pitch, and its absence indicates low pitch); it becomes:

deesi   at the end of a negative construction

déési   dí déési "the medicine"

deésí   mi tá tjá deésí dá dí ómi "I am taking medicine to the man"

déésí   mi tá tjá déésí dá dí ómi "I am taking the medicine to the man".

In syntactical combinations, the presence or absence of a tonemic feature in Saramaccá can make such difference as that between the subject pronoun and the personal possessive construction: for example, /mi gó/ "I went" versus /mí wósu/ "my house".

In the light of the Saramaccá evidence, we must clearly revise previous conclusions concerning the absence of tonemic carryovers from African substratum in pidgins and creoles. The Saramaccá Bush Negroes, being the descendants of slaves who ran away up-country very early in the history of the colony, have been isolated for centuries from virtually all outside contact. Hence, if we find tonemic features in both Saramaccá and African languages, it is highly likely that the former has derived its tonemic characteristics from the latter, through direct transmission from one generation to the next. But Saramaccá and town Sranan are so closely related that it is clear that both are developments from a common ancestral form, seventeenth-century Guianan Pidgin English (which in its turn was a replacement for, and took over a great many features from, an even earlier Guianan Pidgin Portuguese); and these seventeenth-century pidgins must both have had tonemic features in their phonological structure. It is thus quite possible that other creoles that have an African substratum were, at an earlier time, tone languages, whose tonemic contrasts were later lost as the various creoles underwent the influence of the nontonal European official languages that their speakers imitated.

Up to this point we have been discussing the phonological patterns of pidgins and creoles, and emphasizing the joint rôle of the European and the native languages in their formation. In the phonetic realization of phonemic pattern, however, the balance is heavily weighted on the side of the substratum language(s). This is easily understandable: a pidgin has, by definition, no native speakers whose pronunciation might act as a guide or norm for those who learn it, and hence all who use it will pronounce it with whatever articulatory habits, or "accent," they have in their native speech. In normal language-learning, a foreign accent is eliminated to a greater or lesser extent as the learner becomes more proficient in the new language and does a better job of imitating its native speakers; but in the use of a pidgin, any such incentive is absent. Hence the accent of a substratum language can remain in a pidgin and then, when the pidgin is creolized, be transmitted to later generations who learn it as their mother tongue.

The influence of substratum languages on phonetics can easily be documented in any aspect of pronunciation. For instance, although the English tense vowels /i e o u/ are usually pronounced with a certain amount of diphthongization [iʲ eʲ oʷ uʷ], many other languages (including those of Africa, China, and Melanesia) do not have this type of diphthongized pronunciation of their vowels; hence Neo-Melanesian, Neo-Solomonic, and the other English-based pidgins and creoles normally have nondiphthongized vowels in such words as /go/ "go"—['go], not ['goʷ]—or /mi/ "I, me"— ['mi], not ['miʲ]. As mentioned earlier, West African languages have a widespread characteristic of nasalization, both as a phonemically distinct feature and as an aspect of over-all articulation: nasal consonants tend to render adjacent vowels at least partially nasal, and nasalized vowels "infect" neighboring consonants and even syllables, through an anticipation or a continuation of the nasal articulation. These pronunciation-habits are widely reflected in Negro creoles in the Americas, as in Haitian Creole /rēmē/ "to love" [rē'mē], or /ānū/ "let's go" ['ɔ̃'nū]. The Melanesian languages have a widespread contrast between consonants whose onset is nasalized—[ᵐb ⁿd ⁿg]—and those whose onset is not nasalized. The nonprenasalized consonants are, in Melanesian pronunciation, usually voiced—[b d g]—between vowels and voiceless—[p t k]— elsewhere; the prenasalized consonants occur in Melanesian languages only between vowels, but Melanesians have little trouble in articulating them at the beginning of words. These habits are carried over into Neo-Melanesian, so that /bæk/ "back" is phonetically ['ᵐbæk] or ['ᵐbɛk], /tabak/ "tobacco" is often ['taᵐbak], /sɪdawn/ "sit" is ['sɪⁿda̰un], etc.; and /pɪg/ becomes ['pɪk] or ['pik], /rajd/ "ride" becomes ['raḭt], and so forth.

Normally these substratum influences in pronunciation affect only the "accent," that is, the nonsignificant aspects of the way the pidgin or creole is spoken. On occasion, however, as often happens in linguistic change, a non-significant (allophonic) variant may come to acquire significance if the environment in which it occurs is changed. Thus, the contrast between prenasalized and nonprenasalized consonants in Melanesian languages corresponds to that between voiced and voiceless consonants in English and other European languages, in initial position and between vowels; but at the end of a word, the Melanesian has only the nonprenasalized voiceless variety of consonant, so that both /pɪg/ "pig" and /kɪk/ "kick" frequently end in [k]. At an earlier stage, under German rule in New Guinea, this neutralization of the contrast between voiced and voiceless final consonants was reinforced by the pronunciation habits of the German missionaries, who carried over into Pidgin English their own neutralization of the contrast between voiced and voiceless consonants at the end of words; for example, German *bunt* "many-colored" and *Bund* "league" both end in the same consonant phoneme, voiceless /t/. If all speakers of the language treated word-final consonants in this way, then we would have to say that the language had only voiceless consonants in this position, and we would have to transcribe the word for "pig" as /pɪk/, etc. However, the situation is complicated by two factors: first, many Europeans who use Neo-Melanesian do make the contrast between voiceless and voiced consonants in word-final position and have done so from the beginning; and, second, many, though by no means all, Melanesians have been able to imitate the Europeans in making this contrast, and an increasing number are doing so. Under these circumstances, the best formulation is to set up a contrast between voiceless and voiced consonants in all positions, and to note that some speakers neutralize it at the end of a word.

REFERENCES

Phonology of Neo-Melanesian: Hall, 1943a (chap. i), 1956a.
Phonology of Haitian Creole: Evans, 1938; Hall, 1953 (chap. i).
Nasalization in Haitian Creole: Hall, 1950e.
Tonemic features in Saramaccá: Voorhoeve, 1961d.

Orthography

U P to now, we have been discussing the pidgin and creole languages themselves, that is to say, as they are spoken, without regard to the way they are written. Our culture lays so much stress upon writing, and so neglects the facts of language, that people often ask: "But are these languages written? Do they have orthographies? Is there literature written in them, or can literature ever be written in them?"—as if such questions were important in evaluating a language. It can immediately be answered that pidgins and creoles can perfectly well be written, and that if a pidgin or a creole has no orthography, one can easily be provided to represent the facts of the language just as well as any other orthography does for its particular language. Similarly, literature—which can exist without being written and actually has done so throughout most of human history—can be created in pidgin or a creole language as well as in any other. Yet, due to historical accidents involving nonlinguistic factors, the situation is considerably more complicated; we cannot simply say that orthographies have been or can be provided, and let the matter go at that.

Like almost all languages, pidgins and creoles come into existence without orthographies. (We must say "almost all," because artificial languages, like Esperanto and Ido, are usually invented and constructed together with their orthographies from the start.) Pidgins arise to meet elementary needs, and develop in more or less casual contact situations; hence, at first, they function as purely oral media of communication. Creoles likewise normally originate among humble folk of the lowest classes, who—like the Negro slaves in the Americas, or the New Guinea natives—are almost always illiterate. In this respect, pidgins and creoles are just like the majority of human languages, for which no orthographical tradition as yet exists, or for which spelling-systems have been devised only in the last few decades.

Historically, the first persons to feel the need of writing down pidgin or creole languages were nineteenth- and twentieth-century travelers, novelists, and other members of the European speech-communities on whose languages the modern pidgins and creoles are based. Such writers used the pidgin simply for giving local color, to add authenticity to the scenes portrayed in their memoirs or tales. Both the writers and their public looked upon pidgins or creoles as mere "corruptions" or "degradations" of the great "languages of culture." Hence the first graphic representations of pidgin and creole languages, intended for readers who were already familiar with Western European standard orthographies, were based on these orthographies, with no change beyond a few slight alterations to represent some presumed "defect" in pronunciation or in grammar. For example, we find sentences like Beach-la-Mar *Wha' for you put 'im diss long fire, now fire he kaikai?* "Why did you put the dish in the fire, and the fire devoured it?"—presumably standing for /wɔfɔr ju putɪm dɪs lɔŋ fajr, na fajr i-kajkaj?/; or Haitian Creole *Douvant poul', ravètt pas jamais gaignin raison* "in front of the chicken, the cockroach is never right", for /duvã pul, ravèt pa žãmē gēnē rèzõ/.[1] Obviously, a transcription based on a European orthography is helpful only to a European reader; even so, it affords nothing but a confused or inexact idea of the pronunciation of the pidgin or creole involved. The inaccuracies and irregularities of such an orthography, however, make it worse than useless for those who speak the pidgin or the creole and need it for serious purposes.

At the opposite extreme from these dilettantish transcriptions are phonemic transcriptions prepared by linguistic analysts, on the basis of as complete and accurate an analysis as possible. Such phonemic transcriptions have been provided, for instance, by Agard and Harris for Papiamentu, by Taylor for Dominican Creole, by Morgan for Louisiana Creole, by Voorhoeve for Sranan and for Saramaccá, etc. However, such phonemic transcriptions normally

---

[1] For further examples of this type of orthography for Beach-la-Mar (South Seas Pidgin English), see the novels and short stories of Jack London; for Haitian Creole, see the versions of La Fontaine's fables made by Georges Sylvain.

serve only the scholarly public, and do not have much influence on developments in the practical world. This is due, undoubtedly, to their excessively consistent character; most persons who have learned to write in our West European orthographies are unhappy unless a spelling-system has irregularities and inconsistencies. Furthermore, strange-looking symbols such as ŋ, ɛ, ɔ, ə, etc., usually disorient the man-in-the-street, who has been brought up to believe that the twenty-six letters of the Roman alphabet are permanently and definitively sufficient for all possible orthographical needs.

However, a phonemic transcription is extremely useful as the basis for an ethnophonemic orthography, that is, an orthography which follows the principle of having each grapheme (unit of written shape) correspond to a phoneme of the language and vice-versa, but which makes free use of compound graphemes and other orthographic devices found in the official language dominant in whatever region is involved. This facilitates the natives' later learning of the official language and its orthography. Thus, in a region where Spanish is the dominant cultural language, for a native language that has a phoneme /č/, an ethnophonemic orthography will use ch, rather than č, but will represent /u/ by u, since Spanish orthography has ch and u in these respective values. In a region where French is the official language, however, ch will be used for /š/, tch for /č/, and /u/ will be represented by ou (rather than by u, which in French orthography is reserved for the phoneme /y/), to accord with the principles of French spelling.

Most practical orthographies for the use of natives in spelling pidgins and creoles have been of the ethnophonemic variety. At first, such spelling systems were usually the product of missionary efforts, aimed at using the language for gospel work and for conversion. Thus, in New Guinea, the Roman Catholic Societas Verbi Divini (S.V.D.)—or "Society of the Divine Word"—has prepared an extensive series of publications: biblical tales, stories of saints, newspapers, and most recently a version of the Sunday Gospels and other parts of the Bible. The S.V.D.'s orthography for Neo-Melanesian was developed principally at their missionary center at Alexishafen (whence it is known as the Alexishafen orthography), chiefly by German missionaries in the period before 1914. As already pointed out, these speakers of German had no background of English language or spelling habits to distort their view of

Melanesian Pidgin; they treated Pidgin seriously and as a completely foreign language, they did a systematic job of analyzing it, and the resultant orthography was the best so far developed for Neo-Melanesian. In the Alexishafen spelling the Beach-la-Mar question quoted earlier in this chapter would read: *Wofor you putim dish long fair, na fair i kaikai?*.

A similar orthography was developed for Haitian Creole between 1940 and 1945 by the Protestant missionary McConnell, following the International Phonetic Alphabet (IPA) very closely; it was then revised, on the advice of the literacy expert Frank Laubach, to make certain adaptations to the local official language, French. The resultant McConnell-Laubach orthography gave a closely phonemically-based representation of Haitian Creole pronunciation, and at the same time could be written on any French typewriter or set up in any French-language print-shop. In this orthography the Haitian Creole sentence quoted earlier would read: *Douvâ poul, ravèt pa jâmê gêgnê rézô*. Note the use of *ou* for /u/ and of *j* for /ž/, in accordance with French spelling habits; the circumflex, which in present-day French orthography has virtually no function in representing any phonological feature, is given the function of representing nasalization. Since Haitian Creole has a phonological contrast between /ĩ/ (as in /pĩga/ "take care!") and /ẽ/ (as in /zẽga/ "black-and-white striped"), these two nasalized vowels are represented by *î* and *ê*, respectively. The McConnell-Laubach orthography also used *w* for the phoneme /w/, as in /wè/ "see" *wè*.

Certain prejudices on the part of those literate in French, however, led to opposition to the McConnell-Laubach orthography, because of its use of the circumflex for nasalization and of the letter *w*, which was thought, erroneously, to be "made in the U.S.A." and to indicate a desire to "Anglicize the language"! A further adaptation of the McConnell-Laubach orthography, made by Charles-Fernand Pressoir, replaced *w* by *ou* and represented /Ṽ/ by *Vn*, /Ṽn/ by *Vnn* or *Vn-n*, and /Vn/ by *V-n*: for example, /wè/ "see" *ouè*; /tõtõ/ "uncle" *tonton*; /tãn/ "wait" *tan-n*; and /le^ogan/ "Léogane [town-name]" *Léoga-n*. Although it is more cumbersome and less easily learned by the monolingual native speaker of Haitian Creole, the Pressoir adaptation had greater appeal to persons already literate in French, because it collided less with their established orthographical habits; and it appealed to national feelings, since it bore the name of a Haitian. Hence it received greater favor with the élite and was ultimately established by the Haitian government in 1961 as the officially recognized orthography for Haitian Creole. In this spelling, our sample sentence would read: *Douvan poul, ravèt pa janmin gignin rézon.* Chiefly as a result of the work of missionaries, literacy is becoming more and more widespread among the speakers of those languages for which orthographies have been provided. But in the course of its diffusion, the orthography of any language (not only pidginized or creolized, but also full-sized) inevitably undergoes change, due especially to dialect mixture. The Alexishafen orthography for Neo-Melanesian presupposes a phonemic contrast between voiced stop consonants (*b, d, g*) and voiceless ones (*p, t, k*); this contrast is in fact present in the usage of many, perhaps a majority, of the users of Neo-Melanesian, both natives of New Guinea and Europeans. However, as we have seen, there are also many speakers who carry over into Neo-Melanesian the contrast between prenasalized consonants—[^{m}b], [^{n}d], [^{ŋ}g]—and non-prenasalized consonants—[b] ~ [p], [d] ~ [t], [g] ~ [k]. These speakers are likely to write *gut* for *gud* "well", *dok* for *dog*, etc., and also *siupim* for *siubim* /sjʊbɪm/ "shove". Similarly, as we saw in Chapter 3, footnote 6, a number of speakers merge /p/ and /f/, /b/ and /v/; such speakers are likely to write *paitim* "strike, beat" instead of *faitim* /fajtɪm/, *gutpela* "good" instead of *gudfela* /gʊdfɛlə/, and so forth. Furthermore, speakers of European languages, on hearing such pronunciations as ['ta^{m}bu] for /tabu/ "prohibition" or ['sɪ^{n}daʊn] for /sɪdawn/ "sit", are likely to write them as *tambu, sindaun,* and the like. Some of these spellings have found their way into the Alexishafen orthography—for instance, *kirap* for /girəp/ "arise", *tambu,* and *sindaun.* The result is of course an orthography that reflects a mixture of dialects and of orthographical habits. It is no more mixed—in fact it is probably rather less so—than those of our familiar West European languages in the Renaissance and even nowadays; but just the same it causes unhappiness to those who have been taught that in matters of language and especially of writing there is only one right way to say or to spell any given word.

A government or some official agency like UNESCO normally takes an interest in literacy, and hence in providing an orthography for a pidgin or creole, only after private agencies, especially missionaries, have become interested. This has been the case in New Guinea, in Haiti, in Curaçao (with Papiamentu), in Dutch Guiana (with Sranan), and probably elsewhere as well. This delay is due principally to the low social position of native languages, particularly of those that are considered "bastard" or "corrupt." In many situations, such a negative attitude can even induce a speech-community to refuse to be interested in reading and writing a creole, even if it is the native language of the entire group. On the island of Mauritius (a British territory), it is reported that public opinion insists on children learning to read and write, from the first year of school on, not in Mauritian Creole (of which they all have an excellent knowledge on entering school), but in English or French (of which they do not know a single word when they begin their schooling). Naturally, an educational process carried on in a language of which the students do not know a word is sure to encounter difficulties and to risk failure from the start. But when governments begin campaigns against illiteracy, they normally use the orthographies provided by missionary or similar groups. Here again, literacy-campaigns are usually subject to all kinds of outside influences that are irrelevant to education or to language problems —as when, in Haiti, one administration began a literacy-campaign; then there was a revolution, and another administration took over and abandoned the campaign, fearing that it might be too closely associated with the previous régime. The success of such literacy-campaigns has been quite good in many regions (for example, in New Guinea and—as long as it lasted—in Haiti), but it is of course correlated with the accuracy of the phonemic basis on which the orthography has been prepared.

Unfortunately, neither the accuracy of the orthography nor the success of literacy-campaigns has as much influence on the general public as have other factors that have little or no relevance for the language itself. Among these, the most influential is the spelling of the mother language (English for Neo-Melanesian, French for Haitian Creole, etc.) or of the official language (Dutch, in the case of Papiamentu or Sranan). Many naïve persons want to introduce spellings that are not functional, but that reflect more or less faithfully the extravagances of traditional orthography. (Such people, naturally, do not recognize these features as extravagances, but think them to be the "real" language.) They think that they are thereby "improving" the pidgin or creole, or bringing it "closer" to the mother language, or helping the natives to learn the official language at a later stage. To this group we must add also a growing number of natives who, when they have received a certain amount of schooling in a European language, think that the orthographical irregularities of the "language of culture" have more prestige than do the more simple and regular, but less elegant and showy, spellings of the pidgin or the creole. In this, as in many other orthographical and linguistic phenomena that may at first sight appear inexplicably irrational, there is a strong element of what Thorstein Veblen called "conspicuous waste" and of "trained incapacity."[2]

Hence we find, especially in the mimeographed regional newspapers put out by territorial departments of education—for instance, the *Rabaul News* or the *Lae Gaeramut* in New Guinea—a host of Anglicisms in the spelling of Neo-Melanesian. Often, these Anglicisms consist of entire words or phrases written in conventional English spelling (*council*, say, instead of Neo-Melanesian *kaunsil*), giving the same impression as the Latin expressions that used to be inserted in the midst of Romance texts in the Middle Ages.[3] In many instances, the spelling of words is changed only in part, producing an orthographical mish-mash which is neither wholly English nor wholly Neo-Melanesian: for example, *heppi* or *heppy* for *hepi* "happy" and *walkebaut* for *wokebaut* "walk". The result is a weird mixture, as in sentences like *Today i bikpela de bilong ol i welcomim Duke of Edinburgh i kamap long aerodrome bilong city Rabaul* "Today is the great day for the welcome of [*literally*, for them to welcome] the Duke of Edinburgh, who will arrive at the Rabaul city airport". In normal Neo-Melanesian, this would be *Tude i bikpela de bilong ol i heloim Dyuk bilong Edinboro i kamap long ples balus bilong siti Rabaul. Dyuk* "Duke" and *Edinboro* "Edinburgh" would presumably be inevitable loanwords in any case, but the phrase *Duke of Edinburgh* is a crass Anglicism, as are also *welcomim* for normal *heloim* "to greet", and

[2] For a discussion of these Veblenian concepts, see Hall, 1960.

[3] For example, in a ninth-century Old French sermon on Jonah (the Latin words and their translations are italicized): *Habuit misericordiam* si cum il *semper* solt haveir de *peccatore* e *sic liberat* de cel peril quet il *habebat decretum* que *super* els metreiet "*He had pity*, just as he *always* is accustomed to have, on the *sinner* and *so he freed* [them] from that danger which he *had decreed* that he would put *upon* them". I once heard, in 1949, a sermon in Haitian Creole which mixed Creole and French in exactly the same way as the ninth-century preacher mixed early French and Latin.

aerodrome for *ples balus* "airport"; and *today* and *city* are Angli-
cized spellings for normal *tude* and *siti*. The New Guinea native is
normally disoriented by this type of unnecessary Anglicism; I have
heard such a native read off *council* as /saunsıl/—on the highly
rational assumption that, if *c* stood for /s/ in one place, it ought to
stand for /s/ everywhere else—and then, understandably, fail to
identify the resultant word with what he would normally have both
pronounced and spelled as *kaunsil*. Orthographical irregularities of
this type not only do not help the native to learn English, but they
confuse him and act as downright hindrances to his understanding
of both written Neo-Melanesian and English.

Still other linguistically irrelevant factors are often at work to
confuse the relationship between language and spelling: factors of
a religious, political, or social nature. On occasion, missionaries of
differing denominations have extended their religious rivalry to the
orthographical sphere. For instance, at an earlier stage the Luth-
eran missionaries in New Guinea, in the orthographies that they
prepared for native languages and later extended to Pidgin, used
the character "ŋ" for the velar nasal, whereas the Roman Catholics,
not having this letter available in their type fonts, used the combination *ng* in the same value. It is of course irrelevant, in a practical orthography, which of these two graphemic representations is
used for the phoneme /ŋ/, provided it be used consistently; but at
least for a time the use of the one or the other was a kind
of shibboleth in the rivalry between the two groups. Differences
of this type can easily be overcome provided there is a reasonable
amount of good will on both sides; in recent years, the various
missionary groups and the government in New Guinea have agreed
to establish a single, fairly uniform Neo-Melanesian orthography,
which was used, for instance, in the dictionary published in 1957
by Father Francis Mihalić, S.V.D. Similarly, in Suriname, a spell-
ing-compromise was reached in 1957, combining most of the best
features of the orthographies of three groups: the Moravian
Brethren, the Roman Catholic Church, and the cultural-nationalist
movement *Wie Eegie Sanie* (/wi éxi sáni/ "Our Own Things").

If socio-economic and political interests are at stake, however,
the outlook for a rational, easily learned orthography can be considerably darker than it would be if only intellectual considerations
are involved. In Haiti, Creole was for a long time strongly dis-
favored socially; its use was not allowed in any official connection

(neither in school nor in court nor in Parliament, etc.), even though the entire population of the country learn Creole from earliest infancy. The upper classes (perhaps 10 per cent of the population) are primarily mulatto, and are bilingual native speakers of Creole and the provincial standard French of the region;[4] the rest of the population are almost pure African, and only a relatively small proportion of them (perhaps another 15 per cent of the population) have any extensive command of French. The ruling élite were opposed to any recognition of Creole, because its official use would have transferred power from the currently ruling minority to the people as a whole.

Because of this fear on the part of those who were literate in French, the McConnell-Laubach orthography, as one of the major instruments whereby literacy could be spread and the truth (on all matters) could be made better known, was made the object of attack and distortion by its upper-class opponents. In order to render public opinion hostile to the literacy-campaigns, various rumors were spread: for example, that the McConnell-Laubach orthography was an instrument of Protestant propaganda (as if it could not be used by Roman Catholics as well); that it was a trick of Yankee imperialism and colonialism (McConnell was born in Ireland, and was a missionary of the British Methodist church) designed to detach Haiti from its century-old relations with France and French culture (which have never been allowed to mean anything to at least 75 per cent of the population); or that it was a Communist device aimed at gaining the support of the lower classes by means of an easily learned orthography. Conservative laymen and the ecclesiastical hierarchy favored a rival orthography which was much more difficult to learn, because it was full of etymological and pseudo-etymological spellings imitating French (for example, *prend'* for /prã/ "take", *zétoile* for /ze^twal/ "star") and other orthographies (as in the spelling *llo* for /jo/ "they", "them", because of a supposed derivation of this form from Spanish *ellos*, suggested by dilettantish amateurs). It is to be hoped that, with

[4] One of the major reasons that the Haitian upper classes cling so desperately to French language and culture is their extreme insecurity vis-à-vis their partly African origin. Upper-class Haitians will often go to great lengths to deny anything African in their national culture or behavior-patterns, as when some of them maintain that vaudoun dances and ceremonies have no African origins at all, but are simply indigenous developments of seventeenth-century Breton folk-dances.

the adoption of a government-sponsored national orthography, this type of obscurantism has disappeared for good.

Such difficulties are not limited, of course, to pidgins and creoles; they occur wherever an upper class has a vested interest in preventing the mass of the population from easily becoming literate and from gaining access to sources of information—in Mexico and in Africa, for example. In the case of noncreolized languages, however, a factor is lacking that is especially important with pidgins and creoles: the crushing weight and continually increasing cultural prestige of the mother language, which usually serves also as the official language. For this reason, it is not unlikely—in fact it is very likely—that the irrational influence of European spelling habits on the orthographies of pidgins and creoles will not only continue but increase. The final result may well prove similar to those produced by the influence of Graeco-Latin spellings on the orthography of French and English from the Renaissance down to modern times. In situations where there are few or no vested interests at stake, a fairly rational ethnophonemic orthography can often be decided upon by the missionary and educational agencies involved, and can spread with official support; but where a conservative upper-class minority wishes (even if quite subconsciously) to keep itself in power by denying the benefits of a rational spelling-system to the speakers of an indigenous creole, there is little that can be done as long as political power remains in the hands of the minority group.

REFERENCES

Graphemics of pidgins and creoles: Hall, 1959c.

"Conspicuous waste" and "trained incapacity" in linguistic and graphemic behavior: Hall, 1960.

Table of Neo-Melanesian orthographies: Hall, 1957b.

Sranan orthography: Voorhoeve, 1961a.

Saramaccá orthography: Voorhoeve, 1959.

Haitian Creole: McConnell-Laubach orthography exemplified in Hall, 1953; Gallicizing orthography in Faine, 1937, 1939. Sylvain, 1936, uses phonemic transcription. Discussion of Haitian Creole orthographies in Hall, 1949d; table of orthographies in Hall, 1953 (§1.9, pp. 25–27).

Morphology

THE "grammar" of a language is usually thought to involve primarily its morphology, or the variations in linguistic form, which it manifests in such alternations as those between singular and plural in English nouns (*book, books; man, men; child, children*) or between the simple form, the past, and the past participle in English verbs (*sing, sang, sung; drive, drove, driven*). We usually, though often unreflectingly, set up the morphology of Latin as a standard against which to measure that of other languages. Ever since the sixteenth century, it has been common to say that a language has "no grammar" if it does not have, say, gender, number, case, tense, or other features of Latin in its morphological patterning. From this point of view, it has become a commonplace to consider pidgin and creole languages as devoid of grammar.

A broader view of grammar leads us to recognize, however, that it includes not only morphology but syntax, and that it is not to be restricted to a Latinizing model. Not only variations in linguistic forms, but also the order and the types of combinations in which the forms occur—the *syntax* of a language—are part of grammar. Many languages show little or no variation in their forms, but have extensive and often complicated syntactic structures; this is the case, for example, with English and Chinese. Each language has its own grammatical pattern, which we must always describe in terms of its own structure, not in those of any other language—Latin, say —or of any aprioristic pseudo-logical considerations imposed on it from outside.

In dealing with a language of an unfamiliar kind, therefore, our

49

first task is to find what its forms are, which forms occur with which, and what classes of forms must therefore be recognized. (We have intentionally used the term *form*, rather than *word*, because often we shall be dealing with morphemes—functional units of linguistic form—that are smaller than single words: for instance, prefixes and suffixes like the *mis-* of *misuse,* the *-s* of *hats,* and the *-ing* of *working.*) Here, we must establish a highly important distinction between two types of forms: *free* and *bound.* In most languages, some morphemes can occur independently, and others normally cannot. So, for instance, the forms *talk, read,* and *hear* can be used with or without added elements in English; but the elements we add to them—such as *-s* in the present third singular, *-(e)d* in the past, or *-ing*—cannot be used alone. If a form can be used independently of others, we call it a *free form;* if it has to be used in conjunction with some other form, it is called a *bound form.* The distinction between free and bound forms is crucial in linguistic analysis, and we shall find that it is one of the keys to understanding the grammatical structure of pidgins and creoles, as well as that of other languages.

When we examine any pidgin or creole, we immediately find that it does not consist (as many people mistakenly think) of words thrown together without rhyme or reason, nor yet wholly of independent words with no grammatical changes at all. We can use Neo-Melanesian as our example of the procedure to follow in finding the form-classes of a pidgin language. Tables 1, 2, and 3 contain examples of three bound forms that serve as inflectional suffixes, and of one that is prefixed to third-person predicates. With the help of these bound forms we can arrive at a satisfactory classification of the other forms of Neo-Melanesian. The three suffixes are: /-fɛlə/, with the meaning of "more than one"; /-fɛlə/, without plural meaning and serving only to mark one particular form-class of the language; and /-ɪm/, meaning "a direct object is involved". The prefix is /i-/.

On examining first the examples in Table 1, we find the suffix /-fɛlə/, with the meaning "plural", added to two morphemes— /mi/ "I, me" and /ju/ "you" (singular)—thus forming the plurals /mifɛlə/ "we, us" and /jufɛlə/ "you". These four forms are close enough in form and meaning to the customary definition of "pronoun" that we can apply this label to them. In addition, there are two other forms—/ɛm/ "he, him; she, her; it" and /ɔl/ "they,

TABLE 1

mi go "I go"
mi kajkaj "I eat"
ɛm i-fajtɪm mi "he hits me"
ju lʊkɪm mi "you see me"
haws bɪlɔŋ mi "house of me, my house"
papa bɪlɔŋ mi "my father"
lɔŋ mi "to me"
wəntajm mi "with me"

mifɛlə go "we go"
mifɛla kajkaj "we eat"
ɛm i-fajtɪm mifɛlə "he hits us"
ju lʊkɪm mifɛlə "you see us"
haws bɪlɔŋ mifɛlə "house of us, our house"
papa bɪlɔŋ mifɛlə "our father"
lɔŋ mifɛlə "to us"
wəntajm mifɛlə "with us"

ju go "you [sing.] go"
ju kajkaj "you [sing.] eat"
ɛm i-fajtɪm ju "he hits you [sing.]"
mi lʊkɪm ju "I see you [sing.]"
haws bɪlɔŋ ju "your [sing.] house"
papa bɪlɔŋ ju "your [sing.] father"
lɔŋ ju "to you [sing.]"
wəntajm ju "with you [sing.]"

jufɛlə go "you [pl.] go"
jufɛlə kajkaj "you [pl.] eat"
ɛm i-fajtɪm jufɛlə "he hits you [pl.]"
mi lʊkɪm jufɛlə "I see you [pl.]"
haws bɪlɔŋ jufɛlə "your [pl.] house"
papa bɪlɔŋ jufɛlə "your [pl.] father"
lɔŋ jufɛlə "to you [pl.]"
wəntajm jufɛlə "with you [pl.]"

them"—which do not follow the same formal pattern as /mi/, /mifɛlə/, /ju/, and /jufɛlə/, but which do parallel them in meaning and function: that is, they can be used the same way in sentences, occurring as subjects, direct objects, and after such forms as /bɪlɔŋ/ "of", /lɔŋ/ "to, at", and /wəntajm/ "with". In addition to these six pronominal forms, Neo-Melanesian also has a special form, /jumi/ "we" = "you and I, you and me". This form is often called "inclusive," because it includes the hearer, as opposed to /mifɛlə/ "we" = "the other person(s) and me, but excluding you, the hearer". Melanesian languages have exactly the same kind of distinction between inclusive and exclusive in their pronoun-system, and Neo-Melanesian /jumi/ represents a direct carry-over from Melanesian patterns of grammar in its semantic structure, but not in its form.

We have now established one class of Neo-Melanesian forms, the pronouns, partly on the basis of form (the possibility of adding the plural suffix /-fɛlə/ to /mi/ and /ju/) and partly on a syntactic basis. Table 2 gives us the means of distinguishing another class. We notice that /-fɛlə/, without any separate meaning, is suffixed to a number of one-syllable elements like /gʊd/ "good", /bɪg/ "large", /blæk/ "dark-colored", /smɔl/ "little" (and many others

TABLE 2

gʊdfɛlə mæn "(a) good man"
bɪgfɛlə meri "(a) big woman"
blækfɛlə mæn "(a) dark-colored man"
smɔlfɛlə haws "(a) little house"
nufɛlə hæɳjkɪčɪf "(a) new handkerchief"
wənfɛlə məŋki "one boy, a boy"
tufɛlə məŋki "two boys"
trifɛlə məŋki "three boys"
forfɛlə məŋki "four boys"
fajvfɛlə məŋki "five boys"
sɪkɪsfɛlə məŋki "six boys"
dɪsfɛlə məŋki "this boy, these boys"
səmfɛlə məŋki "some boy, some boys"
plɛntifɛlə məŋki ⎫
plɛnti məŋki   ⎬ "many boys"
                 ⎭

BUT

lɪklɪk haws "(a) little house"
lɔŋlɔŋ mæn "(a) crazy man"
rəbɪš mæn "(a) man without wealth or standing in the community"
ɔlgedər mæn "all (the) men"

that we have not listed here). It also occurs after /wən/ "one", /tu/ "two", etc. (including in this group also /sɪkɪs/ "six" and /sɛvɛn/ "seven") and after /dɪs-/ "this", /səm-/ "some", /nədər-/ "another", and, optionally, /plɛnti/ "many". These forms to which our second suffix /-fɛlə/ may be added can safely be labelled "adjectives," with the special subdivisions of "numerals" for /wənfɛlə/, /tufɛlə/, etc., and "demonstratives" and "indefinites" for /dɪsfɛlə/, /səmfɛlə/, /nədərfɛlə/, and /plɛnti(fɛlə)/. As with the pronouns /ɛm/ and /ɔl/, we find likewise among the adjectives a number of forms that do not have the morphological characteristic of the group—that is, they do not take the meaningless suffix /-fɛlə/— but they behave like the others when they occur in syntactical combinations: for example, /lɪklɪk/ "little", /lɔŋlɔŋ/ "crazy", /rəbɪš/ "without standing in the community".

Our definition of adjectives for Neo-Melanesian, therefore, is: a class of forms that (1) when monosyllabic or numeral or demonstrative-indefinite, take the meaningless suffix /-fɛlə/ and can stand before such words as /haws/ "house", /mæn/ "man", /meri/

"woman", /məŋki/ "boy", etc.; and (2) when of more than one syllable (not numeral or demonstrative-indefinite) do not take /-fɛlə/ but in other respects behave like those of Type 1 just mentioned. Notice, by the way, that the old traditional pseudo-philosophical definition of adjectives as words "denoting a quality or accidence" has vanished; it is both less accurate and less helpful than a definition in terms of linguistic form and function in whatever language we are dealing with, in this instance Neo-Melanesian.

In Table 3, we have a number of forms that can occur both with and without the suffix /-ɪm/. The feature of meaning common to all the occurrences of /-ɪm/ can be summed up as "presence of a direct object in the situation", whether there is a further element in the sentence telling us what that direct object is (as in the middle column) or not (as in the right-hand column). We can borrow two terms from Hungarian grammar, and call the forms without /-ɪm/ "subjective" and those with /-ɪm/ "objective." There is a close parallel between Hungarian and Neo-Melanesian in this matter of subjective and objective conjugations:

	"I read"	"I read the book"	"I read it"
Neo-Melanesian	mi rid	mi ridɪm bʊk	mi ridɪm
Hungarian	olvasok	olvasom a könyvet	olvasom

TABLE 3

mi rid "I read"	mi ridɪm bʊk "I read a book"	mi ridɪm "I read it"
mi lʊk "I look"	mi lʊkɪm mæn "I see a man"	mi lʊkɪm "I see him"
ju fajt "you fight"	ju fajtɪm birua "you hit the enemy"	ju fajtɪm "you hit him"
ɛm i-sɪŋawt "she calls"	ɛm i-sɪŋawtɪm meri "she calls the woman"	ɛm i-sɪŋawtɪm "she calls her"
ɔl i-krɔs "they are angry"	ɔl i-krɔsɪm dɪsfɛlə bɔj "they are angry at this native"	ɔl i-krɔsɪm "they are angry at him"
mašin i-bəgərəp "the machine is wrecked"	ɛm i-bəgərəpɪm mašin "he wrecked the machine"	ɛm i-bəgərəpɪm "he wrecked it"
abus i-kʊk "the food cooks, is cooked"	fajr i-kʊkɪm abus "the fire cooks, burns the meat"	fajr i-kʊkɪm "the fire cooks, burns it"

BUT:

	mi gat tufɛlə hæn "I have two hands"	mi gat "I have it"

One especial pecularity of the suffix /-ɪm/ is that when it occurs with a word already provided with an adverbial suffix like /-əp/ "up", it is, at least in older usage, repeated both after the word itself and after the suffix: for example, /fʊləp/ "be filled", but /fʊlɪməpɪm/ "to fill [something]". In more recent usage, however (perhaps because, as has been suggested to me, Melanesians noticed Europeans' amusement at this formation and concluded that it was intentionally ridiculous), the objective suffix /-ɪm/ is used only once with such forms, either before or after the abverbial suffix, as in /fʊlɪməp/ or /fʊləpɪm/.

The presence of the objective suffix /-ɪm/ enables us to set up a third Neo-Melanesian form-class, which we can of course label "verbs." There is one exception, however, to the general principle that verbs take the suffix /-ɪm/: at the bottom of Table 3 is given the one verb that never, in normal usage, takes this suffix, namely /gat/ "have". (To say /mi gatɪm/ "I have it" is a Europeanism that no normal Melanesian speaker would ever use at the present time.) The very fact that pidgin languages show little pecularities like this is evidence that they are normal languages; no linguistic structure is water-tight in its organization, and pidgin and creole languages conform to this rule.

Often, there are divergences of meaning between the subjective and the objective forms of Neo-Melanesian verbs. The most outstanding example of this is /kajkaj/ "eat". At first glance, it would seem that /kajkaj/ should have been mentioned in the preceding paragraph along with /gat/ as a verb that does not take /-ɪm/ with a direct object,[1] since we find sentences like /mi kajkaj abus/ "I eat meat", or /ɔl i-save kajkaj mæn/ "they are in the habit of eating men, they are cannibals". But, on looking farther, we find that /kajkajɪm/ does occur, relatively rarely, with the meaning "bite", as in /snek i-kajkajɪm mi/ "a snake bit me", and /kajkaj/ is in fact a subjective form meaning "feed on". Often, a verb in the subjective has passive meaning, whereas the objective is necessarily active: for example, /stɪk i-brok/ "the stick is broken", but /mi brokɪm stɪk/ "I break the stick".

With the exception of these three classes—pronouns, adjectives, and verbs—the other forms are all invariable. Nevertheless, we can distinguish several different classes among them, by observing the

[1] It was treated this way in Hall, 1943a, §2.13.2, pp. 20–21, but wrongly so.

combinations in which they occur with the classes that we have
already established:

1.   A type of word like /mæn/ "man", /haws/ "house", /bɔj/
"native", and many others, which occur after adjectives and as the
subjects and objects of verbs: for example, /gʊdfɛlə mæn/ "a good
man"; /dɪsfɛlə bɔj i-stap lɔŋ haws kʊk/ "this native was in the
kitchen"; /mi kɪčɪm stɪk/ "I took a stick". These can be labelled
"nouns."

2.   A group of forms that normally occur only before others,
usually nouns, pronouns, or verbs: /bɪlɔŋ tebəl/ "of the table";
/bɪlɔŋ mi/ "for me; of me; my; mine"; /lɔŋ ples/ "to (in, at) the
village"; /lɔŋ ɛm/ "to him, to her, to it"; /wəntajm ju/ "with
you." "Preposition" is the obvious name for this class of forms, since
their use closely parallels that of our English (French, Latin) forms
we are accustomed to calling prepositions.

3.   Still another type of word comes after verbs and adjectives,
modifying them: for instance, /tuməč/ "greatly, very", as in /plɛnti
tuməč/ "very many";/tru/ "indeed", as in /nəmbərwən tru/ "indeed excellent"; or /nogʊd/ "badly; with undesirable results", as
in /ɛm i-fajtɪm mi nogʊd/ "he beat me badly, he gave me a bad
beating". "Adverb" is clearly the appropriate label for these.

4.   Such words as /gɔdæm/ "drat it!", which occur only alone
in independent utterances, can be called "interjections."

5.   The two forms /spos/ "if" and /na/ "and, or", which introduce full clauses, can be termed "conjunctions." These are the
only two conjunctions in normal use in Neo-Melanesian: /æn(d)/
"and", /ɔr/ "or", and /bɪkɔs/ "because" are recent importations
from English, still not really acclimatized in Neo-Melanesian. Occasionally, in somewhat Europeanized use, certain nouns are used
with the force of conjunctions, as in /tajm hɛrodɛs i-kɪŋ bɪlɔŋ
juda/ "(at the) time (when) Herod was king of Judaea".

In its earlier stages, Melanesian Pidgin had no definite or indefinite article—for which it was condemned by purists, who for-
got that such eminently respectable languages as Latin, Russian,
and Chinese also lack articles. Similarly, it was criticized because
its verbs show, in their form, no contrast between present, past,
or future tense. Thus, /kanæka i-stap lɔŋ ples/ might mean "a native (natives, the native, the natives) is (are, was, were, will be) in
a village (villages, the village, the villages)". No harm was done,
since the context normally gave whatever indication might be

needed as to the number or definiteness of the noun, or the tense-reference of the verb. In more recent days, however, /ɔl/ has come to be used very widely as a kind of plural article, as in /ɔl kanæka/ "the natives". So far as I have observed, though, /ɔl/ is normally used to refer to four or five or more, not to two or three; therefore, when one finds in a local mimeographed newspaper an expression like *ol Territory—Papua na New Guinea* "the Territories of Papua and New Guinea", it seems strange, and one is inclined to suspect a Europeanism. In some regions, too, especially the Sepik valley, /ɛm/ is used as a singular definite article, as in /ɛm luluwaj i-tɔk/ "the luluwai [village government head man] spoke". For a singular indefinite article, /wənfɛlə/ "one" is sometimes used—as in /wənfɛlə bɔj/ "one native, a native"—but this, too, is rather a Europeanism. The situation with regard to the article is at present clearly one of transition, and (chiefly under pressure from speakers of English, who feel unhappy without articles) Neo-Melanesian seems to be developing a set—much as the Romance languages developed theirs out of Latin *ille* "that person" and *ipse* "he himself" for the definite article, and *ūnus* "one" for the indefinite.

When we work through the grammatical structure of a pidgin or a creole, we do indeed come out with a set of form-classes or "parts of speech." We can do what we wish about labeling them: either we can call them "nouns," "verbs," and so forth; or, if we dislike these traditional grammatical terms, we can simply speak of them as "Class A," "Class B," etc., or perhaps give them arbitrary names such as "red" form, "blue" form, or the like. However, no matter what name we give the form-classes that we find, the linguistic characteristics by which we identify any given form-class are not the same as those by which we identify similar form-classes in other languages, even in other pidgins or creoles. In other words, there is no such thing as a "noun" or a "verb" in the abstract, definable in such a way as to apply to many or to all languages; each part of speech has to be reanalyzed and redefined for each separate language. The categories that we discover will, of necessity, differ from language to language, often unexpectedly so.[2]

Hence we find that, in other pidgins and creoles, the bound forms are by no means the same as those of, say, Neo-Melanesian,

---

[2] Thus, English nouns and pronouns have no grammatical gender; our pronouns have sex-reference, which is something quite different; cf. Hall, 1951a.

and the parts of speech that we can first identify (and then use to help defining the others by the positions in which they can occur —what the technical linguist would call "privileges of syntactic occurrence") are not the same. Without going into the matter in as much detail as we did for Neo-Melanesian, we can observe briefly that, on looking into Chinese Pidgin English, for example, we find that there are five bound forms, all suffixes, which help us to identify certain form-classes.[3] In the following list, we use the traditional names for the parts of speech, but it is of course to be understood that, in determining the form-classes, we go through the same kind of procedure that we have just outlined for Neo-Melanesian:

1.   /-fæšən/ "in . . . manner", added to adjectives and to certain adverbs: for example, /mɛ́rɪkənfæšən/ "in the American style"; /sófæšən/ "in such a manner, thusly"; /háwfæšən/ "in what manner?, how?".

2.   /-pisi/, a suffix without dictionary meaning, added to numerals and to the indefinite pronoun /ɔ́l/ "all": for example, /wɔ́npisi/ "one"; /túpisi/ "two"; /θrípisi/ "three"; /ɔ́lpisi/ "all".

3.   /-tajm/, indicating time when, added to nouns and to numerals, indefinites, demonstratives, and interrogatives: for example, /nájttajm/ "when it is night, /at/ night-time"; /tútajm/ "twice"; /ɔ́ltajm/ "all the time, always"; /dístajm/ "this time"; /hwátajm/ "at what time?, when?".

4.   /-sajd/, indicating place where— "at . . . , at . . .'s place" —and added to nouns, personal pronouns, and certain adverbs or adverbial stems: for example, /dɔ́ksajd/ "at (to) the docks"; /májsajd/ "at my place"; /tápsajd/ "at the top, above".

5.   /-əm/, indicating the condition into which something has gotten as a result of the action referred to by a verb, and added to the verb-form: for example, /bɔ́jləm/ "boiled", /spɔ́jləm/ "spoiled, rotten"; /brókəm/ "broken". In sentences, these forms in /-əm/ function as modifiers of nouns or as predicate complements: for example, /ték kǽr ðæt spɔ́jləm tlí/ "watch out for that rotten tree"; /mít blɔ́ŋ bɔ́jləm/ "the meat is boiled".

When we work out the form-classes of Neo-Melanesian, Chinese Pidgin English, Sranan, Gullah, and the various Caribbean creoles in Jamaica, etc., we find that, in the end, they correspond

<hr />

[3] There are other suffixes in Chinese Pidgin English, but these are the ones that are important in determining the form-classes; cf. Hall, 1944a.

to the form-classes of English. This is one of the reasons that, from the point of view of linguistic history, we cannot go along with those who say "Pidgin English is simply a native language [Chinese, Melanesian, West African, etc., as the case may be) spoken with English words." We observe the same type of basic correspondence between the form-classes of the French-based creoles (in Louisiana, Haiti, Dominica, Martinique, etc.) and those of French; and between those of Papiamentu and Spanish. We therefore come inevitably to the conclusion that the former are derived structurally, from French, and the latter from Spanish. The surface characteristics of the various pidgins and creoles may often be quite far from those of English, French, or the other Indo-European languages; but, on a deeper level of grammar, all varieties of Pidgin English and creoles that have grown out of them have an underlying identity of structure with English, and similarly for the French-based, Spanish-based, and Portuguese-based pidgins and creoles. No matter how much they may have changed and have been brusquely restructured near the surface, they still maintain a basically Indo-European pattern. This observation, incidentally, forces itself on the observer even against his will: three times I have begun work on a pidgin or creole language (Neo-Melanesian, Sranan, and Haitian Creole) with the determination to find in it a non-Indo-European structure, and each time the language itself has compelled recognition of its basically English or French pattern, as the case might be.

Not only in grammatical markers, but also in categories of inflection, do we find marked differences between pidgins and creoles, on the one hand, and on the other, the languages we are accustomed to think of as normal. Pidgins and creoles often fail to show many of our familiar categories of grammatical inflection—especially number, case, gender, and tense. This was, in the formation of pidgin languages, one of the major types of simplification that speakers of European languages considered necessary in order to make themselves understood by the natives with whom they came in contact. But these particular categories are far from universal or essential, and pidgins and creoles develop new categories on their own (often, though not always, carried over from the native languages of the region where they are spoken or from which their speakers originally came). In Haitian Creole, for instance, all contrasts of number, person, and tense have been lost in the verb, and every verb has only one form used in inflection: for example, /gade/ "keep, kept, will keep, etc."; /dòmi/ "sleep, slept, will sleep, etc."; /bwè/ "drink, drank, will drink, etc.". Samples of complete sentences containing such verbs are: /li mãže tròp/ "he eats (ate, will eat) too much"; mwē gade-1/ "I keep it"; /ki sa u bwè?/ "what do you drink?". However, Haitian Creole has developed a new set of inflectionally bound prefixes, whose occurrence with a form is our criterion for determining whether or not that form is a verb. These prefixes show, not tense, but aspect, that is, the type of action that is involved: whether it is going on and not yet finished (imperfective, durative), or is finished and completed (perfective, completive):[4]

1. The imperfective-durative prefix /apr-/, /ap(e)-/—in southern dialects often /pe-/—indicating action that is going on, continuing, not yet complete, or future. Examples: /m-apr-ale/ "I'm going"; /m-ap-ba u jū kal/ "I'll give you a beating"; /n-ap-šāte/ "we're singing"; /l-ape-mēnē-l kaj zõbi/ "he was taking her to the zombie's house".

2. The perfective-completive prefix /fèk-/—extended or emphatic form /fèk-rēk-/—"to have just [done something]" = venir de [faire quelque chose]. Examples: /m-fèk-rive/ "I've just arrived"; /li fèk-rēk-šita/ "he has just sat down this minute".[5]

Other French-based creoles have much the same aspect-system, although in some instances the markers are different. For instance, in Dominican Creole the imperfective-durative prefix is /ka-/, not /ap-/: for example, Dominican Creole /ka-bat/ "(be) beating" versus Haitian Creole /ap-bat/.

However, Haitian (Dominican, etc.) Creole is not devoid of inflectional means of indicating tense, as are, for instance, most English-based pidgins and creoles: but for this purpose, it uses, not verbally bound prefixes, but prefixes that can occur before any type of predicate. In Haitian and other French-based creoles a predicate is defined as any sequence of elements that can be pre-

[4] The category of aspect is best known from Russian and the Slavic languages. Latin, likewise, had a contrast in aspect that pervaded its verbal inflection fully as much as the category of tense: for example, dīcō (imperfective) "I am saying, the action of saying on my part is still going on", vs. dīxī (perfective) "I'm through saying, the action of saying on my part is over and done with".

[5] In Hall, 1953, §2.142.3, p. 31, the form /ānu/ "let's go" is also listed as an aspectual prefix; it does not belong here, however, since it is not bound but can occur alone.

ceded by the negativizer /pa-/ "not". A predicate can contain, as its central element, either a verb or a noun, a pronoun, an adjective, an adverb, or any other free form: for example, /u pa-gasõ/ "you [are] not a regular fellow"; /vãt li plē/ "his belly [was] full"; /se-li-mēm/ "it's he himself"; /li pa-isit/ "he [is] not here". The time to which the predicate refers can be specified by certain prefixes which, if they occur, come between /pa-/ "not" and the rest of the predicate:

1. The past-tense-sign /t(e)-/. Examples: /mãmã-m te-bã-m ti-plat/ "my mother had given me a little dish"; /li-mēm te-pitit/ "he himself was small"; /jo pa-t-isit/ "they were not here".

2. The future-tense-sign /a-/, /ava-/, /va-/. Examples: /m-ava-todje ku u/ "I'll twist your neck"; /madãm-la va-riš/ "the lady will be rich"; /prezidã-ã va-isit/ "the president will be here".

By combining a future-tense-sign and a past-tense-sign, a conditional is formed in Haitian Creole. Examples: /u t-a-lage-m/ "you would leave me"; /li t-a-kapab/ "he would be able".

The development of aspectual prefixes for verbs in these creoles is unquestionably due to a carry-over from West African languages, in which aspect is far more important than tense so far as verb-inflection is concerned. Thus, in Yòruba, the progressive is formed by prefixing a nasal to the verb-stem, the habitual by prefixing /maa-/, and the perfective by prefixing /ti/: for example, on /wa/ "come", we have /mo ŋwa/ "I am coming", /mo maa-wa/ "I usually come", and /mo ti waa/ "I have come".[6] But the forms of the prefixes themselves have developed out of French elements that have been given new structural functions: /ap(r)(e)-/, imperfective-durative, from French /aprè/ *après* "after";[7] /fèk-/ and /fèk-rēk/, perfective-completive, from French /n(ə)-fè-k(ə)/ *ne fait que* "does only, only . . . , just . . ." and /n(ə)-fè-rjē-k(ə)/ *ne fait rien que* "does nothing else but, only . . . , just . . ." . The predicatively bound tense-prefixes represent a merger between French and African forms: thus, Haitian Creole /te-/, past tense, goes back to French /ete/—representing both *était* "was" (imperfect) and *été* "been" (past participle)—and it also corresponds to the Yòruba perfective prefix /ti-/ just mentioned. Similarly, Haitian Creole /(a)va-/, future tense, clearly reflects French *va* "is going [to . . .]", and also the

---

[6] Cf. Ward, 1952, pp. 76–87.

[7] Cf. the Anglo-Irish construction with *after*, with imperfective-durative meaning: *What's he doing?—He's after eating* "He's engaged in eating = il est en train de manger".

Ewe future prefix /(a)va-/, corresponding to a Bantu root /bia-/ "come" whose derivatives are widely used as future-tense-indicators in West African languages.[8]

This instance of the aspect and tense prefixes is a good example of the way in which chance similarities among forms often favor the development of a given feature in a pidgin language. It is, historically speaking, a matter of pure accident that French /(e)te/ "was" and Yòruba /ti-/, the perfective indicator, happened to resemble each other in phonemic shape and in sense, and the same is true of French /va/ and Ewe /(a)va/ in the future. In the same way the (now archaic) French verb-root /baj-/—in *bailler* "to give [someone something, especially a blow]"—merged with African forms such as Wolof /ba/ "cede, leave" or Hausa /ba/ "give" in the form /ba(j)/ "give", widespread in French-based creoles.[9] The formation of Russonorsk seems to have depended on the chance similarity of the preposition /pɔ/ "on, in" in both Norwegian and Russian. From this type of evidence we are justified in concluding that the source of much of the grammar and also some of the vocabulary of a pidgin language lies in those features that the two "ancestor" languages have in common. To represent the relationship diagrammatically, we can draw two circles, each of which will represent (see Figure 1) the totality of the structure of one of the

[8] Cf. Sylvain, 1936, p. 143; Goodman, 1964, pp. 86–88.
[9] Cf. Sylvain, 1936, p. 144; Goodman, 1964, pp. 61–63.

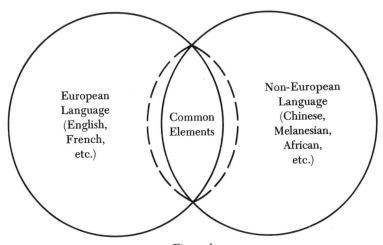

Figure 1

two languages (European or native) involved; we shall have the two circles overlap somewhat, because between any two languages there are always some points of structural similarity and also some words that, by pure chance, will be similar in form and meaning.[10] The structural resources of the pidgin are likely to be drawn in large part from the features common to the two languages (in our diagram, the area where the two circles overlap), with also some features peculiar to each side (indicated by dashes on the diagram).

In addition to inflection, there is another level in morphological structure, known as derivation. The difference may be illustrated in English by such a set as *organize, organizes, organized* (inflection) versus *organize, organizer, organization* (derivation). In derivation a given word, of a given form-class, is used as the basis for the formation of a new word, not merely for an inflectional form of the same word; the new word may or may not belong to the same part of speech as the word on which it is based. In English, we have extensive derivation by means of prefixes (*con-ceive, de-ceive, re-ceive*) and suffixes (*organ-ize, organiz-er*); since both prefixes and suffixes are attached or affixed to words, they are often referred to together as affixes. Another type of derivation is compounding, that is, placing two independent words together and unifying them in some way or other; in English this is done by putting only a single full stress on the resultant compound, as in /ǽr + krǽft/ *air-craft,* /sə́rvɪs + mǽn/ *service-man,* /háws + kòt/ *house-coat,* /ǽnti + sə́bmərìn/ *anti-submarine,* /nɔrwìdžən + bɔ́rn/ *Norwegian-born.*

In pidgins and creoles—at least the modern ones based on European languages—derivation by affixation is relatively rare; when it is found, it is usually in words borrowed recently from European languages. In a few instances, there are suffixes that are freely used in forming new derivatives: for example, in Neo-Melanesian, /-əp/ "up",/-awt/ "out", /-dawn/ "down", and /-we/ "away". (Note that these elements, although independent words in English, never occur alone in Neo-Melanesian and hence have to be classified as suffixes.) Thus we get such formations as /kəməp/ "come up, arise" on /kəm/ "come"; /kəmdawn/ "come down, descend"; or

---

[10] Many more similarities between languages are due to chance than is normally recognized; for example, Malay /mata/ "eye" and Modern Greek /mati/ "eye", which historical research shows to be completely unrelated. Cf. the discussion in Bloomfield, 1933, §18.1.

/gowe/ "go away" on /go/ "go". In most instances, however, the distribution of the suffixes is very scattered, in a way which is parallel to the occurrence of prefixes and suffixes in our English and French learnèd words borrowed from Latin or Greek: thus, in Haitian Creole, we find such terms, taken directly from French, as /kõtãplasjõ/ "contemplation" and /kõtribisjõ/ "contribution". The speakers of pidgins and creoles seem to treat their learnèd borrowings as single units, without breaking them up into separate elements.

Compounding is rather more widespread as a grammatical process in pidgins and creoles. Where there is a phonological feature such as stress (as there is in Neo-Melanesian) which can differentiate a compound from a sequence of independent words, it is often used to convey a difference in function. Thus, in Neo-Melanesian, there is a compound-type consisting of NOUN + NOUN, in which the first noun tells some characteristic or feature of what is referred to by the second: for example, /hawsbɔj/ "house-boy"; /nilfɪš/ "needle-fish (a kind of fish having sharp fins)"; /hɛdmæn/ "head-man, leader". We have this type of compound in English also (though it is often masked, in writing, by failure to mark it with a hyphen on all occasions).[11] In Neo-Melanesian, such compounds contrast with a type of combination involving two nouns in a phrase, in which each noun keeps its own separate accent, and in which the second noun tells some characteristic or purpose of what is referred to by the first. There is a marked difference, for instance, between /hawsbɔj/ (one word, one stress) "house-boy, native who helps around the house" and /haws bɔj/ (two words, two stresses) "house for the 'boys,' house for the native workers".

Compounds consisting of ADJECTIVE + NOUN are also very frequent in Neo-Melanesian; they differ from phrases consisting of ADJECTIVE + NOUN, with regard both to stress (the compound has only a single stress, always on the first syllable) and to meaning (the compound always has a transferred or figurative meaning).

---

[11] It is of course irrelevant for our discussion here whether the resultant English compound word is written with a hyphen or not; for example, /strít + kàr/ can be written *street car*, *street-car* or *streetcar* without making the slightest difference in the meaning of the word or in the "correctness" of its spelling; the same is true of the other compounds listed here.

Contrast the compounds in the left-hand column with the phrases in the right-hand column:

/bɪgmaws/	"insolent person"	/bɪgfɛlə maws/	"large mouth"
/wəntɔk/	"person from the same village [literally, having the same language, compatriot]"	/wənfɛlə tɔk/	"one language"
/blækmæn/	"Melanesian"	/blækfɛlə mæn/	"dark-colored man"
/wajtmæn/	"European"	/wajtfɛlə mæn/	"light-colored man"

An enlightening story, from both the linguistic and the cultural points of view, is told of a Negro anthropologist who once went to Melanesia as a member of an American team. He was all prepared to identify himself emotionally and culturally with the Melanesians, and was quite taken aback when the Melanesians treated him as a European. The following dialogue ensued:

NEGRO ANTHROPOLOGIST: /ɔlsem wɔnem? mi blækmæn ɔlsem ju./ He meant to say, "What is the matter? I am a black man like you," but failed to realize the difference between /blækmæn/ and /blækfɛlə mæn/.

MELANESIAN: /no, mastər. ju no blækmæn. ju blækfɛlə wajtmæn./ "No, sir. You are not a Melanesian. You are a dark-colored European."

Such compounds are not limited to forms functioning like nouns. For instance, Chinese Pidgin English had a type of adjective-compound consisting of two nouns, meaning "having . . . as one's . . .": for example, on /ǧɔs/ "god" and /píǧɪn/ "business" was built the adjective /ǧɔ́spìǧɪn/ "having a god as his business", so that /ǧɔ́spìǧɪn mæn/ "a man having a god as his business" was the normal term for "priest". Haitian Creole has an interesting type of verb-compound consisting of the verb /mānē/ "touch > only, just, a little bit" plus another verb: for example, /li mānē-maže/ "he's eating a little, nibbling"; /m-mānē-grāgu/ "I'm a little hungry"; /l-ap-mānē-gei kò-l/ "she's amusing herself a little, she's having a little bit of a good time". That these combinations of /mānē/ + VERB are compounds, not phrases, is shown by their occurrence preceded by inflectional prefixes—like /ap-/, indicating duration, as in the example just given (/ap-mānē-gei/ "is just enjoying")—coupled with the fact that stress, which always comes on the last syllable of any word, occurs in these compounds only on the last syllable of the second verb. Forms are frequently reduplicated, with various kinds of semantic overtones. The West African languages have many reduplicated words, reflected in such carry-overs as Jamaican Creole /bó-bò/ "a foolish person", /prá-prà/ "gather up", or /njáka-njàka/ "untidy, slovenly" (all from Twi). We find even more derivational reduplication, however, in forms of non-African origin: for example, Jamaican Creole /wás-wàs/ "wasp", /máta-màta/ "matter, pus"; Neo-Melanesian /šipšip/ "sheep", /wilwil/ "wheel > bicycle"; Cameroons Creole /drəŋk + drəŋk/ "continually drunk". Reduplication serves various semantic purposes, indicating, for instance, superlative quality, as in Jamaican Creole /wí-wì/ "very small", /flát-flàt/ "very flat", or Haitian Creole /rõ-rõ/ "very round", /pike-pike/ "very piquant"; or repetition or continuation, as in Jamaican Creole and Neo-Melanesian /lúk-lùk/ "look", Jamaican Creole /báta-bàta/ "beat repeatedly", Haitian Creole /tire-tire/ "shoot a great deal"; or intensification, as in Jamaican Creole /fə́s-fə̀s/ "first of all" or Neo-Melanesian /lıklık/ "small"; or diminution, as in Jamaican Creole /jǽlə-jæ̀lə/ "yellowish", Haitian Creole /píke-pike/ "somewhat piquant" (with emphatic stress and pitch-gliding). Many of these reduplications, in word-formation as in syntax, are undoubtedly of West African origin; but in many other instances they reflect European baby-talk, as in the Neo-Melanesian examples just cited or in Neo-Melanesian /sıŋsıŋ/ "ritual festival < singing" and /nætnæt/ "mosquito".

Another type of derivation that is widespread in pidgins and creoles, just as it is in English, involves simply the passage of a word from one part of speech to another, without any suffix or other formal outward indication of the change in form-class. In English, we can use many words as nouns, verbs, or adjectives: we can fall in a *faint*, we can *faint*, or we can feel *faint*. Likewise, in Neo-Melanesian, such a word as /glas/ "glass; mirror; telescope" can serve as the base for a verb /glasım/ "look at something in a glass (telescope)" and also "find with the naked eye, but with difficulty; give a short glance at something; observe from a hiding place". The form /nogʊd/, as an adverb, means "badly, undesirably, with undesirable results"; as a verb /nogʊdım/ is "to harm". The adverb /ɔlsem/ "thus, so" can pass to the status of a preposition, meaning "like, as", as in /ɔlsem mi/ "like me". In Haitian

Creole, almost any verb can be used as a noun (and can have the formal characteristic of a noun, the power of taking the diminutive prefix /ti-/): thus, /mãže/ "eat" can also mean "food, meal", and the form /ti-mãže/ is "little food, little meal". Yet this does not mean that all Haitian Creole verbs and nouns are interchangeable. Not all verbs can be used this way, nor can most nouns be used as verbs: on /tab/ "table" one can form the diminutive /ti-tab/ "little table", but not a progressive verb-form °/ap-tab/ "being a table". Many linguists like to describe this type of derivation as being performed by the addition of "suffix zero," as contrasted with derivation performed by adding an actual suffix in other instances; if we use this device of analysis, we can say that pidgins and creoles make an extensive use of the zero-suffix in word-formation.

By and large, as contrasted with the "major" languages of Western Europe, pidgins and creoles have relatively little morphological variation in their structure; and many grammatical concepts that, in our familiar languages, are expressed by morphological (especially inflectional) features, find their expression in syntactical combinations (as we shall see in the next chapter). This absence of morphological complication is one of the main reasons why those who do not like pidgins and creoles cry "No grammar!" and call them "formless" or say that they obey only "Rafferty's rules of grammar." However, when we look at the whole gamut of grammatical structures attested in the languages of the world, we find that there is a much wider range of difference in grammar, and especially in the relation of morphology to syntax, than we are accustomed to thinking possible. Some languages, like Eskimo or those of the Iroquois family, are far more complicated in their morphology than any of our Indo-European languages, even in the earlier stages of, say, Greek or Sanskrit; others, however, like Chinese and Ewe, have virtually no inflection at all. There is no correlation between type of linguistic structure and level of cultural development; as the linguist-anthropologist Edward Sapir put it, colorfully but accurately: "Both simple and complex types of language of an indefinite number of varieties may be found spoken at any desired level of cultural advance. When it comes to linguistic form, Plato walks with the Macedonian swineherd, Confucius with the head-hunting savage of Assam."[12] In the range of possibilities

[12] Sapir, 1921, chap. X ("Language, Race, and Culture").

of morphological variation, the simplified inflectional and derivational structures of pidgins and creoles are on that end of the spectrum that tends towards simplification, but are far from having gone to the extreme of "abolishing" all morphology.

REFERENCES

Form-classes in Neo-Melanesian: Hall, 1943a (chaps. ii and iii), 1955a (chap. v).

Form-classes in Chinese Pidgin English: Hall, 1944a, (§2).

Form-classes in Haitian Creole: Hall, 1953 (chap. ii), 1962b.

Aspect and tense in Haitian Creole: Hall, 1952a.

French and African elements in Creole morphology: Sylvain, 1936; Hall, 1950f.

Repetition in Jamaican Creole: Cassidy, 1957.

Syntax

CHAPTER 6

THE combinations in which the free forms of a language occur constitute its syntax, as was mentioned at the beginning of Chapter 5. There are various approaches to syntactic description; the one we shall use here distinguishes principally between two syntactic levels: phrase-structure and clause-structure. A phrase is any longer combination of free forms that takes the place of, and has the same function as, a single free form of some given form-class. Consider the following English sentences:

> Boys run.
> The boys run.
> The fat boys run.
> The eight fat boys run.
> The eight fat American boys run.
> Boys run quickly.
> The boys run quickly.
> The boys run quickly down the street.
> The boys run when they see a policeman.

The first of these sentences consists simply of a noun, *boys*, plus a verb, *run*. In the second, the single free form *boys* is replaced by the combination *the boys*, which has a slightly different meaning, conveyed by the addition of the definite article *the* ("certain specific boys, known to speaker and hearer"), but which fulfills the same function in the sentence (acting as the subject of the verb *run*). In the third, fourth, and fifth sentences, this combination is expanded still further by the addition of other elements—*fat,*

68

eight, and *American.* The main word in the combination still remains, however, the noun *boys,* since it is the presence of this plural noun that determines, all along, the use of the unsuffixed verb-form *run.* For each of these sentences, therefore, we use the term noun-phrase to refer to those combinations that have a noun as their chief element. The main or determining element of a phrase we call its head; the other elements, which are subordinate to or modify the head, we term modifiers or attributes of the head. In the sixth, seventh, and eighth sentences, we have a similar expansion of the verb *run,* by the addition of the modifiers *quickly* and *down the street;* the resultant combinations are, of course, verb-phrases, with *run* as their head and *quickly* and *down the street* as attributes—or, as we often call modifiers in verb-phrases, "complements". An attribute can, in its turn, consist—as in the case of *down the street*—of a phrase, or—as in the last sentence above—of an even larger construction of the type termed a "clause" (*when they see a policeman*).

The phrase-structure of pidgins and creoles, like that of English and other languages, is made up largely of combinations that take the place of individual forms belonging to one part of speech or another—nouns, pronouns, adjectives, verbs, prepositions. But the structure of the phrases themselves differs considerably from that of the corresponding combinations in our familiar European languages—which is presumably what has led to the complaints that pidgins and creoles "disregard the rules of syntax," "have no syntax," and the like. The best way to treat these different types of combinations is simply to take them in a given order (such as that in the first sentence of this paragraph) and to enumerate the various elements that we find in them. A convenient starting-point for phrasal analysis is the relative position of head and attributes.

In Neo-Melanesian, we find that noun-phrases occur both with the structure of ATTRIBUTE + HEAD and with that of HEAD + ATTRIBUTE. However, the only type of attribute that precedes the head is the adjective: for example, /gudfɛlə mæn/ "(a) good man"; /bɪgfɛlə haws/ "(a) large house"; /lɪklɪk bɔtəl/ "(a) small bottle"; /səmfɛlə kajkaj/ "some food"; /trifɛlə pusi/ "three cats"; /dɪsfɛlə blajstɪk/ "this pencil"; /nədərfɛlə ples/ "another village". If the adjective has a modifier, this latter is separated from the adjective and comes after the noun: for example, /gudfɛlə kajkaj tuməč/ "very good food"; /lɪklɪk bɔtəl tru/ "a very small bottle". All other modifiers in a Neo-Melanesian noun-phrase come after the head, and a free form of any class other than adjectives can serve as attribute in this position. Thus, in /haws kʊk/ "room [for] cooking, kitchen", /kʊk/ is a verb; in /haws məni/ "house [for] money, bank", /məni/ is a noun; in /papa tru/ "real father [as opposed to one's mother's brothers]", /tru/ is an adverb.

"Why," someone may ask, "is /tru/ called an adverb? Isn't *true* an adjective?" So it is—in English; but the structure of a pidgin or a creole must always be analyzed in its own terms and according to its own inherent organization. In Neo-Melanesian, we never find /tru/ with the suffix /-fɛlə/, which (as we saw earlier) is the marker of one-syllable adjectives, and without which a one-syllable form cannot be called an adjective; and we never find /tru/ before a noun, which is where adjectives normally stand. Since /tru/ is not a noun, a pronoun, or a verb, nor yet a preposition or a conjunction, we have to place it in the only category left, that of the adverb—keeping in mind, of course, that the term "adverb" as applied to Neo-Melanesian does not mean what it does in English grammar. This decision is confirmed when we find that /tru/ can modify adjectives in Neo-Melanesian, a function normally reserved for adverbs: for example, /gʊdfɛlə tru/ "really good"; /nəmbərwən tru/ "really, truly excellent".

The criterion of position in Neo-Melanesian noun-phrases helps us also in classifying doubtful cases, especially when an attribute in a noun-phrase consists of more than one syllable. If a word of more than one syllable follows the noun it modifies, it cannot (by our definition of adjectives in Neo-Melanesian) be an adjective, and, if it belongs to no other class, must be an adverb. So, in a phrase like /mæn nogʊd/ "(an) evil man", /nogʊd/ is an adverb meaning "undesirably"; this observation is confirmed when we find /nogʊd/ introducing negative commands, as in /nogʊd ju mekɪm ɔlsem/ "don't act that way [*literally*, with undesirable results will you do thus]".[1] Similarly, with the element /nətɪŋ/ in

---

[1] There are interesting parallels at many points between Melanesian Pidgin English and Old French in syntax; here, there is a close similarity between Neo-Melanesian /nogʊd/ and Old French *mar* "in an evil day; with sad results". Thus, in Old French, *mar lo fereiz* "in an evil day you will do it" is equivalent to a negative command "don't do it", just like Neo-Melanesian /nogʊd ju mekɪm ɔlsem/. Cf. also the verse from the *Song of Roland* (v. 1731): *Vostre proȩece, Roḑlanz, mar la veḑimes* "'Twas a sad day for us, Roland, when we saw that prowess of yours".

such expressions as /səmtɪŋ nətɪŋ/ "a thing of no importance; a trifle" or /kanæka natɪŋ/ "an unindentured native on a plantation; a bush-native", we find on further investigation that /nətɪŋ/ is an adverb, with the basic meaning "occurring outside of the normal environment or circumstances in which it is usually found; with something missing".

In addition to single forms, we often find phrases, predicates, and clauses acting as modifiers in Neo-Melanesian noun-phrases. The most frequent kind of phrasal attribute is that which consists of PREPOSITION + OBJECT: for example, /haws bɪlɔŋ mi/ "house of me, my house"; /mastər bɪlɔŋ wokɪm gol/ "miner [literally, European for digging gold]"; /sɪŋsɪŋ bɪlɔŋ lotu/ "hymn [literally, song for worship]". This is the only way of indicating possession in Neo-Melanesian, even with pronouns, and is an obvious parallel to the French or Spanish construction with de "of": for example, /haws bɪlɔŋ papa bɪlɔŋ mɪsɪs/ "the house of the father of the mistress, the lady's father's house = la maison du père de madame = la casa del padre de la señora". Predicates and clauses acting as modifiers fulfill the same function as do English relative clauses, since Neo-Melanesian (like virtually all pidgins) has no relative pronouns, adjectives, or adverbs. In other words, the English construction in the book he gave me, with no relative element and involving simple juxtaposition of a clausal attribute to its head, though optional in English, is obligatory in Neo-Melanesian and other pidgins. So, for example, "the knife (which) this gentleman gave to me" is /najf dɪsfɛlə mastər i-gɪvɪm lɔŋ mi/; "the meat (which) you ate" is /abus ju kajkaj/. Where there would be a relative pronoun subject in English, Neo-Melanesian uses only a predicate as attribute, with no subject of its own: for example, "the man (who) came" is /mæn i-kəm/, and one of the most widely read texts in Neo-Melanesian, the Liklik Katolik Baibel, describes manna as kaikai i-kamdaun long heven "food (which) came down from heaven".

Being a pidgin, Neo-Melanesian has a relatively simple structure in its phrases. When a language becomes creolized, however, in order to meet the needs of its speakers for a complete means of communication, its syntactical structure becomes enlarged again, with the addition of further types of attribute and hence the development of new subtypes among the various kinds of phrase. The phrasal structure found among the various French-based

TABLE 4

Structure of Haitian Creole Nominal Phrase

$$(/\text{tut}/\ \text{``all''} \text{ or } /\text{sak}/\ \text{``each''}) \pm \left[\text{(\textit{ssée} \; DEMONSTRATIVE)}\right] \pm (\text{INTERROGATIVE}) \pm \left[\begin{array}{c}\text{(INDEFINITE ARTICLE or}\\ \text{NUMERAL or INDEFINITE)}\end{array}\right] \pm (\text{ADJECTIVE}) \pm (\text{NOUN})$$

$$+ \textbf{NOUN head} \pm (\text{ADJECTIVE}) \pm (\text{ADVERB}) \pm \left[\begin{array}{c}\text{(NOUN indicating}\\ \text{characteristic,}\\ \text{partitive, rate, or extent)}\end{array}\right] \pm \left[\begin{array}{c}\text{(NOUN indicating}\\ \text{possessor)}\end{array}\right] + \left[\begin{array}{c}\text{(DEFINITE ARTICLE)} \pm \text{(PLURALIZER /jo/)}\\ \text{or}\\ \text{(DEMONSTRATIVE} \pm \text{DEFINITE ARTICLE} \pm \text{/jo/)}\end{array}\right]$$

$$\pm \left[\begin{array}{c}\text{(VERB indicating}\\ \text{purpose)}\end{array}\right] \pm \left[\begin{array}{c}\text{(EXOCENTRIC PHRASE}\\ \text{introduced by}\\ \text{preposition)}\end{array}\right] \pm (\text{CLAUSE})$$

creoles is quite complicated, as exemplified in Haitian Creole (see Table 4, "Structure of Haitian Creole Nominal Phrase"). The elements that precede the noun are much the same as those found in the corresponding position in French noun-phrases, and some of them—for example, the demonstrative /se-/ "that", as in /se-momã/ "that moment"—are clearly recent Gallicisms. The positioning of the adjective, also, is like that of French, in that some adjectives such as /bõ/ "good", /grã/ "large", or /piti/ "little" normally precede the noun; most others normally follow; and if the order of adjective and noun is reversed, this gives emphasis to the adjective: thus, /jū bõ pitit/ "a good child", /sulje nwa/ "black shoes", but /jū pitit bõ/ "a *good* child".

After the noun, however, there are quite a number of different types of complement, with ramifications in their semantic development that go well beyond those found in, say, Neo-Melanesian. This is especially true of the second (modifying) noun in a NOUN + NOUN combination, where the second noun can indicate either a characteristic, a purpose, the whole of which a part is being taken, the extent, or the rate of an activity: for example, /lafjèv vomismã/ "fever characterized by vomiting, vomiting fever"; /bwat alimèt/ "box for matches, match-box"; /jū pil ti-ròš žòn/ "a pile of yellow pebbles"; /jū pje ãturaž/ "one foot in circumference"; /jū kal šak žu/ "a beating every day". In the position indicating "possession," we can find either a noun or a pronoun, as in /māže lòt ti-mun/ = /māže/ "food" + /lòt ti-mun/ "(of) the other children", or /māmã li/ "his mother [*literally*, mother him]". Several nouns, or pronouns, can follow in succession, indicating possessive relationships, as in /pòt kaj māmã li/ "the door of his mother's house". Nouns indicating "property" or "possession" are used with following possessive attributes to form a kind of possessive noun-phrase, equivalent to our English or French possessive pronouns: for example, /pa/ "share, property" (in the west and south of Haiti) or /kin/ (in the north, with the definite article /a/ between /kin/ and the possessive attribute): thus /pa-m/ "mine" = le mien (la mienne, les miens, les miennes) versus the northern /kin-a-m/; /pa jo/ versus northern /kin-a-jo/ "theirs" = le leur, etc. In the same way, emphatic or reflexive phrases are formed with the nouns /kò/ and /kadav/ "body" and /tèt/ "head": for example, /su tèt Lalin/ "against Laline herself [*literally*, against the head of

Laline]"; /pu kò-m/ "for (by) myself "; /jo rēmē kadav jo/ "they love themselves".[2] Verbs, likewise, can form nominal attributes in Haitian Creole with no intervening element: for example, /dwa mãže diri/ "the right to eat of [*literally*, in] the rice"; /tā ašte tol/ "time to buy corrugated iron".

In their origin many of these constructions are the result of the omission of certain linking elements, particularly prepositions, which are present in the corresponding phrase-types of the European language on which the pidgin or creole is based. Thus, for Neo-Melanesian /mæn buš/ "man [of the] bush, backwoods native", the obvious English model was the phrase *man of the bush;* and in Haitian Creole /jū pil ti-ròš žòn/ "a pile of yellow pebbles", the preposition *de,* which would normally intervene in French before the modifying element (*une pile de petites roches jaunes*), has been left out. In some instances phonetic contraction in popular speech in the European language has helped this process, especially the reduction of English *of* to *o',* so that a lower-class English pronunciation *man o' th' bush* ['mæn ə ð 'buš] could easily be heard by the Melanesian (whose ear would not be accustomed to and hence would not hear the sound [ð]) as simply ['mæn] plus ['buš], with an intervening glide vowel. By a similar process, the English phrase *along of,* common in lower-class English with the

<hr/>

[2] This usage, too, has a parallel in the Old French emphatic reflexive construction with *cors* "body", as in *son cors* "himself ", or *lo cors Rodlant* "Roland himself [*literally*, the body of Roland]" (*Roland,* v. 613), or *Jo conduirai mon cors en Rencesvals* "I shall betake myself [*literally*, I shall lead my body] to Roncesvalles" (*Roland,* v. 892). Mme. Sylvain-Comhaire (1936, p. 65), followed by Goodman (1964, pp. 57–58), doubts that the Haitian Creole construction represents a continuation of the Old French one, and therefore ascribes the Haitian Creole phrase-type with /kò/, /kadav/, and /tèt/ wholly to African influence. It is quite possible, however, that phrases with *cor(p)s* "body" might have survived into the seventeenth and eighteenth centuries in French dialects and thus have been taken over into the nascent Haitian Creole. (In general, studies of the relation between Creole and French, whether their authors are "pro-African," or "anti-African," tend to be based too exclusively on the history of the standard language and on the modern dialects, to the exclusion of the dialectal situation as it may have existed in the sixteen- and seventeen-hundreds, at the time when the new Pidgin French was being formed.) As Mme. Sylvain-Comhaire points out, /kadavr/ is synonymous with /kòr/ "body" in Picard; furthermore, its use in Haitian Creole sounds like a piece of "Galgenhumor" which may well have arisen or been strengthened among native speakers of French who heard /kò/ in a construction that seemed either strange or humorously old-fashioned to them.

meaning "in connection with, or account of ",[3] and reduced in rapid everyday speech to [əˈlɔŋə], was reinterpreted by the South Sea Islanders as if it consisted of GLIDE VOWEL + [ˈlɔŋ] + GLIDE VOWEL, and thus gave rise to the preposition /lɔŋ/ "connected with, related to; at, in, on, etc.", common to all the South Sea varieties of Pidgin English. As a result of this ellipsis, the message of grammatical relationship is conveyed in the new construction, not by any overt structural marker such as a preposition or a case-suffix, but simply by the order of the words relative to each other.

However, by no means all the constructions that we find in pidgins and creoles can be traced back to European sources, even assuming an ellipsis of one word or another. Of this type is the Haitian Creole noun-phrase when a definite article is present: in Haitian Creole the definite article and the pluralizer /jo/ come at the very end of any noun-phrase, and in fact they make into a noun-phrase any group of words that they follow. Even a·long expression, containing any number of dependent elements, can take the definite article at its end: for example, /twa pè sulje nwa papa-m te-ašte-m Pòt-o-Prẽs a jo/ "the three pairs of black shoes which my father had bought for me at Port-au-Prince". Likewise, in Jamaican Creole a noun-phrase is pluralized by adding a plural demonstrative at the end, as in /hím tiit dém/ "his teeth". There is no basis for this type of word-order in English or in French, or in Western European languages in general.[4] A number of West African languages, however—Ewe, Wolof, Mende, etc.—have determinative elements that are normally placed after nouns or noun-phrases, and in Ewe the determinant or definite article has

---

[3] Cf. such examples as *You see, he was wet . . . along of washing the dog* (P. G. Wodehouse, *Sam the Sudden* [London, 1925], chap. xxii); *Isaac here wur knocked out by his missus along 'a her* (E. and M. A. Radford, *Death of a Frightened Editor* [London, 1959], p. 163); *I won't have you getting your feet wet along of that horrid moat* (R. J. White, *The Smartest Grave* [London, 1961], p. 195).

[4] In Roumanian the definite article is suffixed to the noun it modifies, as in /ómu-/ "man" + /-1/ "the" = /ómul/ "the man". This does not constitute a parallel with the Creole situation, however, since in Roumanian the definite article is added to the noun, not to the entire phrase; if a modifier follows the noun, the definite article is still on the end of the noun itself: for example, /ómul čél mái bún/ "the best man [*literally*, the man, that-one most good]", not °/óm mái búnul/ as it would have to be in order to parallel the Haitian Creole construction /nòm bō-a/.

the form /la/, so that the resultant constructions are similar to those of Creole, as in the following:[5]

	Ewe	Creole
"the tree"	ati-la	pje bwa-a
"the beautiful tree"	ati-nyui-la	bèl pje bwa-a
"that beautiful tree"	ati-nyui-sia-la	bèl pje bwa sa-a
"the one (he) who came yesterday"	amesi va etso-la	sa ki vini ayè-a

The phrases that function as expansions of pronouns are not too different, either in Neo-Melanesian or in Haitian Creole, from the types we find in English, French, and other European languages. In the verb-phrase, however, we find many interesting phenomena, especially in the core or central part of the phrase, in the combinations of verbs that can take the place of a single verb. One feature that is widely found in pidgins and creoles is the repetition of the verb to indicate continued action: for example, Neo-Melanesian /mi fajnɪm fajnɪm fajnɪm/ "I searched and searched and searched for it"; Haitian Creole /li maše maše maše/ "he walked and walked"; Sranan /didíbri náki náki náki náki/ "the Devil kept on knocking." This type of repetition often occurs with other parts of speech as well, indicating emphasis or intensification, as in the Haitian Creole adjective phrase /bèl bèl/ in /jō bèl bèl fi/ "a very beautiful daughter", or the Sranan adverbial phrase /wàntém wàntém/ "at once, immediately [*literally*, once once]". In the formation of such repetitive phrases, as in that of many other features of pidgins, a considerable rôle is played by "baby-talk," that is, the way naïve people think they have to talk to children (or to native peoples, who in earlier centuries were considered child-like), leaving out connecting elements in order (supposedly) to make themselves understood. In baby-talk, this type of repetition is very common, as when we say *Baby no touch, stove hot-hot*, or *Look, Daddy jump jump jump!*. But West African and other substrata have unquestionably also played a rôle in the use of repetition in derivation and in phrase-structure.

Often a verb is followed by another verb that serves as a complement of purpose, result, or condition: for example, Neo-

[5] Examples from Sylvain, 1936, p. 60. She does not give the tones in her transcription of words from African languages, but this fact is not relevant in this particular connection.

Melanesian /mi kəm lʊkɪm ju/ "I came to see you", or /mekɪm daj mašin/ "cause the machine to cease, stop the machine"; Haitian Creole /li mete-m šita/ "she put me to sit", /pu mõtre-l maše/ "to show her how to walk", /m tõbe krie/ "I fell to crying", /li fin tire bèf-la/ "he finished milking the cow"; Sranan /tígri féti gó na-tápu/ "Tiger fought his way [*literally,* fought to go] up", /mi lóbi dyómpo dyómpo/ "I like to jump and jump"; /anánsi bigín bári/ "the spiders began to call", etc., etc. Such phrases are frequently derived from combinations of MODAL VERB (such as English *can, make, must,* or French *devoir* "be supposed to", *pouvoir* "be able to", *savoir* "know how to", *vouloir* "want to") + DEPENDENT VERB: thus, English *you can work* > Neo-Melanesian /ju kæn wók/, Chinese Pidgin English /ju kǽn wɘ́rki/; English *the story must + can go* > Sranan /a tóri mús kán gó/ "the story must be able to go on"; French *vous pas devoir jurer lui comme ça* > Haitian Creole /u pa-dwè žure-l kõ-sa/ "you oughtn't to curse him like that". More often, however, the sequence of MAIN VERB + DEPENDENT VERB results from the ellipsis of a preposition, as in English *you like [to] kill him + pig* > Neo-Melanesian /ju lajk kɪlɪm pɪg/ "you want to kill a pig"; English *he* must want [to] spit > Chinese Pidgin English /hi mɘ́s wɘ́nči spít/ "he has to vomit". There are a number of such phrases in Haitian Creole: French *moi fais que finir [de] manquer [de] tomber* "I do nothing [but] finish missing falling" > Haitian Creole /m-fèk-fin māke tõbe/ "I've just now almost slipped"; or French *moi commencer [à] aider lui [à] planter* "I began to help him to plant" > Haitian Creole /m-komāse ede-l plāte/. Here, too, baby-talk played a large role in the ellipsis of the intervening prepositions; compare our *Baby go sleep now, Mama help you try hold spoon,* and similar expressions, which are far more common than we sometimes think.

The semantic content of these VERB + VERB combinations, however, is often of markedly non-European type, reflecting the substratum of African (Melanesian, etc.) speakers. This phenomenon is especially noticeable in the Central American creoles, which have a common West African substratum, and in which there is a common semantic pattern in the use of verbs of motion followed directly by verbal complements. Thus, in Haitian Creole we have /u te-mõte vin fisi/ "you had gone up [to] come to Furcy, you had come up to Furcy", /l-a-žābe al Sātjag/ "he will cross [to] go to Santiago, he'll cross over to Santiago", or /u te-desān rive Bakõnwa?/

"Did you go down [*literally*, descend (to) arrive] to Baconoir?"; in Sranan /ju mu tjári ju gón kóm/ "you must bring your gun [*literally*, carry your gun (so that it) comes]"; in Jamaican Creole *I will carry you go*.[6] In West African Pidgin English, we find the same type of construction, as in Nigerian Pidgin *he run come in from inside de hole;* Dahomean Pidgin *he sell 'um go way* "he sold him off"; Gold Coast Pidgin *sen' pikin go* "send the child away" or *I mus' kare* [*carry*] *dis fiah go home*.

Often, several verbs occur in a series, each as the complement of the preceding one: for example, Haitian Creole /mama-m vin rive sòt lavil/ "my mother came [to] arrive [after leaving town, my mother came home from town"; Sranan /den sordáti den-hári hem tjár gó trowé na-líba/ "the soldiers were taking him to the river to throw him in [*literally*, haul him, carry go throw in river]"; or Jamaican Creole *let me kyar de basket come show you.* An almost exact parallel is found in such African sentences as Ewe /eji dagbe jevune ve nam medu di wo/ "he gathered a nut for me to eat and I was satisfied [*literally*, he went arrived gathered coconut came gave me I ate, was satisfied]", or Twi *fá kɔ'* "take away [*literally*, take go]" and *djuane kɔ'* "run away [*literally*, run go]".[7] It must be added that similar phrases are also found in Melanesia, where there is no African substratum: for example, Neo-Melanesian /briŋɪm i-kəm/ "bring it hither [*literally*, bring it (so that) it comes]" or /kartɪm i-go/ "take it away [*literally*, carry it (so that) it goes]". The South Seas pidgin expressions may have originated independently of those that have an undoubtedly African base; or they may have been introduced into the South Seas by sailors and traders who had picked them up directly or indirectly from African contacts.

A widespread African peculiarity is the use of verbs meaning "give" as complements of this type, indicating the person to whom something is given or for whose benefit something is done. Thus we find Haitian Creole /ba(j)/ "give" in such a sentence as /pòt veso bã-m tire bèf-la ba u/ "bring a vessel for [*literally*, to give] me to milk the cow for [*literally*, give] you". In Haitian Creole, the form

---

[6] These and similar examples cited from Herskovits, 1936, pp. 117–135, are given in conventional English spelling because of the absence of any phonetic or phonemic indication in the source; in any case, the important thing here is the semantic sequence of the morphemes.

[7] Examples from Sylvain, 1936, pp. 141–142.

/ba(j)/ is still a verb, as shown by the fact that it can take the aspectival inflectional prefixes, as in /m-a-ba u jū kal/ "I'll give you a beating". The same situation prevails in various English-based creoles of the New World; for example, Bahaman *they fry fowl egg, many cake, give him* or Gullah /dɛm də ca əm ɟi dɪ ɲʊŋ pipl/ "they carry it to [*literally,* give] the young people"; and in Nigerian Pidgin English *and her mother took one give her pikin* "and her mother took one for her child". In Sranan, however, /gíbi/ "to give" (often with an alternative short form /gí/) has remained as a verb, as in /mi sa-gí(bi) ju tín sénsi/ "I'll give you ten cents"; but in the meaning "to, for", only the short form /gi/ is used, and is always unstressed, as in /a wáni tjári drí bón bígi néŋgere gi hém/ "he wanted to bring three good big slaves for him". Here again, the African substratum is obvious: many West African languages use the verb for "give" in combinations with the meaning "for", as in sentences meaning "they bring to the king [*literally,* they take go give the king]"; and in Fanti the verb /ma/ is so widely used in introducing clauses as to have become a quasi-conjunction: for example, /oyéè ma waani' a si' ka/ "he did it to [*literally,* give] make money".

In a number of instances pidgins and creoles show a drastic restructuring of various words, in their assignment to different functions from those they had in the languages from which they came: compare the split of English *give* into two separate words in Sranan, /gí(bi)/ "give", stressed, as a verb, and /gi/ "to, for", unstressed, as a preposition. Likewise, in South Seas Pidgin English, we find /bɪlɔŋ/, clearly from the English verb *belong*, but functioning as a preposition meaning "of, for" (for example, /ɔl bɔrata bɪlɔŋ dɪsfɛlə mæn/ "all the brothers of this man" or /wara bɪlɔŋ waśwaš/ "water for washing"); and /spos/, from English *suppose*, but acting as a conjunction meaning "if" (for example, /spos ju mekɪm ɔlsem/ "if you act like that"). We find /blɔŋ/ in Chinese Pidgin English, too, but this time as a copulative verb equivalent to our "be": for example, /máj mísi hí blɔ́ŋ plénti fǽt/ "my mistress is very fat"; /ðǽt blɔ́ŋ máj/ "that is of me, that is mine".

These are the same type of structural shift that we find in the history of "normal," full-sized languages, as when the Old English noun *dūn* "hill" became Modern English *down* (adverb), or the Old French noun /ɔm/ "man (*nominative singular*)" became the Modern French indefinite pronoun /õ/, indicating an indefinite person ("one"). In "normal" languages, however, such shifts take centuries to complete, whereas they come about in only a few years or decades in the formation of a pidgin. Such a change always pivots around the use of the form in a crucial phrase-type, where its meaning and structural function are ambiguous, and the non-European can reinterpret it in a different way from what was meant by the European speaker. Usually we just have to guess at the type of situation; sometimes, though, as in the case of /spos/ "if ", we have direct attestation. The explorer Florence Coombe, writing in 1911 of her travels in the Solomons, relates her trip with a native guide, and at one point says: "When we had travelled some five hundred yards I came tentatively to a halt with a 'S'pose me stop here'." For Miss Coombe, *suppose* was a verb, and *stop* meant "to cease motion"; but her native guide could take the sentence as meaning "if I were to remain here . . .", and the way was open for the pidgin reinterpretation of *spos* as "if " and of *stap* as "remain", hence "be located continually", practically equivalent to Spanish *estar*.

Auxiliary verbs occur in the verbal phrases of many pidgins, especially those based on English: for example, Chinese Pidgin English /hǽb/ "have", forming a phrase with a past meaning, as in /máj nó hǽb kǽči bǽskɛt/ "I didn't bring a basket". We find *been* in this function in regions as widely separated as Suriname and Australia, and also *done* in the southeastern United States: for example, Sranan /a-ben kísi/ "he received"; Australian Pidgin English /tumə́č mí bín slíp ələ́ŋə ím/ "I slept with him too much"; Gullah /ʋɪ dʌn tɛl dɛm/ "I told them", and similar expressions in the Negro English of Joel Chandler Harris' stories. Probably of African origin is the auxiliary /de/, /də/, which serves widely both as a copula "to be" and as an indicator of continuing action, as in Sranan /a de áksi/ "he is asking"; in Gullah /dɪ rustə də kro/ "the rooster was crowing"; in Cameroons Creole /i də-go sɔfli-sɔfli/ "he is going very slowly". In New Guinea and the Solomons, no such auxiliaries are found in the "classical form" of Melanesian Pidgin English, which has no indication of tense by means of verbal inflection or auxiliary verbs; but /bɪn/ is beginning to spread into the Territory of New Guinea, as a past-tense-indicator, under the influence of Australian administrative officials who have met it in popular representations of Australian Pidgin and who think /bɪn/ one of the most characteristic features of Pidgin English.

TABLE 5

Order of Elements in Neo-Melanesian Verb Phrase

		Noun	Direct Object
Verb ± (Verb) ± (Adverb) ±		or	or
		Adjective	Equational Complement

$$\pm \text{ Adverb} \pm \frac{\text{Exocentric}}{\text{Phrase}} \pm \text{(Predicate)} \pm \text{(Clause)}$$

Since so many prepositions and connecting elements are often left out in the development of pidgin phrase-structure, the verbal phrase in pidgins and creoles often involves complements of types unknown to the languages out of which they develop. Table 5 shows the structure of Neo-Melanesian verbal phrases; Table 6 shows that of verbal phrases in Haitian Creole. Naturally, the types of complement will differ from one pidgin or creole to the next. Thus, not only a number of English-based pidgins and creoles, but also Haitian Creole and other French-based creoles, have the syntactic type VERB + INDIRECT OBJECT + DIRECT OBJECT: for example, Chinese Pidgin English /nó kǽn pé dóg číkən-bón/ "you can't give a dog a chicken-bone"; Sranan /a-gí bófr a pagára/ "he gave Buffalo the basket"; Haitian Creole /li bā mwē jū ti-plat/ "she gave me a little plate". Although this type of verbal phrase is normal in English, it is nevertheless absent from South Seas Pidgin English in general, where we find only the phrase-type /lɔŋ/ "to" + OBJECT to indicate the direct object, as in /ɛm i-gɪvɪm lɪklɪk plet lɔŋ mi/ "she gave me a little plate". Here again, only through recent European influence do we find the English type of indirect object introduced, as when a house-boy once said to me in Rabaul: /mastər, gɪvɪm mi mɔni bɪlɔŋ lukɪm pɪkčər/ "Sir, give me money to go to the movies". In most pidgins and creoles, however, we find a notable extension of the possibilities for verbal

TABLE 6

Order of Elements in Haitian Creole Verb Phrase

Verb ± (Adverb or Exocentric Phrase, emphatic) ± (Noun or Pronoun, indirect object) ± (Noun, Pronoun or Clause, direct object) ± (Noun or Adjective, result of action) ± (Verb) ± (Adverb or Adjective, manner) ± (Exocentric Phrase) ± (Noun, place where or time when) ± (Clause)

complements, to include predicates and full clauses, both as direct objects and as adverbial modifiers: for example, Neo-Melanesian /mastər i-rajt i-stap/ "the master is continually writing [*literally,* the master is writing, it is continuing]", or /fajtɪm kokonʊs i-fɔldawn/ "hit the coconut [so that] it falls down"; Sranan /a-presíri a-no fo-táki/ "she was pleased beyond words [*literally,* she (was) pleased (so that) she (was) not for talking]"; Haitian Creole /li voje ti-mun-a l-di papa-m li mete māže su-tab pu-li/ "she sent the child to tell [*literally,* he should tell] my father she had put the food on the table for him".

Perhaps the clearest case of a specifically African substratum feature is found in the comparative phrase, in which one element is compared with another by means of an adjective or an adverb, followed by an element corresponding to English *than* or French *que*. In West African languages, the regular way of expressing such a comparison does not call for a preposition like *than* or a conjunction like *que*, but involves instead a verb meaning "pass, surpass", as in Twi *wo turo no yɛ fɛ sɛŋ me de no* "your garden is more beautiful than mine [*literally,* your garden is beautiful, surpasses mine]" or in Fanti *míhū ye din kin-nu* "I am stronger than he [*literally,* I am strong, surpass him]" (in Fanti *ye din* form one of a number of series of verbs indicating consecutive actions, motions, etc.). This use of a verb meaning "pass, surpass" to introduce a term of comparison is found in virtually all the pidgins and creoles that have an African substratum, regardless of their European base: for example, West African Pidgin English *Aboma long pass dis tick* "Abome was longer than this tick"; Dahomean Pidgin English *he fine pass all woman* "she was finer than all [other] women"; Gullah /i-tɒl pas mi/ "he is taller than me"; Haitian Creole /li lèd pase u/ "she is uglier than you"; Martiniquais Creole /gasō mwē grā pase fi mwē/ "my boy is older than my girl". In Sranan, /p(a)sá/ "pass" can be used, as in /pasá tén lítri/ "more than ten liters"; or also /móro/ "(be) more", in such sentences as /abóma láŋga móro dísi tíki/ "Aboma was longer than this tick".

In the clause-structure of English and French, we are accustomed to consider the subject as an essential part of the sentence, as much so as the predicate, even in such a sentence as *It is raining*. (If someone asks us "What is raining?", we cannot give any sensible answer; but *it* is nevertheless an essential part of this sen-

tence in English, just like *il* in French *il pleut,* and it would
be impossible to omit the subject and say simply *Is raining* or
Pleut.) However, in many of the world's languages, the subject is a
much less important part of the sentence than is the predicate, and
can often be omitted, as in Spanish *él canta* "HE is singing", which
can be reduced to simply *canta* "he is singing". With some verbs,
in the Romance and other languages, it is not possible to use a subject,
as in Spanish *llueve,* Italian *piove,* and Latin *pluvit* "it is raining".
This is the situation we find in some pidgins and creoles, in which
a predicate can stand alone: for example, Neo-Melanesian /i-ren/
"it is raining" (for the element /i-/, see the next paragraph);
Chinese Pidgin English /hǽb gát lénɪŋ kə́m dáwn/ "there is rain
coming down"; Sranan /dán tjári na-fóru néki kóm gi-kónum/
"(he) brought the bird's neck to the King"; Gullah /tɛl mi aftə sɛ
de kɛc bʌdz/ "(they) told me afterward that they caught birds".

The greater independence of the predicate in many pidgins
and creoles is also shown by the fact that it is often set apart from
what goes before, by some special syntactic marker. South Seas
Pidgin English, in general, has a "predicate-marker" /i-/, which is
normally used when the subject (if there be one) is not of the first
or second person: for example, Neo-Melanesian /mastər i-sɪŋawtɪm
mi/ "the master called me"; Neo-Solomonic /hɛm i-tekɪm lɔŋ šor/
"he took it to the shore". The form /i-/ occurs in no other function in the language and therefore cannot be considered a pronoun,
although it unquestionably comes from English *he.* Its use reflects
a merger of the substandard English habit of recapitulating a subject by means of a pronoun—as in *John, he's an idiot* or *my
mother, she always spanks me*—and the Melanesian-Micronesian
feature of morphologically distinct pronouns that recapitulate subjects and introduce predicates, as in Marshallese /ládrik e-ğérabal/
"the boy, he works".

Haitian and the other Central American French-based creoles
have a series of predicate-prefixes, which indicate negation (/pa-/
"not") and tense (/te-/ past, /(v)a-/ future, and a combination of
the two, /te-va-/ or /t-a-/ conditional); in fact, in these creoles the
predicate is to be defined as that part of the sentence that can be
negativized by placing /pa-/ before it. Thus, we find Haitian
Creole /pipirit pa-di ājē/ "Pipirite didn't say anything"; /rwa
te-gē jū bèl fi/ "the king had a beautiful daughter"; /mašā siro-a
pa-te-gā mēm jū sapat/ "the syrup vendor didn't have even one

shoe"; /u t-a-lage-m/ "you'd leave me". It will be noticed that these elements are all French in origin: /pa-/ < *pas* "not", /te-/ < *était* "was" (imperfect) or *été* "been" (past participle), and /va-/ < *va* "is going".[8] At first, their order seems decidedly non-French, with regard both to the position of the negativizer at the beginning of the predicate and to the occurrence of the tense-signs as prefixes rather than suffixes, a procedure found in many African languages (for example, Ewe, Yòruba, Gã). However, ellipsis of intervening elements in French, especially in usage of the baby-talk variety, could have produced a convergence of African and reduced-French syntactic types: for example, *lui pas bon* "him not good" > /li pa-bõ/; *moi va chanter* "me go sing" > /mwe va-šāte/; *vous été manger* "you been eat(ing)" > /u te-māže/.

In almost all pidgins and creoles investigated so far, there is a much wider choice of elements that can be used as the principal element or center of the predicate than we are accustomed to finding in our familiar West European languages. If we go somewhat farther afield in the European languages, we find some widening of the structural possibilities of the predicate: in Hungarian and Russian, for instance, the predicate can contain not only a verb, as in Hungarian *ez az ember olvas* "this man is reading" or Russian /ón xóṭet kófi/ "he wants coffee", but also a noun or an adjective, as in Hungarian *ez az ember jó* "this man [is] good" or Russian /éta kníga/ "this [is a] book". Such constructions, from the fact that the predicate refers back to or is equated with the subject, are usually called *equational*. In the predicates of most pidgins and creoles, we find, not only nouns and pronouns standing in equational constructions, but virtually any type of free form or phrase, without any verb. Here are a few examples of nouns, pronouns, and adjectives as predicate-centers: Neo-Melanesian /ɛm i-mæn bılɔŋ nədərfelə bænıs/ "he [is a] man of another totemic group", /ɛm i-husæt?/ "who [is] he [*literally,* he who]?", /dısfɛlə mæn i-kræŋki/ "this man [is] stupid, queer"; American Indian Pidgin English *Englishman much foole* (1641); Gullah /i min tıd dat/ "he [was] mean to do that"; Jamaican Creole *when a man belly full;* Sranan /anánsi kóni mán/ "Anansi [is] a clever man", /a-no mí/ "it [is] not me", /anánsi kóni/ "Anansi [is] clever"; Haitian Creole /jõ fi pa-jõ-bõ-dje/ "a girl [is] not a god", /vãt li plē/ "his belly [was]

_____
[8] Perhaps fused with a like-sounding African element (Ewe [a]*va-, a-*) indicating the future (Sylvain, 1936, p. 143).

full", /mwē te-žèn ākò/ "I was still young". Modern Chinese Pidgin English does not have this type of predicate, but it was present in nineteenth-century Chinese Pidgin English, as in /ðǽt jú wájfu?/ "[is] that your wife?". Such constructions are less infrequent, even in standard English, than we are sometimes inclined to think; I remember a widely publicized advertisement in Australia in 1954 which began with the question, addressed to the reader: *You a woman?*.

Examples of other types of predicate-center include those containing adverbs or adverbial phrases: Neo-Melanesian /tɪŋktɪŋk bɪlɔŋ mi i-ɔlsem/ "my opinion [is] thus, this is what I think"; Chinese Pidgin English /tumə́či də́st tébəl tápsajd/ "there is a lot of dust on the table"; American Indian Pidgin English *cache up thur* "the cache [is] up there"; Sranan /tigri dia/ "Tiger [was] there"; Haitian Creole /jo-bjē nā-figi, mē jo pa-bjē nā-ke/ "they were good [*literally*, well] in their faces, but they weren't good in their hearts", /li pa-isit/ "she [is] not here". Phrases introduced by prepositions, acting as centers of predicates, are exemplified by: Neo-Solomonic /wənfɛlə bɪgfɛlə šɛ́l lɔŋ sɔlwatər/ "a big shell [is] in the sea", or Haitian Creole /li avèk-lafjèv-la/ "she [was] with fever, she had a fever" or /nu te-ā-rekreasjō/ "we were at recess". Even full clauses can occur as centers of predicates in larger clause constructions, as in Haitian Creole /sa k-fè-m pa-t-gē admirasjō pu-li, m-te-vin rēmē jū lòt ti-fi/ "that which made me not have any admiration for her [was that] I had come to love another girl".

In Haitian Creole and the other French-based creoles, an interesting problem arises in this connection: the classification of the element /se-/ "it is",[9] found in such sentences as: /se-mwē/ "it's me", /se-pa-mwē/ "it's not me", /se-te-mwē/ "it was me", /se-pa-te-mwē/ "it wasn't me", /se-jū ti-fi/ "its a girl", /se-lapli ki tōbe pādā lanwit/ "it was rain which fell during the night", /se-pa-pu-li, se-pu-mwē/ "it's not for him, it's for me". Clearly, this element is from French *c'est* /se/ "it is", but its structure and function are different in Creole from what they are in French. The French *c'est* is a combination of PRONOUN + VERB, which functions as SUBJECT + CENTER OF PREDICATE, in such sentences as *c'est moi* "it's me", *c'est la pluie* "it's the rain", and also with other

[9] Not to be confused with the Gallicism /se-/ "this, that", found as a demonstrative element preceding the head of a noun phrase (cf. p. 102).

tenses of the verb *être* "to be"; for example, *était* "was" in *c'était moi* "it was me". But in Creole, the element /se-/ is indivisible and always comes before the predicate (which we have defined as whatever can be negativized by the prefixation of /pa-/ "not"); /se-/ must, therefore, be a predicatival element, and wholly a part of the subject in any sentence in which it occurs. It is best classified as an equational subject-particle, which serves simply for the identification of any predicate that follows it.

This type of construction, with an element other than a verb as the center of the predicate, is not traceable to African, Melanesian, or other substratum influences. Since it is present in the very earliest attestation of American Indian Pidgin English (1641), and is so widespread in many different pidgins and creoles, it is rather to be ascribed to the intentional simplification of European languages by their speakers when conversing with supposedly childish natives, on the model of European baby-talk, as suggested earlier. This is another instance of the borrowing, often widespread, of substratum elements that are relatively near the surface of grammatical structure (for instance, the various phrase-types discussed earlier in this chapter, and the morphological features treated in the preceding chapter), along with the retention (frequently in simplified form) of the fundamental structural types of the European base language. Hence it cannot be said that pidgins and creoles are simply "native languages spoken with European words," or that they have "a lexical material which is, so to say, neutral, and which is realized in speech as nouns or as verbs in virtue of the function conferred on it by various processes, especially by the use of aspectival particles."[10] The modern pidgins and creoles are, rather, simplified versions of fundamentally European linguistic structures, to which have been added extensive carry-overs of patterns from the substratum (native) languages.

Sentence-structure, in pidgins and creoles, tends in general to be quite simple. In their earlier stages, while they have not as yet been exposed to the influence of European standard languages, pidgins and creoles are characterized by straightforward sentences, without complex structure or extensive subordination. Sequences of sentences tend to be co-ordinated: for example: Neo-Melanesian /kundiaŋ i-marsalaj ɔlsem mæn. ɛm i-save kajkaj mæn. ɛm sɔdawara

---

[10] Zumthor, 1957.

i-stap dawmbılo. mifɛlə stap lɔŋ namɛl. sɔdawara i-bænısım mifɛlə./ "Kundiang is a spirit like a man. He often eats men. The sea is down below. We are in the middle. The sea encloses us" (this is the beginning of a Melanesian fairy story). If subordination occurs, it is normally without special relative or conjunctional elements; a subordinate predicate or clause is simply placed directly after the element it modifies, and the position is enough to indicate the subordination.[11] In Neo-Melanesian, we find such sentences as: /ɔl meri i-kraj lɔŋ dısfɛlə mæn i-daj/ "the women cry for the man [who] has died", /dısfɛlə mısıs, ɛm mi wok lɔŋ ɛm/ "this white woman, she for whom I worked [literally, she I worked for her]"; in Sranan, /mi na-mán móro ála mán/ "I am the man [who] surpasses all men" or /wán méjtji na-wán kóndre, nòwán mán a-no fíti hem/ "a girl in a certain country, whom no-one suited her [literally, no man suited her)"; in Haitian Creole, /tut ti-dezòd m-kõnē fè/ "all the little naughtinesses I used to do".

On occasion, nouns or other elements modified by predicates or clauses in this way come to be almost subordinators in their own right, especially when they refer to place or time: for example, Neo-Melanesian /tajm/ "time; when", as in /tajm ɛm i-kəməp/ "the time he arrives, when he arrives"; or Haitian Creole /lò/ or /lè/ "hour; when" or /kote/ "place; where", as in /kote lãž rete-a/ "[the place] where L'Ange lived". True subordinating conjunctions— that is, forms functioning exclusively as introductory elements in clauses, like Neo-Melanesian /spos/ "if "—are relatively rare; it is only at a later stage, when the pidgin or the creole has been exposed to learnèd influence from a European language, that the sophisticated habit of using extensive subordination becomes widespread, and such conjunctions as /bɪkɔ́s/ "because" are introduced from English into Neo-Melanesian and Neo-Solomonic, or /kã/ "when" and /paske/ "because" from French into Haitian Creole. When we find such sentences as Neo-Melanesian /maws bɪlɔŋ ju

---

[11] This procedure is optional but very frequent in English, when a relative clause contains a relative element (pronoun or adverb) that may be omitted at will: *the man (whom) I saw, the movie (which) we went to last night*, etc. (The only relative element that cannot be omitted in English is the subject pronoun, as in *the man who did that*.) Old French had even closer parallels, with the addition of predicates and clauses as relative modifiers without any intervening subordinators, as in *Il l'aiment tant ne li faldront nient* "They are so fond of him [that] they will not fail him in any respect" (Roland, v. 397); *Nen aṭ celui ne·l greḍant ed otreit* "There is not a man [who] does not concede and grant it" (*ibid.*, v. 3805).

i-fæs i-stap ɪnəf lɔŋ tajm meri bɪlɔŋ ju i-karɪm pɪkɪnɪni/ "your mouth will remain closed until your wife bears her child", or Haitian Creole /ženeral kapwa, ke jo te-rele kapwa-lamò/ "General Capois, whom they called *Capois-la-mort*"—we can be sure, because of the conjunctional elements /ɪnəf lɔŋ tajm/ "until" or /ke/ "whom", that these sentences are in relatively learnèd, sophisticated style.

REFERENCES

Phrase- and clause-structure: Hall, 1950a (chap vii).

Neo-Melanesian syntax: Hall, 1943a (chaps. iv and v), 1955a (chap. vi).

Haitian Creole syntax: Hall, 1953 (chaps. iii and iv); table of Haitian Creole nominal phrase-structure, *ibid*. (p. 46); of Haitian Creole verbal phrase-structure, *ibid*. (p. 57). Relation of Haitian Creole syntax to African substratum: Sylvain, 1936 (*passim*).

Sequences of verbs in Negro creoles and African languages: Herskovits, 1936 (pp. 118, 131); in Fanti, Welmers, 1946 (chap. iv. 7).

Use of "suppose" > Melanesian Pidgin *spos* "if": Coombe, 1911 (pp. 164–165).

Use of words meaning "pass, surpass" in meaning "than" in Negro creoles and African languages: Herskovits, 1936 (pp. 132–133); in Fanti, Welmers, 1946 (chap. iv. 7.12).

Vocabulary and Idiom

CHAPTER 7

THE "man-in-the-street" is, in general, more interested in the vocabulary of a language than in its structural patterns (phonology, morphology, syntax), because the most obvious meanings are those conveyed by independent words. Morphological and syntactical features also convey meanings, but not (in general) the kind which are listed in dictionaries and which are easily grasped without extensive, subtle analysis. For this reason, some analysts of linguistic structure tend to neglect the study of vocabulary, deeming it superficial and not worthy of their attention. Such an attitude is not justified, any more than that of the naïve person who thinks that language consists only of words; as Edward Sapir said, "The linguistic student should never make the mistake of identifying a language with its dictionary."[1] Although it is not as highly organized as the patterns of linguistic structure, the vocabulary of a language tells us, through its meanings, a great deal concerning the society that uses it as a vehicle for communication.

On first coming in contact with a pidgin language, the observer is often struck by its apparent mixture of words from different sources. Neo-Melanesian, for instance, has such words as /siraŋ/ "cupboard" (from German *Schrank*), *malolo* "rest" (from Kuanua, the language of the Gazelle peninsula in New Britain), and /kajkaj/ "eat, food" from some Polynesian language. On this basis, we frequently find a pidgin characterized as a "mongrel jargon" or "a weird mixture of tongues." Yet there are more English words in Neo-Melanesian than there are Anglo-Saxon words in modern English.

[1] Sapir, 1921, p. 234.

89

Of the sixteen hundred or so individual words given in Father Francis Mihalic's dictionary, roughly 75 per cent are of English origin, 20 per cent are from native languages, and the remainder from German, Malay, or scattering other sources. In English, on the other hand, more than 50 per cent of our present-day vocabulary is of French, Latin, or Greek origin.

Pidgin languages do have, as part of their essential nature, a very reduced vocabulary. Yet even if the number of words is small, the range of meaning they convey is wide; each word has a clearly definable meaning, and by combining words into phrases with idiomatic meanings of their own, one can say anything one wants to in the cultural situation in which the language is used. If something further needs to be referred to, new combinations of words can be made, or new words can be introduced from outside sources. As the Florentine philosopher of language G. B. Gelli said over four hundred years ago in his *Capricci di Giusto bottaio* ("Whimsical thoughts of Giusto the cobbler"): "All languages are fit to express the concepts of those who use them; and if they should chance not to be, they [those who use them] make them so."

In a pidgin, many of the words of European origin keep their original meanings: for example, Neo-Melanesian /tebəl/ "table", /lɛg/ "leg", /najt/ "night", /mašin/ "machine", /hæmər/ "hammer", and so forth. Similar examples from Chinese Pidgin English include /tɔ́ki/ "talk, say", /gó/ "go", /kə́m/ "come", /bébi/ "baby"; from Sranan, /djómpo/ "jump", /fútu/ "foot", /tíri/ "still, quiet", /ték/ "take", etc.; and of course the numerals, demonstratives, and similar expressions. The same type of correspondence can be noted in the Haitian Creole material we have been quoting so far: for example, /mãže/ "eat" < French *manger*, /pale/ "speak" < French *parler*, /kò/ "body" < French *corps* /kòr/, etc.

In quite a number of words, however, pidgins and creoles show extensions of meaning which may strike us as queer at first sight, but which, on reflection, are seen to be quite logical. For instance, English *screw* appears in Neo-Melanesian as /skru/—referring, however, not only to the metal object that holds two pieces of wood together, but to anything that acts as a joint; and so "elbow" is /skru bɪlɔŋ arm/ "the joint of the arm", and "knee" is /skru bɪlɔŋ lɛg/ "the joint of the leg". English *grass* appears in Pidgin as /gras/, but refers, not only to the green plant, but to anything that grows outward from a surface in blade-like shape; so "hair" is, quite logically, /gras bɪlɔŋ hɛd/, and "beard" is /gras bɪlɔŋ fes/. In both Neo-Melanesian and Sranan, English *win* has expanded its meaning, so that Neo-Melanesian /wɪnɪm/ and Sranan /wíni/ now can be used transitively with respect to a person and mean "win out over, defeat", as in Sranan /sèkrepátu wíni día/ "Tortoise defeated Deer". Neo-Melanesian /wɪnɪm/ can also mean "earn", as in /mi wɪnɪm tɛn mark/ "I earned ten shillings".

The essential process involved in such extensions of meaning—and we could multiply them a hundred-fold with further examples from other pidgins and creoles—is that the native hears a given word, which to a European has certain connotations, and then the native sees as primary in the situation certain other characteristics that to the European seem secondary. A recent Neo-Melanesian development, that of the word /wajrlɛs/, will illustrate this point. When the English word *wireless* was introduced into Melanesian Pidgin, along with the use of radio-telephony in the practical situation, in the nineteen-thirties, it referred to broadcast transmission and reception without wires. The speakers of Pidgin who heard the word, however, saw in the situation chiefly the fact that speech was being received without any visible means of transmission, and so they applied the word /wajrlɛs/ to other, similar situations: those of gossiping, slander, and the like, which involve secret or underhanded talk. At present, therefore, Neo-Melanesian /wajrlɛs/ has these further meanings, and a sentence like /ɛm i-tɔk wajrlɛs lɔŋ mi/ means "he is conducting a whispering campaign against me"; while, referring to a person, /wajrlɛs/ can mean "a go-between, especially one who carries secrets from one person to another".

This extension of meaning takes place also with regard to words that, for Europeans, have taboo connotations, like our "four-letter words" in English. Some terms that are taboo in standard English are quite harmless in Pidgin; many of these have undergone considerable extension of meaning, of the same type as that discussed in the previous paragraph. We have already mentioned the development of Neo-Melanesian /ars/ to mean "bottom (of anything), cause, source". The verb /bəgərəp/ means simply "to be spoiled, ruined", and /bəgərəpɪm/ is "to ruin, wreck", as in /ɔlsem wɔnem ju bəgərəpɪm dɪsfɛlə mašin?/ "Why did you wreck this machine?". Many of these words were taken over quite unsuspectingly by natives who heard coarse-mouthed sailors and traders use them in every-day speech; others may possibly have been deliberately foisted on the natives by Europeans who thought they would have a bit of fun thereby. No matter; what is important in such a situation is, not the intent of the one who teaches such expressions, but the actual use to which they are put by the borrower. Frequently, the new meanings that European words acquire in pidgins or creoles are related to the organization of native social groups. A favorite remark of uninformed Europeans in the South Seas is that "native women don't know the difference between men and women"—based on the observation that a woman talking Pidgin will refer to her sister as /bɔrata bɪlɔŋ mi/ and to her brother as /sɪsa bɪlɔŋ mi/. Of course, /bɔrata/ comes from English *brother*, and /sɪsa/ from English *sister;* but in Neo-Melanesian these two words don't mean what they do in English. The form /bɔrata/ means "sibling of the same sex", and hence, when a man is speaking, it means "brother", but when a woman is speaking, "sister." Likewise, /sɪsa/ means "sibling of the opposite sex", so a woman will use this term when referring to her brother. The adjective /rəbɪš/ is derived from the English noun *rubbish,* but it means, in Neo-Melanesian, "without wealth or standing in the community"; the writers of the *Liklik Katolik Baibel* made a very good choice of words when they referred to Lazarus as *rabish man.* The Neo-Melanesian word /wənfɪš/ means, not "one fish", but "the last surviving member of a clan". In Haitian Creole, /zõbi/ "zombie" comes from a word in one of the languages of the Congo, /nsumbi/ "devil", but it has acquired its specifically Haitian meaning of "human soul which is neither alive nor dead, and which is in the power of a malignant sorcerer" from the circumstances of New World slavery, the zombie being a symbol of the slave in his status of bondage.

Even such apparently simple and obvious words as *yes* and *no* can have meanings different from those we are accustomed to in our European languages. At a hotel in Rabaul (Territory of New Guinea), I had this conversation in Neo-Melanesian with a house-boy:

> AUTHOR: /bɛlo kajkaj i-no sɪŋawt jɛt?/ "Hasn't the dinner bell rung yet?"
>
> HOUSE-BOY: /jɛs, mastər, i-no sɪŋawt./ "Yes, sir, it hasn't rung."

Had the bell actually rung, he would have answered: /no, mastər, i-sɪŋawt fɪnɪš/ "no, sir, it has rung already". However, if my question had been in the positive: /bɛlo kajkaj i-sɪŋawt jɛt?/, his answer would have been as in English: either /jɛs, mastər, i-sɪŋawt fɪnɪš/ "Yes, sir, it has rung", or /no, mastər, i-no sɪŋawt jɛt/ "No, sir, it hasn't rung yet". This is the type of response that one finds in Melanesian languages and elsewhere, as in Japanese, and that amuses speakers of English, as shown, for example, in the song "Yes, we have no bananas" of the early nineteen-twenties. On occasion, it serves, as do other uncomprehended linguistic differences, as an excuse for obloquy: during the Second World War, it was said in American magazine articles that it was evident from this usage that the Japanese did not even know the difference between *yes* and *no*.

The use of /jɛs/ and /no/ in Neo-Melanesian and in English can, however, easily be formulated as follows:

1. In Neo-Melanesian, /jɛs/ and /no/ refer to the meaning of the preceding utterance, and indicate the speaker's opinion of its accuracy or otherwise. Neo-Melanesian /jɛs/ thus means "what you've just said is right"; /no/ means "what you've said is wrong".

2. In English, *yes* and *no* normally refer to the linguistic structure of the utterance to come and indicate the speaker's intention of producing a positive or a negative statement, respectively. This formulation will hold even for instances like *yes, isn't it?*. Such an utterance is equivalent, with ellipsis of the middle section, to *yes, it is, isn't it?* Hence, in *yes, isn't it?*, the use of *yes* implies that the coming sentence is to have a positive value as a whole.

Up to now, the use of /jɛs/ and /no/ in Neo-Melanesian has been quite clear and unambiguous to anyone willing to take the trouble to learn the language. In recent years, however, uncomprehending speakers of English have, in their attempts to use Neo-Melanesian, introduced the English meanings of *yes* and *no;* native users of Neo-Melanesian, imitating speakers of English because of the latter group's prestige, are currently beginning to use *yes* and *no* as in English. It is too early to tell which usage will win the day; in the meanwhile, ignorance on the part of the prestige-group and naïve imitation on the part of the less prestigious have caused confusion to arise in the meanings of Neo-Melanesian /jɛs/ and /no/ where none existed before.

Of course, with limited vocabularies such as those of pidgin languages, words are likely to have wider ranges of meaning than do the corresponding forms in the European source languages. However, the context normally makes it quite clear what is being referred to, so that no confusion results if both speaker and hearer know the language sufficiently well. Words can be amplified by the addition of modifiers to make any distinction that is needed. For instance, Neo-Melanesian /papa/ refers to both "father" and "mother's brother", since the latter is fully as important as the former (if not more so) in child-raising in Melanesian cultures; if, however, one needs to distinguish, the physical progenitor can be referred to as /papa tru/ "real father", and the mother's brother as /smɔlpapa/—a compound and hence involving transferred meaning, not literally "small father" but something like "substitute father". Nor need we be worried by the discrepancies we often find, when pidgin or creole words cover a different range of meaning from that covered by the corresponding words in European languages: for example, Haitian Creole /lese/ "leave = "go away" ≠ French *laisser* "leave behind, allow", whereas Haitian Creole /kite/ means "leave" = "allow" ≠ French *quitter* "go away from". This is a phenomenon that we always encounter on comparing the vocabularies of any two languages, such as the fact that English has only the one word *know* corresponding to the two French words *savoir* "to know from the inside out" and *connaître* "to know from the outside in"; whereas, on the other hand, French has just the one expression *se promener* "to go for a [relatively short, nonbusiness] excursion" as contrasted with English *take a walk, take a (tram, bus, horseback, train, plane) ride*, etc.

The proportion of words from other than the source language varies from one pidgin or creole to the next. The highest percentage of words from native (substratum) languages that I have come across so far is in Neo-Melanesian, where such words form perhaps 20 per cent of the total vocabulary. To a large extent, these are terms for local phenomena such as fauna and flora: for example, /kapʊl/ "New Guinea tree-wallaby", /lala/ "[a kind of fish]", /kurita/ "octopus", /karua/ "mullet", /lawlaw/ "New Guinea apple", /abus/ "a side-dish [especially of meat, eaten with other food]", and so on. Various words of native origin, however, refer to objects of more widespread occurrence, and presumably entered Melanesian Pidgin as the result of vocabulary-mixture at an early stage, when speakers of native languages would carry over into Pidgin their own terms for things whose English names they did not yet know; so, for instance, /balus/ "bird", /kiaw/ "egg", /buk/ "boil, sore, swelling", /lɪmlɪmbu(r)/ "time off, vacation". With these words, too, extension of meaning has taken place, so that /kiaw/, for example, means "anything of egg-like or spherical shape", including "electric light-bulb"; and, when the Melanesians were introduced to the amenities of "civilized" warfare in the Second World War, /kiaw/ came to mean "bomb" in some regions. In modern times, /balus/ has come to mean not only "bird" but "aeroplane"; /ples balus/ is "place for aeroplanes, airstrip, air-port", and /balus i-troɪmwe kiaw/ means "the aeroplane casts bombs, the aeroplane is engaged in bombing".

In other pidgins and creoles the proportion of native words is rather smaller. In Central America, many of the words of African origin are connected with African religious behavior patterns: for example, Haitian Creole /vodū/ "vaudoun", /ūgã/ "vaudoun priest", /ūfò/ "precincts of vaudoun temple"; Sranan /kina/ "food taboo" (< Loango /čina/), /azemán/ "vampire" (with /aze/ < Dahomeyan /aze/ "witch"), /akra/ "soul" (< Twi). Gullah has a number of other words, such as /ɟuk-/ in /ɟúk-hàws/ "disorderly house" (an element that has passed into every-day American English in *juke-box*), from Wolof /ɟug/ "to lead a dis-orderly life", or /anánse/ "spider" (also found in Sranan and other Central American creoles) < Twi /anánse/.[2] Similarly, Jamaican Creole has such words of specifically Twi origin as *fufu* "mashed starch-vegetables", *nyam-nyam* "food" (widespread in Central America), *kas-kas* "contention", and /kotokú/ "a kind of bag or sack", as well as numerous others.

In outlying regions, such as the remote country districts in Haiti or the bush region in Guiana, there are considerably greater survivals of African words; the Comhaires have told the author that they have discovered over four thousand African words in Haitian Creole in recent years, whereas it used to be thought that

---

[2] In a large group of African folk-tales that have been brought to the Americas, the spider (*Anansi*) is the hero; in the versions of these tales that circulated among American Negroes in the southern United States, many of which were included by Joel Chandler Harris in his "Uncle Remus" stories, the rôle of Anansi and many of his actions have passed to Br'er Rabbit—and that of Tiger, Anansi's perennial rival and enemy, to Br'er Fox—while the name Anansi survives in that of another character in these stories, "Miss Nancy".

this creole had only a handful of such Africanisms. Gullah has an especially interesting group of survivals of African words, in its personal names; Gullah people have, in addition to their official names, a kind of pet name (which they call "basket name"), used only among themselves. Lorenzo D. Turner collected nearly four thousand such "basket names" and tentatively identified them with corresponding African personal names, at the same time demonstrating a close parallel between Gullah and African methods in naming children. Some older Gullahs could count from one to ten or further (even to nineteen) in various African languages, having learned such counting systems through oral tradition; this type of survival is similar to the use of Celtic numerals (as in counting sheep) in parts of England where no Celtic has otherwise been spoken for many hundreds of years. In stories and songs the Gullahs have many set phrases and expressions of African origin (for example, /sa na pon:/ "he is lying far away"), which they often use without knowing their exact meaning. Yet in text-frequency, the occurrence of these substratum elements varies considerably, being, in most instances, rather low in every-day speech (except, of course, for the special instance of the Gullah "basket names"), but rising markedly in special contexts such as those of story-telling, singing, and religious ritual.

Although practically never absent, borrowing may occur to a greater or lesser degree, depending on the circumstances, from the superstratum of the official language dominant in the region where a pidgin or a creole is spoken. In Melanesian Pidgin, a certain number of words were introduced from German during the period 1880–1914, when the present Territory of New Guinea was under German rule as Kaiser Wilhelms Land. The total percentage of German words, in terms of list-frequency, has probably never been very high in Melanesian Pidgin, and yet the superficial observer has the impression that there are a great many German borrowings, because some of them have a very high text-frequency. Certain German words are firmly ensconced in the vocabulary and are likely to remain as long as Neo-Melanesian is spoken: for example, /raws/ "to get out" (from German *heraus!* "out of here!", used mostly as a command-form) and its objective form /rawsɪm/ "to put out, bring out, take away, cut off"; /mark/ "shilling"; /hobəl/ "plane (for smoothing wood)"; /tajs/ "pond" (from German *Teich*); /betən/ "to pray"; /brʊs/ "chest" (from German *Brust* "breast"). A number of German words, however, are on their way out, including some that my anthropologist informants gave me in 1942 as being in normal use in the Sepik valley in the nineteen-thirties: for example, /blajstɪk/ "pencil" (< German *Bleistift*, crossed with English *stick*), now being replaced by /pɛnsɪl/; /laŋsam/ "slow", giving way to /slo/; /blʊt/ "blood, pus, sap", now alternating with /bləd/ from English *blood;* or /hajdən/ "heathen" (< German *Heiden*). The dictionary prepared in the nineteen-thirties by the reverends Schebesta and Meiser gives a number of other Germanisms that by now are either regional or obsolete, such as /brajt/ "broad" (from German *breit*); /gəvér/, /kɪvér/ "rifle" (from German *Gewehr* "weapon"); /kail/ "wedge" (German *Keil*); /pəplú/ "blast it!" (German *verflucht!* "cursed; curse it!". In more modern times, English has taken the place of German as a superstratum language from which borrowings can be made, especially of learnèd words such as /dɪsɛnt(ə)ri/ "dysentery" or /ɛksampəl/ "example", to say nothing of the host of words brought over complete with their irrational English spellings in government mimeographed newspapers: for example, *competition, specialist, private,* and (believe it or not) even *choir!*

In the Americas, however, the superstratum of the official European language which is dominant in the region where a creole is spoken has often exerted a very strong influence, contributing a high percentage of the total vocabulary of the creole, and on occasion, through these loan-words, even introducing new phonemic features into the structure of the language. In Haitian Creole, there are a large number of words, French in origin like most of the basic vocabulary of the language, but very little altered from their shape in standard French: for example, /bibliotèk/ "library", /difikilte/ "difficulty", /ēterõp/ "to interrupt" (< French /ēterõpr/), /ipokrit/ "hypocritical", /kãtite/ "quantity", etc. In some instances, it is possible to distinguish different strata of lexical borrowing according to their phonological characteristics: for instance, earlier borrowings of words containing the French suffix *eur* /-œr/ (indicating agent, etc.) show /-ò/ as in /gadò/ "baby-tender", /mãtò/ "liar" etc.; whereas later borrowings containing this same suffix show /-è/, as in /profèsè/ "professor" or /flãnè/ "lounger, idler". On more or less formal occasions, even people of the lower social strata like to interlard their speech with fine-sounding French words or expressions,[3] and of course modern technology is bringing more and more learnèd terms into every-day use in connection with latter-day mechanical developments, for instance in connection with automobiles, power machinery and the like, such as /radio/ "radio", /šāžmā vitès/ "gear-shift" [< French *change-ment de vitesse* [*literally*, change of speed]". Sometimes, however, in the desire to sound elegant, unlearned speakers are likely to make mistakes in their use of unfamiliar high-falutin' terms, indulging in malapropisms such as /jo pase lānwit nā-kōplezãs zetwal jo/ "they passed the night in the complaisance of the stars": what the speaker means to say is /nā-kōtãplasjō zetwal jo/ "in the contemplation of the stars"! As always happens when learnèd terminology is borrowed from the source language, there arise pairs of doublets, that is, terms that come from the same word but differ in their phonological shape and sometimes also in their meaning or connotation: for example, Haitian Creole /šwal/, the normal term for "horse", as opposed to /šival/ or /ševal/, a later attempt at reproducing the French word /šəval/ *cheval*.

In Sranan (especially the town speech of Paramaribo) and Papiamentu, both of which are spoken in territories that have been under Dutch rule for several centuries, there is a very heavy overlay of borrowings from the official languages. No detailed statistical count has been made, but one can estimate that probably somewhere between 20 and 25 per cent of the words in every-day use in both Sranan and Papiamentu are of Dutch origin. In Papiamentu, we find such common words as /hán-skún/ "glove(s)" (< Dutch *hand-schoon*, literally "hand-shoes", parallel to German *Handschuhe*), /blɔ́w/ "blue", /búki/ "book", /skér/ "scissors", /vérf/ "paint", or /zómər/ "summer". In Sranan, we find /búku/ "book", /dréi/ "turn", /fró/ "wife", /héimel/

---

[3] Cf. the speeches made on formal occasions, like weddings, reproduced in Hall, 1953, §7.12, pp. 212–214, with such sentences as /že-swi kōtā boku pu-vwar mizi mun ki vene isit dã-sèt mariaž de-mõ-neve solvès/ "I am very happy to see the number of people who have come here to this marriage of my nephew Solvès", with such interlardings of (approximative) French as /že-swi/ "I am", /boku/ "much", /vwar/ "to see", /vene/ "come", /dã/ "in", /sèt/ "this" (feminine singular modifying /mariaž/, whereas French *mariage* is masculine, and /de-mõ-neve/ "of my nephew". In normal Creole, the sentence would be something like /mwē kōtā ãpil pu-vwè mizi mun ki vini isit ná-mariaž neve mwē solvès sa-a/.

"heaven", /dómini/ "priest", etc., etc. Since the basic vocabulary of Sranan comes largely from English, and since Dutch and English are closely related West Germanic languages, it is sometimes hard or impossible to tell whether a given word comes from the one or the other; this is the case with /gótu/ "gold", /ríŋgi/ or /liŋga/ "ring", and a number of others. In both Sranan and Papiamentu, the Dutch borrowings contain phonemic features not found in other parts of the language, particularly the phoneme /x/ (which, in Dutch, has developed out of an earlier /g/ and hence often corresponds etymologically to an English /g/), in such words as Sranan /xólde/ "gulden [a coin]", /xolúku/ "luck", /sxádu/ "shadow", or Papiamentu /zax/ "saw", /órxəl/ "organ", and /bráx/ "bridge". Papiamentu seems to have had originally a simple five-vowel system, into which, through loan-words from Dutch, there was later introduced a further contrast between open and close /e/ and /ɛ/, /o/ and /ɔ/, as shown by such a pair as /serbés/ "beer" (< Spanish cerveza) versus /skér/ "scissors" (< Dutch Scheer); and also between the front-rounded vowels /y/ (like the u in French tu or the ü of German müde) and /ə/, in such words as /jýli/ "July", /stýr/ "to steer", and /xáldə/ "(a) gulden". Both Sranan and Papiamentu also show, in their Dutch loan-words, a number of consonant combinations that were not present in earlier strata of the vocabulary, such as /kt/ (Sranan /bikti/ "confess"), /rx/ (Papiamentu órxəl/ "organ"), /ft/ (Papiamentu /beléft/ "polite"), etc.

Even though a language may have a high percentage of its vocabulary derived from foreign sources—like the 25 per cent or more of Sranan and Papiamentu words from Dutch, or the more than 50 per cent of English words that are of French and Graeco-Latin origin—it is nevertheless not changed thereby in its fundamental genetic affiliation. English is still a Germanic language, despite all its loan-words. Chamorro, the language of Guam and the Marianas, derives perhaps 90 to 95 per cent of its vocabulary from Spanish; yet it is basically a Malayo-Polynesian language. Similarly, Papiamentu remains a Romance-based creole, with specifically Ibero-Romance affiliation; and Sranan remains an English-based creole (and hence of ultimately Germanic origin)— despite their heavy overlay of Dutch vocabulary. Our criteria for determining a language's genetic affiliation are, not its lexical make-up (which is very much on the surface of linguistic structure, and can change very rapidly through obsolescence, neologism, and borrowing), but its structural characteristics—in Hockett's terminology, its functors—and its underlying, deep-level grammatical core. This can be proved by considering such nonsense poetry as Lewis Carroll's "Jabberwocky" (" 'Twas brillig, and the slithy toves / did gyre and gimble in the wabe; / All mimsy were the borogoves, / and the mome raths outgrabe"), in which the content-words (in Hockett's terminology, the "contentives") have either no meaning at all or else only a vaguely identifiable one: for example, *slithy* = *lithe* and *slimy*). Such material is none the less English, because its functors are all English. Similarly, a sentence like *Die Funktion der Philologie ist relativ limitiert* is German, not Latin; and Sranan /mi dóifi fréi gowé, ma mi xolúk, dáti tán/ "my dove flew away, but my luck, that stays" is Sranan, despite the presence of the Dutch contentives /dóifi/ "dove", /fréi/ "fly" and /xolúk/ "luck", and the functors in this sentence (and in Sranan in general) are of English origin, despite the survival of the conjunction /ma/ "but" from an earlier Guianan Pidgin Portuguese.

One of the most common words, almost a characteristic word marking a pidgin or a creole, is *savvy* "to know", in its various forms in the different languages: in Romance-based pidgins or creoles, Cape Verde Portuguese *sabi* /sábi/, Indo-Portuguese *sabe* /sábe/, Papiamentu /sabi/, Lingua Franca *saber* /sabér/, and North African Pidgin French /sabír/ (which furnished the very name of the pidgin, *sabir*); and in English-based languages, Beach-la-Mar, Chinese and Australian Pidgin English /sǽvi/, Neo-Melanesian /save/, and Sranan /sábi/.[4] This word was probably borrowed into English and the English-based pidgins and creoles at different times and from various Romance sources: the Chinese Pidgin English word from Cantonese Pidgin Portuguese, the Taki-Taki from Guianan Pidgin Portuguese, and the South Seas forms (including Neo-Melanesian and Australian Pidgin English) through English. Besides "know", these forms mean "know how; be able", and from these meanings they have developed that of "be in the habit of"—a semantic transition which is common to the Romance verbs that have developed out of Proto-Romance /sapé^re/ "to know".

4 Cf. Hall, 1957a.

In several pidgins and creoles, this verb has developed a shortened form, used especially when it is not stressed and stands before another verb: for example, Haitian Creole /sa-/ or Sranan /sab-/. In Haitian Creole, we find only /sa/, meaning "can, may", both as an independent verb—as in /tu sa pa-sa/ "all that can't be [so]", in which the first /sa/ is a demonstrative pronoun and the second /sa/ is our verb—and as a prefix—as in /li sa-šāte/ "he can (may) sing". For "to know," Haitian Creole uses /kōnē/ (< French /kɔnɛtr/) alone; from this fact we may infer that /sa/ had already made the semantic transition to "can, may" before being taken into Creole, thus fitting in with the general pattern of the Romance equivalence of /sapéˆre/ "to know" with "to be able; can, may".

The vocabulary items we have mentioned so far have all come into the various pidgin and creole languages, so far as we know, by normal processes of unreflecting linguistic imitation in real-life situations. On occasion, individuals or groups have made special efforts to introduce words; the most extensive of these attempts has been the borrowing of numerous Latin words into Neo-Melanesian, in Roman Catholic mission-work: for example, /santu/ "holy", /misa/ "mass; go to mass", /eklesia/ "church", /kruse/ "cross", etc. Sometimes such efforts have backfired, due to the natives' taking a given word and extending its meaning in directions not originally intended by the introducer of the word. This happened, for instance, with /paŋaŋar/ "to be open", which was brought into Meianesian Pidgin by the nineteenth-century missionary Parkinson, as in the sentence /dor i-paŋaŋar/ "the door is open". In Melanesian usage, it came to be applied to situations quite different from those the good missionary had intended, as in /meri i-paŋaŋar/ "the woman assumes position for sexual intercourse".[5] Here, as always happens, the speakers of the language used the new word in accordance with their own patterns of behavior and outlook on life.

[5] In Hall, 1955a, p. 97, I referred to /paŋaŋar/ as "a word from a native language." The similarity in phonological shape and meaning to Italian *spalancare* "to open wide" is noticeable, and one wonders whether through some indirect channel of transmission (for example, through borrowing from Italian sailors' usage into Pidgin Portuguese and thence into pidginized Malay) the Italian word might not have been the ultimate source of Neo-Melanesian /paŋaŋar/; to date, however, specific data on this word are lacking.

REFERENCES

Extent of vocabulary of Neo-Melanesian: Hall, 1943d. A rough count of the material in Mihalic, 1957, shows approximately the same proportions as those presented in the earlier study, which was based on Schebesta and Meiser.

Meaning of /wənfɪš/: Sayer, 1943 (p. 91); cf. Hall, 1944b. *Yes* and *No* in Neo-Melanesian: Hall, 1956b.

Gullah "basket-names" and other African lexical elements: L.D. Turner, 1949 (chap. iii).

Neo-Melanesian /save/ and other words from Proto-Romance /sapéˆre/ "to know": Hall, 1957a.

Significance

PART III

Linguistic Significance

CHAPTER 8

PIDGINS and creoles have significance for our modern world in several respects. They have far-reaching implications for our study of language, with regard to the applicability of our techniques of linguistic analysis, to the validity of the theory of linguistic substratum, and to the accuracy of our techniques of reconstructing ancestral or "proto-" languages. Our conclusions with regard to their intrinsic merits have a fundamental bearing on the social attitudes that are held regarding them. In many regions where pidgins or creoles are prevalent, their use has come to be a matter of political concern, and our findings concerning their nature and function are directly relevant to the determination of governmental policy on their admissibility in official and educational activities.

It used to be thought that not all languages had a true "grammar," but that only a few—especially, of course, Greek and Latin—were "grammatical," while the rest had no rules and hence no fixed structure, being (as Dante put it ca. 1295 in his *De vulgari Eloquentia*, "On Poetry in the Vernacular") "imbibed without any rule together with our mother's milk." In fact, during the Middle Ages, the term *grammatica* was virtually synonymous with Latin, and to talk or write "grammatically" was to talk or write in accordance with the rules laid down for Latin in the grammars of Donatus, Priscian, and later scholastic grammarians. In the Renaissance, with the rise of the vernaculars of Western Europe—Italian, French, Spanish, English, etc.—as literary vehicles, the defenders of these latter languages worked hard to demonstrate that they, too, had "grammar"—often, unfortunately, by forcing the facts of the modern vernaculars into the straitjacket of Latin rules, but eventually making enough adjustments to show tolerably well that the modern languages have structures of their own. Even then the idea still persisted for some centuries that although the literary languages might have a "grammar," the local dialects did not; for instance, the sixteenth-century Italian theorist Benedetto Varchi declared roundly that Genoese was such a confused jargon that it had no clearly articulated sounds at all!

In the nineteenth century, scholars recognized that dialects, as well as standard languages, have grammatical structures of their own, even though they may differ in one respect or another from those of the literary language. Towards the end of the last century and the beginning of this, students of the languages of "primitive" peoples—in Africa, Asia, the South Seas, and the Americas—showed conclusively that all languages spoken as the native languages of human speech-communities, no matter how "backward" their speakers may seem to be technologically or in other respects, are nevertheless endowed with complete structures of their own. All stories about tribes whose languages have only three hundred words, who have no articulate sounds and can say nothing but "ugh," whose languages are so deficient that they have to be eked out with gestures, etc., have been shown to be pure myth. It is now recognized that there are no "primitive" languages extant any longer, in the sense of languages whose development has not yet reached the stage of having clearly definable units of sound, linguistic form, and syntactic order. Any such earlier stages must have existed, everywhere in the world, hundreds of thousands of years in the past. In fact, some so-called "primitive languages" are considerably more complicated in many respects than our "languages of civilization"; as we pointed out earlier, however, none of the many attempts at correlating linguistic structure with stages of social or technological development has been at all successful.

The last refuge of the concept of "language without grammar" —that is, of languages that do not have clearly articulated sounds, grammatically patterned forms, or adequate syntactical or lexical resources—has been the popular idea of pidgin and creole languages. It is on this basis that critics of Pidgin, in the debate following the United Nations Trusteeship Council's pronunciamento of 1953, used such expressions as "inferiority made half-articulate" or said flatly:

If the attempt to simplify vocabulary is fraught with difficulties, the attempt to simplify grammar is simply disastrous. . . . The standard grammar has, in fact, been jettisoned, and a new, crude, and incredibly tortuous form of grammar has been built up in its place. . . . So far from being an independent language, pidgin takes over a whole ready-made phonetic and morphological system, crudely distorted by false ideas of simplification.[1]

However, investigations by unprejudiced investigators, using modern techniques of linguistic observation and analysis, have demonstrated conclusively that all pidgins and creoles, even the simplest, are as amenable to description and formulation as are any other languages. Their structures, although in some ways simpler than those of full-sized languages, are nevertheless complete in themselves, and are not "crude," "distorted," or "tortuous." This much is evident from purely objective observation; if we wish to introduce aesthetic (and hence necessarily subjective) criteria of judgment, it becomes a matter of personal preference. Some, including myself, have found pidgins to be most interesting and attractive little languages, and their creole outgrowths to be equally pleasing. The kind of imagination and resourcefulness that have gone into the development of pidgin languages is on a par with that shown in many other material devices and cultural patterns which have been devised to meet short-term but pressing needs, and often reveals great ingenuity and capacity for adaptation.

One of the major problems under discussion in linguistics, for over a century, has been that of the nature and extent of substratum influence. The problem is substantially this: is it possible that a given language, when it is abandoned by its speakers in favor of a new language (as when speakers of Celtic abandoned that language for Latin in Roman Gaul), can leave traces in the new language? If our answer is affirmative, three further questions arise: (1) In what aspects of linguistic structure can substratum influence be manifest? (2) By what mechanisms are substratum features carried over into the language that replaces the earlier substratum, as Latin replaced Gaulish? (3) In what cases should we ascribe a given linguistic change to the effects of a presumed substratum? That

[1] French, 1953.

a language can preserve traces, often numerous traces, of a previously spoken substratum in its vocabulary, is now admitted by everyone: for example, French *alou-ette* "lark" < Celtic *alauda;* Spanish *vega* "flat lowland" < Iberian *baika.* Concerning other levels of linguistic structure, however, there has been extensive debate. Some linguists are disposed to admit the possibility of substratum influence on all levels—phonological, morphological, and syntactic as well as lexical; others deny it completely or (basing their conclusions primarily on conditions prevailing among immigrants to the United States) consider it admissible only in syntax. As for the transmission of substratum traits, it is usually envisaged as taking place in three possible ways: (1) through physical heredity; (2) as a relic of a period of bilingualism; and (3) through a kind of mystical aura, exerting its influence without any relation to the physical world. "Substratomaniacs" see the influence of linguistic substrata everywhere, and ascribe virtually every linguistic change to one substratum or another, whether anything is known about the presumed substratum or not; "substratophobes" deny such influence in almost all instances; and "eclectics" wish to distinguish according to the situation prevailing in each separate instance.

In historical linguistics of the traditional type, the discussion of substratum theory has reached a dead center, with substratomaniacs and substratophobes repeating their arguments at each other without effect, principally because of the lack of decisive evidence on one side or the other. Pidgins and creoles can furnish just this type of decisive evidence, as was seen as early as the eighteen-sixties and seventies by Hugo Schuchardt, and somewhat later by Otto Jespersen and D. C. Hesseling. Unfortunately, the data available to these scholars were not as reliable as might have been desired; Schuchardt, especially, relied almost exclusively on material in the conventional orthography of the standard European languages, which was sent to him by travelers without training in the recording of linguistic phenomena or was gathered from humorous columns in newspapers, etc. In more recent years, however, studies carried out according to scientific principles have given us enough dependable data so that we can affirm that a substratum can make its effects felt in all aspects of the structure of a pidgin or creole, as we have seen in chapters 4, 6, and 7. We need only remind the reader of such phonological features as the loss of contrast between English /i/ and /ɪ/, /e/ and /ɛ/, /o/ and /ɔ/, /u/ and /ʊ/ in such words as Neo-Melanesian /leg/ and the Joel Chandler Harris spelling *laig;* the carry-over of tonemically significant pitch on the level of the individual syllable in Saramaccá Bush Negro Creole; or the phonetic realization of voiced intervocalic consonants like /b d g/ as [ᵐb ⁿd ᵑg] under the influence of Melanesian habits of pronunciation in Neo-Melanesian and Neo-Solomonic. In morphology, the entire inflectional system of the Haitian Creole verb with its loss of tense and of person-and-number endings and its use of aspectual prefixes, is straight African; similarly, the presence of a contrast between subjective and objective verb-forms in Neo-Melanesian reflects a widespread contrast between transitive and intransitive verbs in Melanesian languages. The possibility of substratum influence in syntax is shown by many phrase-types, such as the Haitian Creole nominal phrase with the definite article /-(1)a/ and/or the pluralizer /jo/ at the end; by the widespread use of words meaning "give" in the sense of "for" in Haitian Creole, Sranan, Gullah, and other American Negro creoles; or by the comparative phrase with words meaning "(sur)pass", etc.

However, we must not conclude on this account that pidgins and the creoles that grow out of them show nothing but the influence of one substratum or another, or that such languages are, in the current expression, "simply native languages spoken with European vocabulary." In the first place, it often happens that an element of the source language, used at first in a loan-translation—or, to use Haugen's term, in a loan-shift[2]—as the semantic equivalent of a native construction, may eventually be completely restructured and receive a function that does not correspond to anything in either the source or the substratum-language. Thus, Chinese has a number of nouns used as so-called "measures" or "classifiers," coming between numerals and the nouns they modify: for example, *sān jāng jwōdz* "three flat-thing table" = "three tables", *sān kwài chyán* "three hunk money" = "three dollars", *sān-ge lĭbài* "three [-*ge,* of colorless meaning, used as classifier] week" = "three weeks". In "classical" Chinese Pidgin English, two elements, /-pisi/ and /-fɛlə/, were added to numerals, forming, semantically speaking, an exact parallel to the Chinese construction: /-fɛlə/ was used only with animate nouns, as in /θrífɛlə mǽn/ "three men"; whereas /-pisi/ was used with inanimates, as in /θrípisi tébəl/

---

² Following Hockett, 1958, chap. xxix.

"three tables". In the twentieth-century stage of Chinese Pidgin English, however, the distinction between animate and inanimate was lost, /-fɛlə/ went out of use, and /-pisi/ remained as the only element added to a numeral, so that one could say, for example, /θrípisi mæ̀n/ "three men". Note that, on the one hand, /-pisi/ came to be semantically an equivalent of the Chinese element -ge, a meaningless element added to a numeral; but, on the other hand, it came to be used universally, in a way that Chinese -ge is not used, and became simply a numeral suffix, whose meaning is not related (as is, in most cases, that of the Chinese numeral classifiers) to that of the following noun. From this point of view, the Chinese Pidgin English element /-pisi/ is derived historically from the source language (English), was originally used in a loan-translation of a construction in the substratum language (Chinese), but ended by being restructured into a function (pure numeral suffix) that is not present in either the source or the substratum language.

We must also distinguish, here, between relatively surface grammar and deep-level grammar.[3] Most of the features, on all levels of linguistic structure (phonology, morphology, syntax), that are ascribable to substratum influence—and there are plenty of them— are relatively superficial; the more fundamental features derive from what we have been terming, for this reason, the source language. There are different levels of structure involved in, say, specific inflectional categories and processes, as opposed to the fundamental form-classes of a language as a whole; and the latter are surely more basic than the former. Similarly, derivational patterns are more basic, closer to the core of linguistic structure, than are inflectional patterns. Thus, for example, the facts of Haitian Creole force us to recognize Romance-type conjugational differences in verbs, even though every Haitian Creole verb has only one form used in inflection, which we may call its "simple form." Table 7 shows the derivational pattern of forms built on verbs, especially with the suffix of agent /-ò/, which, it will be remembered, belongs to an early phonological stratum in the history of Haitian Creole; thus, this type of derivational relationship dates from the early stages of the language, and cannot be dismissed as having come in only with latter-day learnèd borrowings from standard French. We notice immediately that the pres-

---

[3] Cf. Hockett, 1958, chap. xxix.

TABLE 7

Haitian Creole Verbs Classified according to Derivational Patterns[4]

"Simple" form of verb	Derived noun	"Simple" verb-form broken into root + stem	Stem-vowel	Class
gade "watch"	gadò "baby-tender"	gad-e	e	I
māti "lie"	mātò "liar"	māt-i	i	II
dwè "owe"	—	dwè	zero	III
vomi "vomit"	vomismā "vomiting"	vomis- + ↓	zero with ↓	IV

ence of such pairs as /gade/ "watch" and /gadò/ "watcher, baby-tender", /māti/ "lie" and /mātò/ "liar", forces us to peel off the final vowel (if there is one) of the inflectionally "simple" form, and to recognize the existence of bound forms within the verb. These may be termed "roots" (as in /gad-/ and /māt-/); their existence becomes evident only when we have examined the entire structure of the language, taking derivation as well as inflection into account. This leads us to the conclusion that the Romance conjugational system is still present, and in a specifically North Gallo-Romance form, in the classes of verb-roots that we have to set up on the basis of their relationships to the vowel (if any) which is added to them in the inflectionally simple form; the Romance origin of the verb-system is still evident, but has been pushed down to a more fundamental but less obvious level of linguistic structure by later accretions from other (African) sources.

The data furnished by pidgins and creoles afford concrete exemplification of the only way in which a substratum can exert its influence—through a stage of bilingualism, in which the new language is learned more or less imperfectly, without a complete control of the new linguistic habits. If the structure and the lexicon of the new language are drastically reduced, the language is pidginized, according to our fundamental definition; then the resultant pidgin may become creolized, thus transmitting features of the substratum language to later generations and transmuting them into permanent characteristics of the creole language's structure. On the other hand, if the structure of the new language is not reduced, it is simply

---

[4] In this table, the symbol ↓ stands for "loss of final consonant" (following Hall, 1948b and 1953): thus, /vomis-/ "vomit" + ↓ → /vomi/.

spoken with a foreign accent and with foreign features in morphology and syntax. This has happened in our days with first- and second-generation immigrants in English-speaking countries, and with English used as a lingua franca among non-native speakers in India and the Philippines. It must have happened in many parts of the Roman Empire as non-native speakers of Latin used that language to converse together and eventually gave up their native languages in favor of exclusive use of Latin.

The extent to which a non-native accent is ironed out in the speech of successive generations is determined, not by heredity, but by the amount of social pressure towards conformity in the speech-community. In the United States and in Canada, even if first- or second-generation immigrants may speak English with a marked accent and other foreign peculiarities, the English of the third and fourth generations shows no trace of such features: it is impossible to distinguish between Americans of Italian, Hungarian, Croatian, German, etc., origin on the basis of their speech. This phenomenon is due to the strong "melting-pot" pressure exerted by American society on all new arrivals, in linguistic as well as other matters. In other circumstances, though, where no such pressure exists—as in India or the Philippines—one or more substratum-features may survive and be transmitted to later generations. If we are to assume the influence of substratum languages in the history of European languages in the last two or three millennia, we must postulate this type of essentially *laissez-faire* attitude towards linguistic conformity on the part of the speech-communities involved.

Under certain conditions, we may speak of a "negative pressure" towards linguistic conformity and effective learning of the complete structure of the new language. This is the case in situations where the master or owner does not wish the servant or slave to learn the full upper-class language, and therefore refuses to speak with him except in a pidgin. This is the situation which has prevailed widely (though not exclusively) on plantations in Melanesia and Australia, and was formerly widespread in the colonies of almost all European powers. It is also notable that even the so-called Negro accent is determined, not by heredity, but solely by environment, in that the majority of Southern whites speak with the same characteristics; and it can be lost, as shown by the growing number of Negroes brought up in the North who speak with purely Northern accents. In short, the weeding-out of "foreignisms" and of features derived from a substratum language is due exclusively to social pressure, and in no wise to physical heredity, or to presumed "spiritual" or "psychological" characteristics whose existence can be proved only on the basis of the effects ascribed to them. It is in general wise to be cautious in assuming the effect of a substratum on the history of a language, unless we have specific and detailed evidence to render such an assumption likely. A *reductio ad absurdum* may be found in so-called "noun-incorporation" in English. Many American Indian languages have a type of word-formation in which a verb is derived from another verb by including in the stem a noun-like element: for example, Fox /pje:tehkwe:we:wa/ "he brings a woman or women" (much as if we could say *he woman-brings*), containing the primary suffix /-ehkwe:we:-/ "woman" (compare the noun /ihkwe:wa/ "woman"); or Nahuatl /ni-naka-kwa/ "I meat-eat", in which /naka-/ represents the noun /naka-tl/ "meat". At present, in English in general, but especially in American English, there is a widespread habit of coining compounds such as *tongue-lash* ("give a lashing with the tongue"), *stage-manage, dress-make, ball-room-dance,* and so forth. Hundreds of such compounds have been attested to date, and more are being coined every day. In North America, English is spoken in much the same territory as that formerly occupied by speakers of American Indian languages, of which many possessed the same type of verb-compounding process, often termed "noun-incorporation".

On the basis of this situation, and if he had records only of American English and of American Indian languages, a linguistic analyst of the year 4000 might be tempted to see in this phenomenon the effect of an Amerindian substratum in English. How erroneous such an assumption would be, our greater closeness to the situation and more extensive coverage of sources of course enable us to see. English noun-incorporation actually existed before the English language was established in North America (*brow-beat,* 1603); its spread post-dates the period in which any significant number of speakers of English had contact with American Indian languages; there is no attestation of this type of compound in our (admittedly scanty) records of American Indian Pidgin English; and the use of this type of formation is by no means limited to North American English. Our type of noun-incorporation has had its origin in patterns already existing in English, such as *dress-maker, tongue-lashing,* not from any type of loan-translation on non-English models; and the presence of noun-incorporating verbs in both English and the American Indian languages is simply the result of coïncidence.

In the eighteen-seventies a group of historical linguists (later nicknamed "Neo-Grammarians") proclaimed the principle that "phonetic laws have no exception" in historical linguistics. Ever since that time, there has been extensive and apparently unceasing debate over the validity of this principle, and of the comparative method that is based upon it. It must be admitted that, in its original form, this principle was poorly stated, especially by being over-simplified, since it is obvious that in the history of every language there are plenty of exceptions to virtually every "phonetic law;"[5] and the original principle, as stated by Karl Brugmann, was later modified by August Leskien to include the qualification "under like conditions." Essentially what is involved is, not a statement of fact, but an underlying postulate on which to base scientific analysis: that sound-change would be regular if not disturbed by other factors. In recent years, it has been proposed, since the term "Neo-Grammarian" has acquired unfavorable or polemic connotations, to use, instead, the term "regularist" to denote anyone who observes (whether he acknowledges it or not) the principle of the regularity of sound-change.

The major accomplishment of linguistic science in the nineteenth century, the comparative method and the reconstruction of the ancestral forms of related families of languages (for example, Romance, Indo-European, Finno-Ugric), was based squarely on the principle of regularity of sound-change, by which—and by which alone—it was possible to bring order out of chaos in the history of language, and to trace the development of linguistic structures and their gradual differentiation, through time, from a common source in the case of each language family. It is now standard practice, in historical linguistic analysis, to consider two or more languages as "genetically" related if they show systematic correspondences in phonological structure between morphological

[5] In any case, the term "law" is very poorly chosen to refer to sound-changes, which are historical events, not general laws like those of physics or chemistry. It is less confusing to use some such expression as "Grimm's correlation" to refer to a correspondence of sounds on the basis of which a phonetic law is set up; or, for the historical event, some term like "Grimm's phenomenon" or "Grimm's sound-change."

and syntactical phenomena and at least basic elements of vocabulary. If such correspondences are found, we consider that two languages attested contemporaneously must have come from a common source, and that if two languages are attested at different stages of time, they must both have come from a common source, or the one must be a later stage of the other. Note that, on the one hand, this says nothing concerning the means of transmission from one generation to another or from one speech-community to another (as when, for instance, speakers of Etruscan or Gaulish or Iberian learned Latin). On the other hand, it does emphasize that there must be correspondences between all levels of linguistic structure, not merely in phonology and vocabulary (the latter is one of the least reliable indications of linguistic relationship, since words can be borrowed so easily from one language into another), and that these correspondences must be systematic (rather than merely numerous) and attested in morphemes (especially functors) which are, or can reasonably be assumed to have been, alike in form, function, and meaning.

From the languages on which they have traditionally worked (languages of "normal" or "full" size, usually spoken by relatively sedentary populations), and for which they have reconstructed "proto-" or ancestral languages, comparativists have customarily made certain further, corollary assumptions, which are the immediate sources of disagreement: (1) that, among languages related through having come from a common source, the process of differentiation has always been gradual; and (2) that, among such languages, the relationship has always been "pure," that is, there has been little or no introduction of structural patterns (phonemic, morphological, syntactical) from any source outside the language-family concerned. This latter corollary is essentially a survival from Renaissance and neoclassical purism; the extreme case of "historical purism", as we might call it, was the remark made by some scholar that a certain Old Persian inscription containing *būmā* "earth" instead of the "correct" *būmī* must necessarily have been a later forgery, since no pure-blooded Persian would have been so false to his ancestral language!

Even before the current intensification of work on pidgins and creoles, various scholars had expressed doubts as to the validity of these corollary assumptions, and from the evidence of pidgins and creoles it is quite clear that their doubts were justified. The restructuring of English into South Sea Pidgin (from which Neo-Melanesian, Neo-Solomonic, and the other pidgins of Oceania developed) took place in not over half a century, from the eighteen-twenties (when speakers of English first came in effective numbers into the South Sea Islands) to 1860 or 1870. Likewise, the restructuring of English into Chinese Pidgin took place in a short time, from the sixteen-sixties (when the first trading-post or "factory" was opened at Canton) until the first part of the eighteenth century, when our first attestations of Chinese Pidgin occur. The Pidgin French out of which arose the various Creoles must have developed in a similarly short period. Half a century is, if anything, a long time in the time-perspective of pidgin languages: a pidgin can grow up in a few days of trading, or in a few hours of contact between an English-speaking tourist and an Italian cicerone. The restructurings that take place in these instances are very brusque and violent, and take place very fast, as compared with what we customarily consider "gradual" change over the centuries. Furthermore, no linguistic relationship is "pure," whether the change be gradual or brusque; just to remain on familiar ground, we have plenty of instances of Romance languages taking over structural features from territorially neighboring languages (for example, Roumanian getting the high central vowel [ɨ] first in loan-words from Slavic) and vice-versa (for example, Alsatian German getting nasalized vowels from French).

Yet in these latter instances, no-one considers that the basic relationship of the languages is changed by the presence of structural borrowings: we do not classify Alsatian German with the Romance languages because it has nasalized vowels. The question now arises: how far can structural borrowings go before they affect our classification of a language? Can structural borrowings submerge the inherited system so thoroughly that later inspection cannot discern the actual "genetic" affiliation of the language? Is it possible for such borrowings to result in a language that actually has many "ancestors," rather than one? With the traditional type of comparativism, like that which developed in the study of the Indo-European languages, the question did not arise, because it was assumed that genetic relationships were "pure," and that hence a given language must be related genetically to one and only one language-family. However, opposition to the comparative method arose as soon as the Neo-Grammarians had made their pronouncement that "Phonetic laws admit of no exceptions." One of the leading opponents of the principle of phonetic law and of the Neo-Grammarians was the German scholar Hugo Schuchardt (see p. 108). In order to combat the comparative method, Schuchardt and his followers proposed the notion of a "mixed" language in contrast to a "pure" language. Schuchardt's extensive studies on pidgins and creoles were undertaken primarily to demonstrate that these, as "mixed" languages, were related to more than one family, and that therefore the entire concept of necessary genetic relationship, which they thought to be based on linguistic "purity," must perforce be untenable. Since, however, we have by now abandoned as unfruitful the opposition between "pure" and "mixed" languages (we now recognize that all languages are "impure"), the immediate aim of Schuchardt's approach to pidgins and creoles becomes invalid.

But even though all languages are "mixed," some—to paraphrase Orwell's famous expression—are more "mixed" than others. We are left with the question whether, in fact, the more mixed languages are so mixed as to invalidate the assumption of genetic relationship, particularly as applied to languages of whose history we have no detailed knowledge. In theory, a language might conceivably combine elements from two or more sources so that they were perfectly evenly balanced, and so that they would be, therefore, unclassifiable according to our customary assumption. Yet, in practice, such a condition of perfect balance is never found—not even in any of the pidgins and creoles that have been investigated in more detail than, say, Schuchardt or Jespersen were able to do, and not even with their (admittedly extensive) carry-overs, in structure as well as vocabulary, from Chinese, Melanesian, African, or other substrata. In Haitian Creole, the proportion of French structure is both greater and more fundamental than that of African-type structure; and the same is true of Chinese Pidgin English, Neo-Melanesian, Sranan, Gullah, etc., in relation to English and the various substrata involved.

When we speak of "structure," we of course mean all levels of linguistic patterning—phonology, morphology, and syntax—and our criterion for structural origin is that of systematic correspondence in specific linguistic forms. Thus, if a particular phoneme in one language corresponds to some comparable feature of phonemic structure in another language, in morphemes of reasonably similar meaning (for example, *ai* in French *pain, main, bain = a* in Spanish *pan, mano, baño,* with French *ai* and Spanish *a* from Proto-Romance /á/ before a nasal consonant, in forms that can be reconstructed as /páne/, /mánu/ and /bánịu/, respectively), we consider the correspondence to be systematic and the forms to be genetically related. The correspondences between Creole and French, between Sranan or Melanesian Pidgin and English, etc., are all-pervasive—that is, they are found in all branches of linguistic structure—whereas the correspondences between Creole and Sranan on the one hand and African languages on the other (or between Neo-Melanesian and Melanesian languages, etc.) are indeed extensive, but scattered and less systematic.

Even with the data available at present, it is evident that the ancestral form of any given group of related pidgins and creoles can be reconstructed, using the accepted techniques of comparative linguistics, and that the "proto-pidgin" which we reconstruct in this way shows a reasonable correspondence to certain features of the "source" language which we already know from other materials. Table 8 shows sample correspondences between several English-based pidgins and creoles (Neo-Melanesian, Chinese Pidgin English, Sranan, Gullah), on the basis of which a kind of Proto-Pidgin-English can be set up. In following this procedure, we are of course making believe, for the time being, that we have no outside knowledge of the proto-language, and we do not "look in the back of the book" to find the answers until we have made the comparative reconstruction. Even though there is a "back of the book," however, and even if we can compare our reconstructed proto-language with attested materials, it is nevertheless worth the trouble to reconstruct it, in modern pidgins as well as in such groups as the Romance languages. In the first place, our attested materials for earlier stages of languages are not always directly representative of the ordinary linguistic behavior out of which later languages have grown; thus, Classical Latin does not give us a complete picture of popular Latin speech, while the Romance languages afford valuable evidence for the latter. Secondly, the reconstruction of Proto-Romance and Proto-Pidgin-English, where we do have a "back of the book" that we can look into, serves as a means of testing the probable validity of reconstructed proto-languages (for example, Proto-Germanic, Proto-Indo-European, etc.) for which we have no possibility of ever finding direct documentation—and thus of test-

Sample Proto-Pidgin-English Correspondences[6]

Proto-Pidgin-English Phoneme	Meaning of form	Neo-Melanesian	Chinese-Pidgin-English	Sranan	Gullah	Proto-Pidgin-English
/i/	"he, she, it"	i- pred.-mkr.	hí	i-	i-	hí
/e/	"three"	tri(fɛla)	θrí	drí	trí	θrí, drí
	"table"	tebal	tébal	—	tébal	tébal
	"make"	mekim	méki	mék(i)	mék	mék(i)
/ɛ/	"red"	rɛd(fɛla)	rɛd	red	rɛd	rɛd
/æ/	"be able"	kaen	káen	kán	kán	kaen
	"axe"	aekis	—	áksi	áks	aeks
/a/	"hat"	hat	hát	háti	hát	hát
/o/	"no"	no	nó	nó	nó, ne	nó
	"break"	brok(im)	brók	bróko	brɔk	brók
/u/	"good"	gud(fɛla)	gúd	gúdu	gúd	gúd
	"foot"	fut	fút	fútu	fut	fút
/u/	"you"	ju	jú	únu	úne	jú(ne)
	"do"	du((im) "rape"	dú	dú	dú	dú
/m/	"me"	mi	máj	mí	mí	mí, máj
	"mouth"	maws	máwθ, máwf	mófo	máwt	máwθ, máwf
	"time"	tajm	-tajm (suff.)	tém	tajm	tájm
/n/	"name"	nem	ném	ném	ném	ném
	"man"	maen	máen	mán	mán	mæn
	"with"	lɔŋ	lɔŋ	nánja	—	lɔŋ
/ŋ/	"sing"	sɪŋsɪŋ	síŋ	síŋ	síŋ	síŋ

[6] In the proto-language, as reconstructed solely on the basis of this type of comparative evidence, we should have to set up certain alternate forms, for which (if we did not have other attestations to help us to choose between them) we should simply have to say *non liquet* in attempting to choose between them. In cases where both Chinese Pidgin English and Sranan show a final /-i/ vowel, we might consider it desirable to set up alternative Proto-Pidgin-English forms both with and without final /-i/; for the alternate form /drí/ in Proto-Pidgin-English (necessitated by Sranan /drí/), we know from outside evidence that this in reality represents the Dutch numeral *drie*. Further analysis would show us that the unstressed /-ɛm -ɪm/ which we would have to set up as a direct object suffix in Proto-Pidgin-English was simply the pronoun /hém hím/ used in unstressed position after a verb-form.

119

ing the validity of the comparative method as a whole. Despite the current prevalence of the Schuchardtian view-point (especially in Romance linguistics and among workers in the creole language field) that pidgins and creoles furnish arguments against the comparative method, it can be maintained that even from languages of this type, proto-languages can be reconstructed with historic verisimilitude and resultant validity.

It is often thought that the comparative method is not valid unless it enables us to arrive not only at features of the linguistic system of the presumed proto-language, but also at the place of its use and the approximate time at which it was spoken.[7] The example of pidgins and creoles demonstrates that neither of these last-mentioned matters is of the essence of reconstruction. The Proto-Pidgin-English that we reconstruct, on the basis of such correspondences as those shown in Table 8, is essentially an approximation of such features of lower-class seventeenth-century English speech as its speakers saw fit to use in their contacts with non-Europeans in the course of their trading, "blackbirding," and colonizing activities. If we have to assign a specific locality to our Proto-Pidgin-English, it will have to be somewhere in the lower reaches of the Thames, on either bank of the river, in the docks and settlements in such parts of London as Bermondsey, Rotherhithe, Wapping, Shadwell, and Limehouse, and in other English seaports such as Plymouth. This locality could never be guessed on the basis of the world-wide distribution of historically attested English-based pidgins and creoles in the Americas, Africa, the Far East, and the South Pacific. Nor is any physical heredity involved—quite the opposite: the linguistic ancestors of the speakers of present-day Sranan, Gullah, Krio, Neo-Melanesian, etc., were totally unrelated to them physically. In the same way, the speakers of our reconstructed Proto-Indo-European may, very likely, not have been the physical ancestors of any of the speakers of present-day Germanic languages, if Feist's theory of the origin of Proto-Germanic from a creole Indo-European has any validity.

It has been suggested that all modern creole languages have their ultimate origin in the fifteenth-century Pidgin Portuguese of

---

[7] Cf. such remarks as that of Migliorini, 1946, p. 104: "We lack and shall always lack the means of reconstructing what is the fundamental character of a language: its structure as a system, at a given time and in a given place." Cf. also my comments on this point in Hall, 1946, pp. 260–261.

West Africa, which in its turn may have been an imitation of a Mediterranean lingua franca. This suggestion is based on the presence of certain common features in Hong-Kong Creole Portuguese (Macanese) and in other pidgins and creoles based not only on Portuguese but also on French, Spanish, and English in Africa, the Caribbean, and elsewhere. Among these features are: the use of particles preceding verbs to make aspect- and tense-formations; reduplication in derivation and in phrase-structure; the semantic developments "too much, too many" > "much, many" and "excessively" > "very", as in the Philippine contact-vernaculars (Ermitano *masiao*, Caviteño *dimasiado*, Zamboangueño *demasiado*) and Papiamentu /mašá/ (all < Spanish *demasiado* "too much"), Dominican Creole /tro/ < French /tro/ "too much", and Chinese Pidgin English /tuməči/, Neo-Melanesian /tuməč/ < English *too much*; and the presence of /kabá/ indicating completed action and the preposition /na/ "in" in the Philippine contact-vernaculars, Macanese and other Portuguese-based pidgins and creoles, Papiamentu, the French-based creoles, and Sranan.

It has further been claimed that the historical relationship between creoles is not that which is envisaged in the customary view of genetic relationships as set forth above, but that it involves a totally different process, termed "relexification." Sranan and Saramaccá have a certain number of unquestionably Portuguese forms, such as /pasá/ "pass", /kabá/ (indicating completed action), Sranan /grándi/ "big", or Saramaccá /paazóo/, Sranan /prasóro/ "parasol", which are to be taken as survivals of a Pidgin Portuguese spoken when the plantations of Suriname were owned by Portuguese Jews in the seventeenth century. Many other words of Portuguese origin have been replaced by English in modern Sranan: for example, /vívo/ "alive" by /líbi/ "living", /lío/ "river" (< Portuguese /řío/) by /líba/, /kusumí/ "gloomy, sorry" (< Portuguese /konsumido/) by /sári/, or /pakaméntu/ "payment" by /paimán/. Others have been at least partially reshaped under English influence: for example, eighteenth-century Saramaccá /véntu/ "wind' ≠ twentieth-century /wíntu/, Sranan /wínti/. Since the beginning of Dutch rule in 1667, many Dutch words have in likewise come in to replace English words, such as /mói/ "handsome" ≠ /hánson/, or /makándra/ "together" ≠ /tugédre/.

This process of lexical replacement is of course going on in all languages at all times; but some scholars have suggested that in the case of Sranan and other creoles it has been so great as to constitute a complete shift in the genetic affiliations of the language—in this case, from Portuguese to English to Dutch. The proponents of this theory therefore consider it impossible to classify creole languages genetically, since they have presumably changed their affiliation one or more times. Hence it is considered possible to trace, not only the obviously "Portuguese-based" creoles, but all others, back to an original West African Pidgin Portuguese (with an African substratum), which would then have been relexified with English, French, Spanish, or Dutch morphemes.

This view-point is simply a somewhat more sophisticated version of the old notion that a pidgin or creole is simply "a native language spoken with European vocabulary." The argument from relexification assumes that only abstract syntactic patterns are valid criteria for determining linguistic relationships, and that phonological and morphological correspondences are not relevant. Such assumptions are not valid in the light of everything else that is known about linguistic history. English has been extensively relexified, in the last thousand years, with morphemes (primarily contentives) from French, Latin, and Greek; yet it is still to be classified as a Germanic, not a Romance, language, because its fundamental stock of morphemes (especially its functors) show systematic phonological correspondences with the Germanic languages, as do its basic syntactic structures. Coming to a language like Sranan, therefore, we may say that it is specifically English in the historical origin of its structure, but that it has many carry-overs from the earlier Pidgin Portuguese that it replaced; and that its present expansion with Dutch vocabulary does not affect its basically English genetic affiliation.

All the evidence available so far indicates that the type of linguistic change and the mechanisms involved—sound-change, analogy, borrowing of various kinds—are the same for pidgins and creoles as they are for all other languages. The only difference lies in the rate of change—far faster for a pidgin (because of the drastic reduction in structure and lexicon) than for most languages. When a pidgin has become nativized, the history of the resultant creole is, in essence, similar to that of any other language. Hence, whereas a pidgin is identifiable at any given time by both linguistic and social criteria, a creole is identifiable only by historical criteria—that is, if we know that it has arisen out of a pidgin. There are no structural criteria which, in themselves, will identify a creole as such, in the absence of historical evidence. We consider that a language or a group of languages, such as Sranan, Gullah, Papiamentu, or the French-based creoles, have had this type of origin because the extent of restructuring they have undergone, in contrast to the languages from which they are clearly derived, is of the kind that normally takes thousands of years, whereas we know from historical sources that they arose in a century or two; and because we know that pidgins or pidgin-producing conditions existed in the regions where these languages are now spoken. In the instances mentioned, our historical data are such that we can be quite sure; in others, as in the case of Afrikaans, the available evidence does not permit a clear-cut decision.

It is usually assumed that linguistic change, both in structure and in vocabulary, takes place fairly slowly; on the basis of the observed time that elapsed between Latin and the modern Romance languages, or between Old and Modern English, the student of historical linguistics develops a kind of feel for the approximate "normal" rate of change. Various attempts have been made to quantify this rate; for structural features, it is very difficult, especially because it is hard to arrive at a satisfactory weighting to assign, say, to phonological characteristics as opposed to morphological or syntactical features, or to one specific trait as opposed to another. In lexical matters, a fairly widely used modern method is that of "glottochronology," first conceived by Morris Swadesh and developed also by several others. In this method, it is assumed that we can isolate between sixty and two hundred basic meanings that are free from cultural influences, and that the replacement of the words for these meanings proceeds in all languages at an approximately equal rate, which can be stated in a mathematical formula. On the basis of this formula (modified on occasion to meet special conditions of the cultural environment, such as known vocabulary borrowing from other languages), it is presumed that we can compare the lexica of any two or more related languages and calculate the approximate time (to within a few centuries) it must have taken them to diverge from their common source.

Various types of objection have been raised against the validity of the glottochronological method: for example, the impossibility of finding any meanings that are really free from cultural influence, and of sufficiently eliminating the skewing effect of lexical borrowings. Our findings concerning pidgin and creole languages are also significant in this connection, in that they show another way in which glottochronological techniques can give unrealistic results. If we calculate the presumed relationship between Neo-Melanesian and Modern English, using Swadesh's revised basic list of one hundred words, we obtain a figure of two to three millennia of separation between the two languages if we assume that Neo-Melanesian is directly descended from English, or between one and two millennia if we assume that the two are cognates, descended from the same proto-language. Either of these figures is, of course, wildly divergent from what we know to be the actual length of time involved in the formation of Neo-Melanesian—not over a century and a half since its earliest possible beginnings in the eighteen-twenties or thirties. We would probably obtain similar results from calculations of the glottochronological relationships between Sranan and English, Gullah and English, Krio and English, etc., or between the various English-based pidgins and creoles themselves.

It may be objected that Neo-Melanesian, being a pidgin (and an incipient creole), is not to be considered on the same plane as "normal" languages, since its formation took place under special circumstances more similar to those attending the construction of artificial languages than to those of gradual linguistic change. However, for most language families of the earth, we do not know their previous history, and have no way of knowing whether or not—especially in the case of apparently distantly related languages—a stage of pidginization and creolization may have entered into the process of differentiation. This would seem especially likely in certain regions, such as Melanesia, where it is suspected that pidginization may be endemic as a linguistic behavior pattern; but who can tell whether similar processes may not have taken place elsewhere, in places and times no longer accessible to use by historical record?

Even at present, when the scientific study of pidgins and creoles is only at its initial stage, it is evident that it has significant contributions to make to our understanding of general linguistic theory. There is a very extensive field for further research here, and it is to be hoped that, in future decades, new linguistic features will be revealed as further pidgins and creoles are investigated; and that future researchers will uncover still more aspects of these languages which will have a bearing on linguistics as a whole.

REFERENCES

Attitudes towards grammar of vernaculars in Renaissance: Hall, 1936, 1942c, 1958.

Substratum influence: Hall, 1950f, 1952b, 1955b.

Chinese numeral measures (classifiers): Hockett, 1958 (chap. xxvi, p. 224). Their reflection in Chinese Pidgin English: Hall, 1944a.

Noun-incorporation in English: Hall, 1956c.

Relationships of creole languages: Schuchardt, 1884; Taylor, 1956, 1959, 1960, 1961b, 1963; Hall, 1958; Weinreich, 1958; Valkhoff, 1960.

Postulate of regularity in sound-change: Bloomfield, 1933 (chap. xx); Hockett, 1948, 1958 (chap. lii); Hall, 1957c, 1964 (chap. 1).

Comparative method and reconstruction of proto-languages: Bloomfield, 1933 (chap. xxii); Hockett, 1948, 1958 (chap. lvii). As applied to Romance languages: Hall, 1950b.

Pidgin languages and glottochronology: Hall, 1959d.

Social Significance

FROM the point of view of social function, the chief difference between pidgins and creoles is in the type of speech-community whose needs they meet. Unlike "normal" languages, a pidgin language usually comes into existence for a specific reason, lasts just as long as the situation that called it into being, and then goes quickly out of use. "Normal" languages do not have life-cycles; a language is not an organism, but a set of habits, handed down from one generation of speakers to another, so that the customary expressions "mother language" and "daughter language" are, at best, nothing but metaphors. A "normal" language is one handed down from generation to generation through transference to children who learn it as their first language, and its life is conditioned only by the length of time its speech-community lasts. Often the speakers of a language show remarkable tenacity in clinging to it (especially as a symbol of their group identity) long after they have become greatly reduced in number and the apparent usefulness of the language has nearly reached the vanishing point—as has happened with a great many American Indian languages. A pidgin acquires a longer lease on life only by becoming the native language of a group of speakers (becoming creolized), and thereby passes over to the status of a "normal" language. From this point of view, we can speak of pidgins as having "life-cycles", and of their being "inherently weak" in that, not their linguistic structure, but their social standing is normally not hardy enough to enable them to be used outside of their original context.[1]

[1] Cf. Swadesh, 1948, especially the remark on pp. 234–235: "There are no such things as inherently weak languages that are by nature incapable of surviving changed social conditions."

A pidgin normally owes its origin to relatively casual, short-term contacts between groups that do not have a language in common. It therefore does not, properly speaking, have a speech-community of its own. These contacts may be of various types, involving all kinds of social relationships: between equals as when two or more groups meet for trade or similar purposes (as in the Pacific Northwest, in the formation of Chinook Jargon); between sightseer and guide, as in a Florentine or Roman cicerone's simplification of Italian; between master and servant, as in New Guinea and the South Seas; or between owner and slave, as in Africa and on the American plantations. It is not accurate to ascribe the formation of all pidgins to inequality of social relationship and hence to condemn them out of hand, as is often done, as products of colonialistic expansion. Rather, a pidgin can arise—on occasion, even in the space of only a few hours—whenever an emergency situation calls for communication on a minimal level of comprehension. For this reason, Jespersen rightly termed pidgins "minimal" languages and, from their basically improvisatory character, "makeshift" languages. In the contact situation, by our very definition of the term "pidgin," all its speakers already have full-sized "normal" languages which they customarily use in their everyday relationships with the other members of their own speech-communities, and hence the pidgin is socially marginal; Reinecke therefore called pidgins "marginal" languages.

From the structural point of view, a pidgin represents the very first stage of rudimentary language learning, with the development of linguistic structure and lexicon arrested at this level, except for whatever analogical extension is made using the resources of the pidgin itself. (Compare, for example, the Neo-Melanesian phrases /gras bɪlɔŋ maws/ "mustache", /gras bɪlɔŋ fes/ "beard", /gras bɪlɔŋ hɛd/ "hair" as ingenious ways of referring to these phenomena within the limited vocabulary of the language.) The crystallization of structure at this first stage is due essentially to the slightness of contact involved. In noninvidious[2] situations, the slightness of the contacts is due to their brief and relatively infrequent nature—for instance, the tribes of the Pacific Northwest coast coming together only every so often for trading purposes. We can also apply the term

[2] "Invidious" is used here in the special technical sense given it by Veblen, 1899 (chap. ii, at end), to mean "describing a comparison of persons with a view to rating and grading them in respect of relative worth or value."

"slight" to contacts that last for longer periods—for example, those between master and plantation-laborer or house-boy in New Guinea. Here, the slightness of the contact is rather one of continued nonintimacy, because of the desire of at least one side to keep the other at arm's length; in other words, the situation is invidious, involving a social distinction for whose maintenance the continued use of pidgin is one of the means. On occasion, both sides may use the pidgin to keep each other at arm's length, as happened at Canton with Chinese Pidgin English. The sharp reduction in grammar and vocabulary entailed in the formation of a pidgin usually leads to low social status: the pidgin is regarded as a "bastard lingo," a "mongrel jargon," etc., often by both sides using it.[3]

The contact situation in which the pidgin is used may be brief or of longer duration. Normally, it lasts only a generation or two, until closer relationships have been established; this was the case, apparently, with Pidgin English in North America, in New Zealand, and on most parts of the Australian frontier as white settlement advanced. On the other hand, it may last considerably longer—even up to several centuries, as was the case with the original Lingua Franca in the Levant and with Chinese Pidgin English—if the contacts themselves involve a socially conditioned nonintimacy over a long time. Such long survival of a pidgin normally implies that its use has been institutionalized to a certain degree; newcomers to the situation are initiated into the pidgin as one of the distinctive characteristics of the relationships involved. In British public schools such as Winchester, new students must learn their school's argot, and in fact special dictionaries have been prepared to help them; learning Pidgin was one of the first tasks of the young British merchant on arriving at Canton; and knowledge of *tok boi* (Neo-Melanesian) is one of the most prized acquisitions that a New Guinea indentured servant brings back to his native village from the labor-line. The greatest degree of institutionalization so far recorded for a pidgin is in the case of Neo-Melanesian, which, under German rule, was made into the official contact-language for what was in those days Kaiser Wilhelm Land (New Guinea, the Bismarcks, and the northern Solomons); this is also, perhaps the

---

[3] This contempt for a pidginized version of one's language is not restricted to speakers of "languages of culture." At Port Moresby, I was told that speakers of Motu show the same attitude toward the pidginized Motu which is used as a lingua franca in Papua.

widest geographical extent of the use of any pidgin, at least in modern times.

Because of the low social and intellectual status of pidgin languages, their usefulness and necessity are often greatly underestimated. Even in the most casual, short-lived contact, a pidgin serves a function that no other means of communication could duplicate—that of facilitating mutual understanding on a limited range of topics. When it is used on a wider scale, a pidgin is not necessarily a "caste language," and pidgins often come to be indispensable as lingue franche in areas where there are many different, mutually incomprehensible languages. In New Guinea, Neo-Melanesian is used more among Melanesians than it is between Melanesians and Europeans, and has come to be an indispensable "linguistic cement" for the Territory, not a language foisted by European invaders on helpless natives. Its use has spread far beyond the territory usually visited by administrative officials or other Europeans, and Margaret Mead tells of having come across neighboring villages, far up in the mountains, where no white person had ever preceded her, in which mutually unintelligible languages were spoken and between which all communication was carried on in Pidgin; even the children, playing naked in the villages, practiced the language as they had learned it from their elder brothers who had come back from the plantation labor-lines. The mimeographed journals published by the Education Department at such centers as Lae, Madang, Wewak, and Rabaul were proving their worth as disseminators of information far beyond the circle of those who were literate in Pidgin; Mr. Sidney J. Baker reports that he was told by an administrative official, "I myself have seen natives in outlying districts gathering in hundreds to hear one man reading from a single copy." It has well been said that if the use of Neo-Melanesian were to disappear completely overnight, the entire business of the Territory of New Guinea would come to an abrupt halt.

If relationships between the two sides using a pidgin become closer, normally one side learns the other's language, and the pidgin falls rapidly into disuse. In most of the areas touched by European colonial expansion, the natives have ultimately learned the European language, usually in a more or less substandard form. If the previously-used pidgin is based on the European language that the natives learn, the final stages of their use of the pidgin involve heavy interlarding of words and constructions from the European language, for example, from English into Australian Pidgin English. This process takes place fastest in areas of restricted size, where relatively few people are involved, as in individual towns or stations in Australia; usually it has come about as a result of normal processes of acculturation, though there have been instances of deliberate extirpation of a pidgin through pressure from colonial governments, as in the German government in the Carolines and the English government in Papua under Sir Hubert Murray). On the other hand, the process is far more gradual in large areas, such as New Guinea and West Africa, where the pidgin is widely used and serves as a means of communication among many groups of different language-backgrounds, as we have just seen. Usually, since pidgins do not enjoy any degree of social esteem, they go out of use rapidly once the special contact situation which called them into existence has disappeared.

The only way in which a pidgin escapes extinction when the contact-situation disappears is by becoming creolized. In this case, it reaches the status of a "normal" language by expansion of its structure and vocabulary, and by becoming one of the psychological pillars of its speakers' personalities; a creole is just as intimately bound up with the egos of its native speakers as is any other language. Yet a creole languages is often, as in Haiti and Curaçao, the object of strong contempt and social prejudice, which is a major factor in rendering its speakers psychologically insecure. A well-educated Haitian, very fluent in French, once told me that he could express his innermost thoughts and feelings only in Creole; and a Papiamentu informant, on hearing that linguistic scientists consider Papiamentu a "real" language, burst out in strong resentment against a schoolmaster who had taught him and his classmates that Papiamentu was only a "base, corrupted jargon." This same feeling was given intense poetic expression by the Haitian author Léon Laleau:

> This obsessed Heart, which does not correspond
> To my language and my clothing,
> And upon which bite, like a clamp,
> Borrowed emotions and customs
> From Europe—do you feel the suffering
> And the despair, equal to none other,

Of taming, with words from France,
This heart which came to me from Senegal?[4]

In many regions where the indigenous population speak a creole language side by side with an official language, there has developed a situation that might be called "linguistic schizophrenia" —often referred to by a term taken from modern Greek, *diglossía* "being torn between two languages". Edith Efron has summed up the situation as it used to be in Haiti—and as it still is in most other Creole-speaking areas—as follows:

> Faced, on the one hand, by academic French, the language of civilized White world, spoken by few citizens, and by Creole, a language of Black slave origin, spoken by all citizens, Haiti has evolved a characteristic myth of language to deal with the situation. French has become the official tongue, the language of intellect, of social distinction, the language of the *élite;* while Creole has been pushed into the background, receives no formal status at all and is termed the language of the *mass.* . . . The two languages [are not really symbolic of two Haitis, but] actually complement each other in Haitian life, serve a vital function in the split culture of the Haitian people—French being the linguistic vehicle for the formal-public-official European cover of all Haitian institutions, and the lively and popular Creole expressing in all its rich nuances, the living mores of the country themselves.[5]

The result of this *diglossía* is a situation of intense linguistic snobbery, in which all cultural prestige goes to the command and use of French, and only contempt accrues to Creole. All Haitians, upper-class as well as lower-class, have Creole as their native tongue, since children are brought up by *gadò* or baby-tenders, who speak to them in Creole, and even the children of the highest-ranking families know and use Creole from birth. In addition to this, some children (those of the upper 10 per cent of the population) learn French from their parents and hence are bilingual in Creole and

---

[4] Efron, p. 954, p. 199.
[5] *Ibid.,* pp. 199–200.

French. The correlation between language and class status is well described by Miss Efron:

> The significant fact that language strongly implies class status —a total absence of French decidedly placing the Haitian in the unschooled lower classes—intensifies the social snobbery towards the native tongue. The uneducated Haitian feels an immense pride in his child who goes to school and becomes "educated," who can "really" write and speak the French language; and conversely, the French-speaking Haitian who has emerged from the lower classes may feel real shame over his exclusively Creole-speaking family, keeping them out of sight of his more educated acquaintances.[6]

Every culture has a folk-lore about language, and speakers of every language have "images" of their own linguistic behavior which are often very far from the truth. Just as they try to deny that Haitian vaudoun has any African origin, educated Haitians will proclaim their contempt for Creole and even deny that they know it. In Miss Efron's terms:

> Aggressively snobbish towards Creole in public, most educated folk feel impelled to denounce the language, declare that it is vulgar, ugly, crude, that it hurts their ears, and even, in some cases, maintain that they hate it or "never speak it". Interestingly enough, women, who, by and large, speak French far less well than men, seem more inclined to make these charges publicly against the native tongue. Possibly this is felt by them to be a compensation for inadequate French. The collective disdain for Creole undoubtedly reaches its absolute pitch when the educated Haitian travels abroad, even for a few months, and—as so often happens— returns to Haiti, insisting to all who will listen that he has forgotten how to speak Creole![7]

The educated Haitians' use of French tends to be grandiose, flowery, imitated from eighteenth-century models, over-literary— and inexact in comparison with metropolitan French usage. Not

[6] *Ibid.*, p. 200.
[7] *Ibid.*, p. 203.

infrequently, both in conversation and in print, Haitian French contains infelicities and downright malapropisms, as when a dentist advertising in a small-town newspaper proclaimed: *Le Dr. X refait l'oeuvre du Bon Dieu en procurant à sa clientèle une magnifique dentelure nouvelle* "Dr. X redoes the work of the Good Lord by procuring for his clients a magnificent new"—and here he meant to say *denture* "denture", but evidently considered that too unpretentious a word, and so used, instead, *dentelure* "lace-work"! It is very easy for a Haitian to be high-falutin' in French, and hence to be insincere and dishonest. The common man has long since realized that, whereas French is the vehicle of the official, heavily Gallicized national institutions, the only really satisfactory carrier for the common people's real living mores is Creole. For the normal, unpretentious Haitian, use of Creole is the symbol of truth and reality, and French is the language of bluff, mystification, and duplicity, as shown by such expressions as: /se-kreol m-ap-pale ave-u, wi?/ "I'm talking Creole [*that is,* straightforwardly, honestly] to you, am I not?"; /pale frãse/ "to speak French" = "to offer money [*or a bribe*] to someone" the French language itself being used as the symbol of distinguished duplicity, and of the glossing over with respectability of dishonest thoughts and acts; /l-ap-mãde šarite ã-frãse/ "he's asking charity in French [*that is,* in an attempt to deceive the giver as to his intention of returning the money]".

In religious and cultural matters, the linguistic split between French and Creole in Haiti has led to a breakdown of communication between upper and lower classes, and hence to an independence but also a cultural lag on the part of the masses of the population. In religion, as is well known, the people of Haiti show a three-way division: "pure" Catholics, who disavow all vaudoun rites and their African associations; *vaudouisants*, who are officially Roman Catholics, but who also practise vaudoun, in a type of syncretism that views the Trinity and the official Christian figures as distant and unapproachable, and the *loas*, or African deities of vaudoun, as near-at-hand and immediate; and Protestants, who reject both Roman Catholicism and vaudoun. The Roman Catholic hierarchy and priesthood reject virtually all use of Creole, especially in church services:

> One may find, for example, that in a majority of churches, priests are declaiming sermons in French, destined to exalt

and uplift the souls of their audiences, and turn them away from the primitive faith of their ancestors—sermons which might as well be delivered in the purest of Latin, along with the rest of the Mass, for all the comprehension they evoke in most of their hearers. Leyburn remarks that he has met "priests who though they have lived in the country for a generation, have never learned the tongue used by ninety-five out of a hundred of their parishioners all the time, and by a hundred percent of them some of the time".[8]

By thus rejecting Creole, the "pure" Catholics have cut one of the main bridges between themselves and the mass of the population whom they wish to wean from vaudoun, and have relinquished the use of the most direct way to the people's understanding, to the Protestant missionaries, who have been conducting an increasingly successful campaign involving the extensive use of Creole.[9] This attitude contrasts sharply with that of the Roman Catholic missionaries in New Guinea, who used Pidgin, from the beginning of their work, in order to speak most effectively to the plantation-laborers and other natives who had Pidgin as their only language in common.

For purposes of literary creation, many writers, in Haiti and other regions where pidgins and creoles are used, have considered these languages as unsuited for lofty artistic endeavor. Such an attitude is based purely on cultural prejudice; every language is, in and for itself, as suited for use in literary expression as is every other, though naturally each language has its own peculiarities which serve as a base for artistic development.[10] In Haiti and other territories where French-based creoles are spoken, the prestige of French culture and literature has been so strong as to induce a belief that no language but French could possibly be fit for the highest cultural expression.[11] In earlier decades, Georges Sylvain,

---

[8] *Ibid.*, p. 204.

[9] In theological matters, the "pure" Catholic missionaries have told the Haitian peasants that the *loas* are demons, thereby reinforcing the peasants' belief in the existence of the *loas;* the Protestant missionaries, on the other hand, undercut vaudoun entirely by persuading their converts that the *loas* are neither beneficient spirits nor demons but simply do not exist at all.

[10] Cf. Sapir, 1921, chap. xi.

[11] For example, Jourdain, 1956a, especially pp. 234–239, where she sets forth her belief that Creole is unsuited for literature because it lacks abstract nouns (according to her, this lack is an African characteristic).

the author of a number of attractive adaptations of La Fontaine's fables in Haitian Creole, was regarded as a mad eccentric, whose example no sensible person would follow in writing in Creole (even in the Gallicizing orthography which he used). It is only in recent years that any amount of creative writing has been done in Creole. Most of the material published in the McConnell-Laubach orthography in connection with the literacy programs of the nineteen-forties and early fifties was of an informative nature: for example, history of Haiti, a manual of arithmetic, and similar items. More recently, however, poems, novels, and adaptations of foreign dramas, like Sophocles' *Antigone,* have been written in Creole, using the newly recognized official McConnell-Laubach-Pressoir orthography. In Curaçao and Suriname, likewise, Papiamentu and Sranan are now more widely recognized and used than formerly. But in other areas where French- or English-based creoles are in use and where a cultural colonialism is dominant (no matter what the political status of the region may be), either the local creoles are not written at all, or they are used only for newspapers and the like, with little or no effort at creative writing.

Where class distinctions are absent from the local social structure, the standing of a pidgin or a creole is much less subject to snobbery and resultant depression. There is an instructive difference in this respect between the situation in the British Solomons and that in the Territory of New Guinea, where two quite closely related and mutually intelligible pidgins (Neo-Solomonic and Neo-Melanesian, respectively) are widely used. In the British Solomon Islands, the government has taken a markedly hostile position towards Pidgin English, and, although it requires its officers to acquire a practical command of the language for purposes of communication, it has had the firm intention to "keep the language on a purely spoken basis," as one official put it to me. This hostility is due to the intellectual prejudices of the British administrative caste, with their a priori conviction that a pidgin language must of necessity be inferior and hence must be kept in a low-ranking position.

In New Guinea, on the other hand, ever since German days, the government has shown little or no discrimination against Pidgin, and has been forced to admit its use, in written as well as spoken form. Some natives have already begun to write out narratives of their experiences, folk-tales and the like, and to publish them in various of the local mimeographed newspapers. One Assistant District Officer made a collection of accounts and narratives of notable happenings, personal experiences, etc., written by natives of his district, mostly in Neo-Melanesian. Some types of poetry have already begun to arise, such as songs of homesickness, satirical songs, love-songs, work-songs, etc.; and some Europeans, including myself, have made a start on retelling such traditional stories as those of Troy, Roland, Tristan and Isolde, El Cid, etc. One does not need to write down to one's native audience, who, after all, are adults in their own culture. Even such relatively sophisticated subject-matter as the legend of Roland or that of Tristan and Isolde can be handled simply, yet with a reasonable degree of subtlety, preserving the requisite decencies and yet making clear the basic human problems involved: for example, the relation between bravery and foolhardiness and the problem of loyalty versus personal vengeance in the *Roland,* or the conflict between love and honor in *Tristan and Isolde.*

If a situation prevails such as those discussed in the preceding pages, with government and ruling classes hostile to the local pidgin or creole, it is natural for those members of the community who use the standard language to have doubts concerning the value of the vernacular. In the open session of the First Conference on Creole Languages, held at Mona (Jamaica) in 1959, queries of the following type were expressed:

> Was there any utilitarian value in the study of Jamaican Creole? Might that study not have a deleterious effect on the advent of Standard English in the schools? What attitude should school teachers adopt to JC [Jamaican Creole]? Was there anything that could be done immediately to help school teachers—of whom only about half had any training of any kind, let alone a training in linguistics, and who in the primary schools were struggling along as best they could with hardly any printed books to help them; the Department of Education was at the stage of producing cheap readers which at least referred to the West Indian environment—substituting "oranges" for "apples", so to speak; could the linguists help them do more than this? Surely, another questioner asked, in order to use a language for teaching purposes it had to have a grammar—had

Creole a grammar? And if so, did the same grammar hold good throughout the West Indies? Wasn't there in any case a big difference between the West Indies and other Creole-speaking parts of the world, in that the population here was moving steadily towards a more standard English?[12]

Doubts of this kind, although usually unfounded from the linguistic point of view, are widespread enough to warrant serious consideration and patient answers, based on the arguments we have presented in this chapter. It is perhaps not over-optimistic to hope that, in the long run, users of standard languages can be taught enough of the findings of linguistics to help them to understand the true relationship between the standard and the pidgin or the creole. In the last analysis, the social standing and hence the cultural usefulness of any given language, be it a pidgin or a creole or a language of some other type, depend on the attitudes of those who use it. Pidgins and creoles are perhaps somewhat more "behind the eight-ball" than are other vernaculars, because it is so easy for upper-class speakers of European languages, enjoying cultural prestige, to direct especially strong condemnation and vituperation against languages that can be called "corruptions," "degradations," etc., of the very European languages with which they are in competition. Even this disadvantage can eventually be overcome, however—as shown by the example of Indonesian, which has developed from a bazaar-jargon into the standard language of a new nation—provided the speakers of the language have enough faith in it to develop it and utilize the natural resources for cultural expression that are present in every human linguistic system.

REFERENCES

Social strength and life-cycles of pidgins and creoles: Hall, 1962a.

Terms "minimal" and "makeshift" languages: Jespersen, 1922 (chap. xii). "Marginal" languages: Reinecke, 1937.

Migration of Pidgin English with advancing frontier in North America: Hall (with Leechman) 1955d. In New Zealand: Baker, n.d. In Australia: Baker, 1945.

[12] *Creole Language Studies* (1961) 2, p. 118.

Social function of pidgins: Reinecke, 1937, 1938; Bateson, 1943.

Use of Melanesian Pidgin in outlying bush areas: Mead, 1931.

French as symbol of duplicity: Efron, 1954 (p. 211).

Literary use of Haitian Creole: Efron, 1954 (pp. 208–211).

Status of Pidgin English in New Guinea: Hall, 1954b. In British Solomon Islands: Hall, 1955e.

Provision of literature in Neo-Melanesian: Hall, 1954d.

Political Significance

IN any modern country, the government has specific policies with regard to the use of the native language or languages and of foreign languages in official situations over which it has control—that is, in the government itself and its established bureaucracy, in the lawcourts, and in education. The study and analysis of governmental policies concerning language is sometimes called "glottopolitics." In countries where the rulers and the ruled speak the same language, of which there is a recognized standard variety used in literature and cultural activities, there is normally no glottopolitical problem so far as the standard language itself is concerned, since this latter is admitted in the carrying on of all official business. It was not always so, even in the West European countries whose languages now have the most prestige, such as French and English: Latin was the only officially recognized language in the French lawcourts until the Ordinance of Villers-Cotterets, promulgated by Francis I in 1539, required the use of *le langage maternel françoys* ("the French mother tongue"); and an ever-diminishing proportion of Anglo-Norman French has been used in the ritual of the English courts right down to the present day. In countries where the vernacular is different from the official language, glottopolitical problems arise as soon as speakers of the vernacular are given even a nominal share in the choice of the government and the determination of governmental policy, and hence—at least in theory— require to be informed and educated in order to meet their responsibilities. These problems are of course complicated by emotional attitudes connected with invidious distinctions between the official language and the vernacular, usually involving contempt on the part of the dominant classes for the popular speech and its users.

One extreme, that of almost complete neglect and of every possible hindrance placed in the way of a creolized vernacular, was found in Haiti until the law of September 14, 1961, which recognized the existence of Creole and granted it legal and educational status. Formerly, Creole was deliberately barred from virtually all official recognition. In political life, it was occasionally used in speeches made by politicians to popular audiences; normally, however, all announcements, discourses, and policy-speeches were made in French, even though the persons who made these announcements habitually used Creole in their private affairs. In Parliament, French was the only language permitted to be used; in earlier times, Haitians have told me that to use Creole (apart from an occasional quotation inserted into a speech for humorous effect) would have been extremely infra dig for a member of Parliament, and that a formal speech delivered in Creole would have been immediately silenced and its maker severely condemned. (This insistence on standard French did not keep politicians and parliamentarians from making all sorts of mistakes in its use, however, and from grandiose vaniloquence of a kind that they could never have gotten away with in Creole.) The laws themselves were of course always formulated and published in French. Consequently, the ordinary nèg-mòn or "hill-billy" who knows no French was simply excluded entirely from direct knowledge or comprehension of what was done in the government or what it decided for him. Nor did he normally have any newspapers in any language except French, a language which—assuming him to be literate in the first place—is as foreign to him in structure and lexicon as Latin is to the ordinary Frenchman. This state of affairs was, of course, very convenient for the ruling classes in their dominance and exploitation of the mass of the people.

In the Haitian law-courts, likewise, no language was admitted except standard French. The ordinary peasant, therefore, was reduced, when he had any contact with the courts, to dependence on lawyers who could present his case in standard French—and who were thereby enabled to take the fullest advantage of their client's ignorance, with the same lack of scruple that characterized mediaeval lawyers who knew Latin while their clients knew only the local vernaculars (for example, Dr. Azzeccagarbugli in Manzoni's

Promessi Sposi). Haitian folk-lore recognizes this state of affairs, in such proverbs as /de mun õnèt vãn šwal jo sã-lavãt/ "Two honest people make a deal over a horse without [need for] a receipt", since a written receipt would imply unreliability, need for going to court, and resultant dependence on cheating lawyers.

That superiority in dealing with the official language does not necessarily imply superior intelligence is recognized in another proverb, /pale frãse pa-di lespri pu-sa/ "To be able to speak French is not proof of cleverness"—all that a command of French implies is an advantageous position from which to fleece those who do not speak French. Forward-looking, liberal-minded Haitians have expressed to me their hope that a day might come when Creole would be admitted on a parity with French in the formal activities of the government, in Parliament, in newspapers, and in the law-courts; but even the most optimistic of such people recognized that, under the former social order in Haiti, such a hope was almost wholly Utopian.

Underlying the current movement toward more widespread use of Creole in official matters, there is of course a recognition of its status as the native language of the population, and of the desirability of its use in education. Modern linguistic research has shown that, for elementary and advanced education it cannot be said that one language is intrinsically inferior or superior to another; and it is universally recognized that learning should begin in the child's mother tongue, so that he will not have to overcome two difficulties (that of language and that of subject-matter) at the same time. To teach a child in a language he does not know is the best way to kill his interest in both the new language and the subject he is expected to learn. This point has been verified in practice time and time again. In Papua, where great emphasis was laid on exclusive use of English in the schools (in accordance with Sir Hubert Murray's puristic principles), the local Europeans boast of the absence of Pidgin; and yet Dr. Lucy Mair reports concerning the Papuan situation: "Insistence on English has doubled or tripled the difficulties of teachers and pupils."[1] She tells of scenes in which both native teacher and native pupils were repeating by rote a series of English sentences of whose content neither the instructor nor the learners had the faintest idea—a situation strangely familiar to anyone who has observed or has read descrip-

[1] Mair, 1948, pp. 163, 167, 168.

tions of attempts at instruction wholly in a European language in such places as India, Africa, or the Caribbean.

In Haiti, the same type of situation used to prevail: underpaid teachers, who had a relative mastery of French (which was often their only claim to intellectual distinction), conducted their classes in French and thereby awed but did not succeed in instructing their exclusively Creole-speaking pupils. Some enlightened theorists saw the need for using Creole as the basis of instruction, calling for both text-books and teaching in the pupils' native language; but this point of view was held until recently only by a small, rebellious minority, who were quite unable, by the strength of reason alone, to demolish the stone wall erected against Creole by what Miss Efron has termed "the stolid and almost holy conviction of the majority of educated Haitians that French is, by its intrinsic nature, the only possible language of education and instrument of 'culture'; and that, if *Le Peuple* cannot learn French, *Le Peuple* may simply remain illiterate".[2]

To justify their opposition to Creole, the upper-class Haitians have invented an entire folk-lore concerning the merits of French and the demerits of Creole. They have tended to cling to French as an invaluable, irreplaceable vehicle of culture, and have often declared that, if French were in any wise replaced by Creole in the schools, Haiti would lose its language, its "culture," and its connection with the outside world, especially France. The proposition that French is, in reality, a foreign language to 90 per cent of the population, and hence would be more effectively taught to a larger proportion of the people if it were recognized as a foreign language and taught as such on the basis of prior literacy and education in Creole, was felt to imply the deepest cultural insult, and hence aroused extreme hostility from Haitian intellectuals. Creole itself came in for violent condemnation, being denounced in such terms as the "puerile maternal patois" and the "vicious habits of speech" of the people at large. One of Haiti's leading intellectuals, Dantès Bellegarde, has written:

> Creole, having neither grammar nor a written literature, cannot constitute the material of methodical teaching; unstable, subject to continual variations in its vocabulary, its syntax and its pronunciation, it has none of the character-

[2] Efron, 1954, p. 207.

istics of a fixed language, and can neither be transmitted nor conserved save by oral use.[3]

It was of no use for linguistic science to set forth the actual facts concerning Creole, which are, as we have seen in this book, quite different, since pidgins and creoles have as firm and as describable a grammatical structure as any other language, and can be written and used in education as effectively as any other. It was of no use to explain that a straightforward ethnophonemic orthography such as the McConnell-Laubach-Pressoir system would facilitate quick attainment of literacy in the first and second grades, on the basis of which a really effective command of French as a foreign language could be rapidly built up. Any such explanations would meet with and irremovable resistance in the (largely unacknowledged) inferiority complex and resultant cultural colonialism of the Haitian upper classes, whose prejudices are catered to by, and whose support therefore goes to, dilettante writers on language such as those who deny all African substratum and trace Haitian Creole /jo/ "they" to Spanish *ellos!*

As a result of this obscurantist attitude on the part of the dominant classes in Haiti, little or no progress has been made until recent years in literacy campaigns directed at the mass of the population. As we pointed out in Chapter 5, the very simplicity and straightforwardness of even the Pressoir adaptation of the McConnell-Laubach orthography was made an object of attack, since it differs from that of French. An advocate of Creole education, Christian Beaulieu, wrote irritatedly of the fanatical defenders of French:

> To listen to these people, one might think that . . . writing comes before the creation of a language, that the spoken language is somehow the instrument of the written word which has pre-existed since all time—instead of being merely a graphic representation of the auditive image created by the word itself![4]

Yet many Haitians showed such subservience towards the French language and French culture as to consider that any departure from French norms would be inconceivable, would constitute virtual cultural treason. On one occasion, in a discussion with a group

[3] Quoted by Efron, 1954, pp. 207–208.
[4] Quoted by Efron, 1954, p. 208.

of Haitian teachers concerning the merits of Creole and the McConnell-Laubach orthography, a French woman declared that she envied the Haitians the possession of such a rational orthography as the McConnell-Laubach, and that she wished a similar one existed for French. To which one of the Haitian teachers replied, "But, mademoiselle, how do you expect us Haitians to change our spelling before the French themselves have done so?"!

The situation in Haiti is no longer as dark as it was before 1961. Only recently, though, has it come to be as encouraging as that which we find in New Guinea. There, Pidgin has been used as a medium of instruction for the last sixty years, first by Roman Catholic and (less extensively) Protestant missionaries, as a means of teaching primarily religious material, but also for secular subjects. In government schools likewise, Neo-Melanesian has been a lingua franca wherever pupils from two or more language backgrounds have come together in the class-room, and has served successfully as a vehicle for arithmetic, geography, and social studies. Nor has its usefulness been limited to merely elementary subjects; various agencies (missionary and government) have prepared manuals for such subjects as economics, medicine, and handicrafts, and could equally well prepare manuals in any other subjects. There has been criticism of this policy from various sources, particularly from the United Nations Trusteeship Council's missions, and we find references to "the heavy responsibility of those who decided to introduce Pidgin as a medium of instruction" and so on. The best answer to such criticism has been given by Höltker, who makes the following essential points:[5]

1.   Neo-Melanesian is already in widespread use throughout the Territory, and has been since the earliest German colonial days; and it is still spreading.

2.   Neo-Melanesian is the creation and possession of the Melanesians themselves. It shows the force of expansion that characterizes a truly creative language.

3.   Neo-Melanesian corresponds to the way of talking and hence of thinking of the Melanesian. Far from being "harmful" to his psychology (as some well-meaning but ignorant anticolonialists have claimed), it reflects his linguistic and therefore his mental structure.

[5] Höltker, 1945.

The usefulness of Neo-Melanesian in elementary education is attested by a number of teachers, who find it definitely preferable to English. One teacher remarked to me that he much preferred to teach such a subject as arithmetic in Pidgin, rather than in English, because he could thus be sure that the learners knew what they were talking about and understood what they were learning. As he put it, "you can't blether in Pidgin"; you have to be sure what you mean and say it clearly, in which case there is no danger of being misunderstood. Pidgin has no big, empty words, or abstract nouns like English *multiplication* or *division* which the native learner can use grandiosely without knowing what they mean. Talking Neo-Melanesian in class forces both teacher and pupils to talk sense. In general, the extensive use of Pidgin in education in New Guinea has aided the natives of that region to become more easily adapted to European culture, to learn more and to be more sophisticated in their knowledge, than their cousins in the British Solomons, in whose schools British Solomon Islands Pidgin is frowned upon.[6]

In fields outside of formal education, the use of Neo-Melanesian is so widespread that it would be completely impossible to "abolish" it, as the United Nations Trusteeship Council demanded in 1953. Neo-Melanesian is extensively spoken in all types of contacts between natives among themselves, and between natives and Europeans. I have been present at town gatherings, district council meetings, co-operative society meetings, and similar assemblies where Neo-Melanesian was the language in which all the activities of the gathering were carried on; and a great many of the religious services, Catholic and Protestant, are held in Neo-Melanesian, including the readings from the Bible and the hymns sung by the congregations. Consequently, the ordinary Melanesian native has a decidedly better understanding of the immediate environment in which he lives, and even of its relation to the rest of the world, than does his counterpart in the British Solomons, to say nothing of Haiti. Furthermore, the widespread use of Neo-Melanesian as a

---

[6] This does not mean that we are necessarily advocating the use of Neo-Melanesian at all stages of education through the secondary and university levels. As pointed out in Hall, 1955a, pp. 125–126, economic factors alone would make it imperative for English to be taught as a foreign language in the primary schools and used as the main language of instruction in the higher grades. One Assistant District Officer remarked to me, quite rightly: "We can't afford to translate the *Encyclopaedia Britannica* into Pidgin."

lingua franca has a leveling effect, avoiding the disparity of social status which would arise either from the natives' more or less halting attempts to use the language of the ruling colonial power (in this case, English) or from the administrative officials' even more halting efforts to use the native language. As Margaret Mead says:

> The Neo-Melanesian language of New Guinea (formerly called Pidgin English) presents an excellent example of the genuine equalization of status and experience which can be brought about by the introduction of a language used by both speakers as a second and "urban" language. The native from the deep bush and the European are here on a par, proficient and fluent as neither could be in the language of the other.[7]

It can hardly be said that, even in New Guinea, the local lingua franca has achieved complete recognition from the glottopolitical point of view. The most that can be said is that, as far as the situation permits, Neo-Melanesian has been given something resembling a fair chance, and has been demonstrated to be a wholly viable means of communication, on all levels. Lest the reader think I am exaggerating, it should be mentioned that, from time to time, Europeans who have no other language in common and have chanced to meet in New Guinea, talk together in Neo-Melanesian, and find it adequate to discuss everything, including such subjects as theology and international law.

In other regions, the local pidgins and creoles normally fall somewhere along the scale between the nearly total neglect accorded to Creole in Haiti and the other islands of the Caribbean region, and the relatively favorable recognition given Neo-Melanesian in New Guinea. For the most part, such languages labor under considerable difficulty, because of social snobbery and puristic condemnation from conservatives, and, more recently, because of well-meaning but linguistically uninformed anticolonialism on the part of liberals. In very few regions have pidgins and creoles been accorded official recognition, and in most places the possibility of attaining quick literacy in the local pidgin or creole and of basing further education thereon has been neglected, either deliberately or out of ignorance and prejudice.

---

[7] Mead, 1959, p. 33.

Glottopolitics cannot, any more than can any other applied social science, prescribe policy. All it can do is to study and present the facts of the situation, and to point out what will happen if one course or another is followed. Applied anthropology has already been able to contribute to the solution of social problems, wherever it has been permitted to do so (as in the case of the "zoot-suit" riots in Los Angeles in the nineteen-forties); applied linguistics can do the same wherever its findings are heeded, and not—as in the case of Haiti—embedded in reports which are filed and then treated as if they had not been made. In the case of pidgins and creoles, we can say that, whenever they and their speakers are subjected to strong social disfavor, the communities that use them are likely, as a result, to be embittered—as are, say, the speakers of Krio in Freetown—and to be very fertile seed-beds for discontent, anti-Western propaganda, and social strife. If, on the other hand, the legitimacy and the usefulness of pidgins and creoles are recognized, they can be used as channels of communication for the education and betterment of their speakers. A pidgin used widely as a lingua franca, such as Neo-Melanesian, may perhaps eventually be discarded after having served its purpose, to be replaced by some standard language such as English; or it may continue indefinitely, if its use is found advantageous. There would be no reason for rejoicing or sorrowing over either outcome, but the process can be made smooth in either case by applying the findings of linguistic science to the use of the pidgin and by basing further learning (of other languages and of subject-matter) on a sound analysis of the pidgin. Since we are dealing with the native languages of speech-communities, recognition of the status of creoles as such can be expected to prepare a firm foundation, not only for the education, but also for the psychological security, of their speakers, on which more sound linguistic, cultural, and economic relations can be built than would ever be possible if their speakers remain insecure concerning their language.

To sum up: pidginized and creolized languages represent one of the most interesting frontiers of linguistic science, and offer points of special challenge in all respects. The actual work of exploration has only begun, and there are a great many pidgins and creoles still awaiting complete investigation. Their importance for linguistic theory is great, and there is a large field open for the further investigation of their relation to social structure. In the glottopolitical implications of pidgins and creoles, there is still an immense amount of work to be done, of both the expository and the persuasive variety. It is to be hoped that the rest of the twentieth century will see a thoroughgoing expansion and development of this fascinating but hitherto neglected field.

REFERENCES

Political status of Haitian Creole: Efron, 1954 (p. 205).

Results of exclusive use of English in Papuan schools: Mair, 1948 (p. 154).

Use of Neo-Melanesian as basis for teaching English: Hall, 1955a (chap. ix).

Use of Neo-Melanesian in elementary education: Höltker, 1945; Wedgwood, 1953; Hall, 1955a (chap. x).

Sample Texts

ɪN this section are contained texts in various pidgins and creoles, given in phonemic, phonetic, or ethnophonemic transcription. For lack of a satisfactory phonemic interpretation, it has been necessary to exclude material available only in the conventional orthography of European languages; unavoidably, this restriction has led to the omission of a great many pidgins and creoles, especially those based on Portuguese and French, which it is to be hoped will be documented more accurately and fully by future research. The texts are given in the left-hand column, with their English translations in the right-hand column.

I. English-based Pidgins and Creoles

1. Neo-Melanesian. A section of the autobiography of a work-boy, Čavi, collected by Margaret Mead *ca.*1936 and transcribed phonemically by Hall in 1942; reproduced from Hall, 1953a, §7.62.4 (p. 62).

naw mi stap rabawl. mi stap lɔŋ bɪglajn, mi kətɪm kopra. naw wənfelə mastər bɪlɔŋ kəmpəni ɛm i-kɪčɪm mi, mi kuk lɔŋ ɛm gɛn. mastər kɪŋ. mi stap. naw ɔl mastər i-kɪk, naw ɔl i-kɪkɪm ɛm, naw leg bɪlɔŋ ɛm i-swɛl-əp. ɔl mastər tæsɔl i-kɪk, naw ɔl i-kɪkɪm ɛm. naw ɛm i-go lɔŋ sɪdni lɔŋ haws sɪk. mi wənfelə mi stap lukawtɪm haws bɪlɔŋ ɛm. əltəgedər	Then I stayed in Rabaul. I was in the work-group, cutting copra. Then a white man from the company took me as a cook again. Mr. King. I stayed there. Now all the white men were playing football, and they kicked him, so that his leg swelled up. The white men were just kicking, and kicked him. So he went to Sydney, to the hospital. I stayed alone to look

149

səmtıŋ mi lʊkawtım, mi stap. ɔrajt,
naw pæs i-kəm. naw kiap i-lʊkım,
i-tɔk: "o, mastər bılɔŋ ju i-no kæn
kəm bæk." naw mastər—dısfɛlə ɛm
i-kəməp—bılɔŋ kəmpəni tu, ɛm i-save
bajım nufɛlə bɔj lɔŋ ɔlgɛdər ples—
ɛm i-tɔk lɔŋ mi: "ju no kæn go lɔŋ
bıglajn, maski, ju kʊk lɔŋ mi gɛn."
mi stap lɔŋ ɛm. stap stap stap stap.
ɛm i-lajk go lɔŋ kurili, naw mi no
lajk. plɛnti bɔj i-kʊk lɔŋ ɛm. mi no
lajk go wəntajm ɔl, naw mi tɔkım
mastər, mi spik: "o, mi no lajk go
wəntajm ju. plɛnti bɔj tuməč. maski,
mi stap. mi kæn go bæk lɔŋ bıglajn.
ɛm i-tɔk: "ɔrajt. ju kæn stap." mi stap
gɛn. ɔrajt. ɔl kəmpəni i-gowe, naw
i-no mor. ɔltəgɛdər i-go sıdni. nəm-
bərwən bılɔŋ ɔl, ɛm i-go tu. bipi
kıčım stešən bılɔŋ kəmpəni, bænıs
bılɔŋ ɛm. naw mifɛlə ɔl bɔj hir.
ɔrajt, naw mi tɔk lɔŋ mastər bılɔŋ
mifɛlə: "a, ajtıŋk mi brokım tajm,
mi go lɔŋ ples." mastər bılɔŋ bipi
i-tɔk: "no, ɛm i-no holım wok bılɔŋ
jet." ɔrajt, naw mi stap naw lɔŋ bipi.
naw mastər bılɔŋ bipi i-tɔk: "čavi,
mi save ju. ju no wok lɔŋ bıglajn,
ju ɔltajm məŋki bılɔŋ mastər." naw
ɛm i-mekım pepər, naw mi go lɔŋ
mısıs bılɔŋ dısfɛlə kæptɛn bılɔŋ
mirani bıfor.

after his house. I looked after everything, and stayed there. Very well,
then a letter arrived. Then the government official looked at it, and said:
"Oh, your master cannot come back."
Then the master—this one who had
come—he too was of the company,
he recruited new native laborers
from all the villages—he said to me:
"You cannot go to the work-group,
rather you shall cook for me again."
I stayed with him, and kept on stay-
ing. He wanted to go to Kurili, but
I didn't want to. Many "boys" were
cooking for him. I did not want to
go with them, and I spoke to the
master, saying: "Oh, I don't want to
go with you. [You have] a great many
'boys.' I'd rather stay. I can go back
to the work-group." He said: "Very
well. You may stay." I stayed on
again. Very well. All the company
men went away, and they were not
there any more. They all went to
Sydney. Their chief went too. B.P.
[Burns Philp & Co.] took over the
company's plantation and its labor-
line. Now we, the "boys," were there.
Well, now I said to our master: "Ah,
I think I will break my indenture, I
shall go to my village." The B.P.
master said: "No, he has not done
work for me yet." Very well, then I
stayed on with B.P. Then the B.P.
master said: "Čavi, I know you. You
did not work in the work-group, you
were always the master's servant."
Then he made an indenture, and I
went to the wife of this former cap-
tain of the "Mirani."

2. Neo-Solomonic. The beginning of a story told to the author in 1954 by a native of Malaita.

ɔrajt. mifɛlə i-go go lɔŋ sɔlwatər, lukawtım fıš, naw wın i-kəm, naw mifɛlə i-go ɔləbawt lɔŋ kinú, naw bıgfɛlə wın i-kəm naw, mifɛlə i-fafasi ɔləbawtə, rɔŋ tuməs, mifɛlə go, no kæčım ɛni ples i-kwajtfɛlə. mifɛlə go ɔləbawt lɔŋ ɛvri ples, an mifɛlə go lɔŋ sɔlwatər, æn traj go, æn wın i-kəm hart, naw trifɛlə i-go, naw mifɛlə i-go slip ɔləbawt nomor lɔŋ antap lɔŋ sanbič, naw mifɛlə go go go, ən wənfɛlə man i-dajvən, wənfɛlə bıgfɛlə šɛl lɔŋ sɔlwatər, an hɛm i-tekım lɔŋ šor, an mifɛlə askım hɛm, "blɔŋ wɔnem hir?". naw mifɛlə se, askım hɛm ɔlsem, an hɛm i-se: "blɔŋ kajkaj." "o, dıswən ajtıŋk bajmbaj kajkajm, man i-daj hir." na hɛm i-se, "a, hɛm i-ɔrajt. səmtıŋ hir, ɛm i-gud hir, i-gudfɛlə fıš." ɛm i-tɔk ɔlsem, naw mifɛlə i-go, livım hɛm, mifɛlə go ɔləwe. ɔl kæčım wənfɛlə ples mor, mifɛlə fajndım wənfɛlə wumən i-pıkəp wənfɛlə šɛl ɔr tu lɔŋ sɔlwatər. mifɛlə askım ɛm, i-se: "hwıčwe? ju save lukawtım šɛlə, na bajmbaj ju save go lɔŋ ɔlgedər wajtmæn fɔr bajım?" ɛm i-se, "no. i-blɔŋ mi fɔr kajkaj."

Very well. We kept going on the sea, hunting for fish, and a wind arose; now we were going in canoes, and an immense wind arose now, and we were thrown around and ran very fast [before the wind]. We went, and did not come to any place which was quite. We went around to every place, and we went along on the sea, and tried to go, and the wind came hard, and three [canoes?] went, and we went and simply rested on the beach; then we kept going, and one man dived [for] a large shell in the sea, and he took it to the shore, and we asked him, "Why [do you do this] here?" Now we spoke [and] asked him thus, and he said "To eat." "Oh, this one, probably, if one eats it, one will die here." And he said: "Oh, it's all right. This thing here is good. It's a good fish." He spoke thus, and we went and left him, we went away. They came to another place, and we found a woman who was gathering a shell or two by the sea. We asked her, saying: "How come? Are you in the habit of looking for shells, and then of going to the Europeans to sell them?" She said, "No. They are mine, to eat."

3. Australian Pidgin English. Sentences dictated to the author in 1954 by Judge Norman Bell, a resident of the Northern Territory since 1907, and formerly a judge at West Arm. These sentences represent the type of utterances characteristic of an interrogation and a native's response.

tɔ́mi, jú bín sí ðǽtwən lúbra?

Tommy, did you see that native woman?

jú síɪm lɔŋ áj bɪlɔ́ŋ ju?   Did you see her with your own eyes?
jés, mí bín síɪm.   Yes, I saw her.
wɔ́tnem ší bín tɔ́k?   What did she say?
watsəmǽtər jú bín həmbəg lɔ́ŋə   Why did you cheat the Chinese?
    čájnəmən?
ðís púr nígər, ðé bín wə́rk əlɔ́ŋə   These poor black men, they worked
    kə́tɪm wúd.   at cutting wood.
ím bín kílɪm mi.   He struck me.
kílɪm ju? wɔ́tnem? kílɪm ju ɔr kílɪm   Killed you? What? Struck you or
    jú déd?   killed you dead?
ó, ím bín kílɪm mi.   Oh, he struck me.
jú nomór dú ðǽtwən.   Don't you do that.
wasəmǽrə jú həmbəg lɔ́ŋə ðǽt?   Why did you do wrongly with regard
    to that?
mí bín tɔ́kɪm jú dú ðíswən.   I told you to do this.

4. Chinese Pidgin English. A dialogue dictated to the author
in 1944 by Mrs. Kathleen M. Merritt, native of Wu-Hu (middle Yang-
tze valley, Hankow region); the dialogue represents a conversation
between a lady and her tailor.

MISTRESS: télər, máj hǽv kǽči wə́n-   Tailor, I have a very fine [piece of]
pisi plénti hǽnsəm sílka. máj   silk. I want you to make a nice
wɔ́nči jú méki wən nájs ívniŋ-   evening dress.
drés.
TAILOR: mísi hǽv gát búk?   Has missy a [fashion] book?
MISTRESS: máj nó hǽv kǽči´búk.   I haven't brought a book. Let me see
pémi sí jú búk.   your book.
TAILOR: máj búk blɔ́ŋ tú ólə.   My book is too old [out of date].
MISTRESS: máski, jú pémi lúk-sí.   Never mind, let me see it.
TAILOR: máj sǽvi mísi nó wɔ́nči   I know missy doesn't want this kind
ðísfǽšən. səpós mísi kǽn kǽči   [of dress]. If missy can get a
búk, máj kǽn méki. səpós mísi   book, I can make it. If missy
nó kǽn kǽči búk, máj nó kǽn   can't get a book, I can't. Can
dú. mísi kǽn kə́m tumɔ́lo?   missy come tomorrow?
MISTRESS: tumɔ́lo máj nó kǽn kə́m.   Tomorrow I can't come. I'll leave
máj lívi sílka ðíssajd, səpós máj   the silk here, and possibly I'll
kə́m tumɔ́rə néks dé.   come day after tomorrow.
TAILOR: ɔ́rajt, mísi, tumɔ́rə néks dé   Very well, missy, day after tomorrow
kǽn dú. máj méki véri pɔ́pa fɔ́ jú.   is all right. I'll make it just right
    for you.

MISTRESS: jú méki wə́npis ívniŋ-drés   If you make an evening-dress for me,
fɔ́r máj, háwməč jú wɔ́nči?   how much do you want?

TAILOR: spós blɔ́ŋ dǽnsɪŋ-drés, máj
wɔ́nči twɛ́lv dɔ́lər.
MISTRESS: twɛ́lv dɔ́lər blɔ́ŋ tumǽči.
TAILOR: háwfæšən twɛ́lv dɔ́lər blɔ́ŋ
tuməči? mástər hǽv kǽči plɛ́nti
fájn plés, mísi tɔ́ki twɛ́lv dɔ́lər
tumǽči. ɛ́ni mísi ǧə́snaw kǽči
hǽnsəm ívnɪŋ-drés, kǽn pémi
twɛ́lv dɔ́lər.
MISTRESS: spós máj kǽči búk, kə́m
ðíssajd tumɔ́rə nɛ́ks dé, hwátajm
jú kǽn fínɪš fɔ́r máj?
TAILOR: mísi, ǧə́snaw máj plɛ́nti bízi.
mə́s wɔ́nči tɛ́n dé mór.
MISTRESS: tɛ́n dé mór blɔ́ŋ tú lɔ́ŋ
tájm. máj wɔ́nči vɛ́li kwɪk.
TAILOR: fɔ́ jú, mísi, máj kǽn dú wə́n
wík.
MISTRESS: ðǽt blɔ́ŋ vɛ́li gúd.

If it is a dancing-dress, I want twelve
dollars.
Twelve dollars is too much.
How is it that twelve dollars is too
much? The master has gotten a
very fine job, [and yet] missy
says twelve dollars is too much.
Any missy who gets a fine evening-dress at present can pay me
twelve dollars.
If I get the book and come here day
after tomorrow, when can you
finish it for me?
Missy, at present I'm very busy.
It'll take more than ten days.
More than ten days is too long a
time. I want it very quick.
For you, missy, I can do it in a week.

That is very good.

5. Sranan. Beginning of a folk tale taken down in Surinam by
the Herskovitses, and reproduced in Herskovits, 1936 (p. 286).

wán kónde bén dé, en wán fóru bén
dé bári. ɛf' a bár só, na hér kóndre
e trúbu. kónu pót táki, wán súma
kír na-fóru, a-sa-tró nána wán úman
pikín fo-éŋ.

anánsi jére. a-go táig kónu táki, éŋ
sa-kíri na-fóru. mék kónu gí-em móni
en bái sáni, dán éŋ sa-gó kír eŋ. dí
anánsi gó, a-tán tú wíki. a-kír wán
pómpom, a-tjár kóm. kónum nó bríbi
eŋ táki na na-fóru dáti de-bár só.
kónum táig hem, táki, éfu na-fóru
nó bári báka wán mún, dán a-sa-tró
nána na-pikín. ma bifós wán mún,
dán na-fóru bári. dán kónum séni
ték anánsi, mék srót eŋ.

There was once a kingdom, and
there was a bird which screeched. If
it screeched so, the whole kingdom
was disturbed. The King announced
that the person who killed the bird
would marry a daughter of his.
Anansi heard this. He went to tell the
King that he would kill the bird. Let
the King give him money to buy
things, then he would go and kill it.
When Anansi went, he remained
away two weeks. He killed a Pom-
pom and brought [it]. The King did
not believe him, that this was the
bird which screeched so. The King
said to him that if the bird did not
screech again within a month, then
he could marry the girl. But before
the month was up, the bird screeched.
Then the King sent for Anansi and
had him imprisoned.

6. Jamaican Creole. Beginning of a story entitled "William Saves His Sweetheart," transcribed by DeCamp and reproduced in LePage and DeCamp, 1960 (p. 143).

nóu, a úol táim anánsi-in stúori, wi gwáiŋ at nóu. nóu wánts dér wáz, a úol wíč líedi lív, had wán són, níem av wíljəm. wíljəm wór ingjéj, tu a jóŋ líedi, frám a néks úol wíč séksən hú waz hár mádar in láa. nóu dát gjól fáda, had dát gjól wid iz fós wáif. an áfta di wáif disíis, hii iz mári a néks wúman, wíč is a úol wíč an dát wúman bíer túu dáataz bisáidz. nóu di tríi sístaz líviŋ gúd, bót di máda in láa dídn láik dat wán dáata atál, fi-di mán. him prefár fi-ar túu. bót, jét di tríi gjól wor ğúobial wid wán anáda. wel dát wán gjól, frénz wid dís jóŋ mán, níem av wíljam. wíljam máda iz a úold wíč. di gjól mádaanláa iz a úold wíč. súo, ju gwain fáin óut, wá de gó hápm nóu.

Now, a old-time Anancying story we going at now. Now once there was a old witch-lady live, had one son, name of William. William were engage to a young lady from a next [another] old witch's section who was her mother-in-law [stepmother]. Now that girl's father had that girl with his first wife. And after the wife decease, he is marry a next [another] woman, which is a old witch. And that woman bear two daughters besides. Now the three sisters living good [got along well together], but the mother-in-law didn't like that one daughter at all, the man's. She prefer her own two. But yet the three girls were jovial with one another. Well, that one girl was friends with this young man, name of William. William's mother is a old witch. The girl's mother-in-law is a old witch. So, you going to find out what is going to happen now.

7. Gullah. The first paragraph of a religious narrative, /sikɪn/, dictated to Turner by Hester Milligan (Edisto Island, South Carolina) and reproduced in Turner, 1949 (pp. 270–271). (For typographical reasons, Turner's upside-down ɒ has been replaced by ɔ, and his upside-down a by ə, as well as long ʃ by š.)

mɔi masa šo mi ɔl kɔin ə tɪŋ. ɔi tɪŋk ɪt bin ə frəidɪ, in Julɑɪ. i šo mi hɛl; i šo mi hɛwm; i šo mi hɔu tu Jɪt rɪlɪJən. an wɛn i Jɪt tru, i ʌpm ə bɪg bɔibl; an dɛn i blɛs mɔi sol. dɛn i tɛl mi—i sɛ: go in pis n sɪn no mo. unə sol də set fri. an aftə wɔil ɔi kʌm əut dɛ,

My Master show me all kind of thing. I think it been a Friday, in July. He show me hell; he show me heaven; he show me how to get religion. And when he get through, he open a big Bible; and then he bless my soul. Then he tell me—he say: "Go in peace and sin no more. Your soul set free. And after while I come out there,

an ɔl wɛrəs tɪŋ ɔɪ si. di mɔrɪs ɔɪ si bɪn ə ɲɔŋ manz, n ə Jal, n cɪlən, n mɔɪ faṛə, n pipl—ɔl ʌp in ə bɔndl. dɛn ɔɪ si ə Jadn n flɔwəz wɪd ə fɛnc rɔun. ɔɪ si fɔɪw kɔu n ə caf, sɔɪd ə pədl ə wɔtə. de də ɲam fɔṛə. dɛn ɔɪ si hɛl; ɔɪ si hɛwm; ɔɪ si ɔl kɔɪn ə tɪŋ.

peace and sin no more. Your soul is set free." And after while I come out there, and all various thing I see. The most I see been a young mans, and a girl, and children, and my father, and people—all up in a bundle. Then I see a garden and flowers with a fence round. They been work hard. I see five cow and a calf, beside a puddle of water. They were eating fodder. Then I see hell; I see heaven; I see all kind of thing.

II. French-based Creoles

1. Haitian Creole. The first paragraph of a folk-tale, "The Lion and the Donkey," from Hall, 1953a (p. 146), retranscribed phonenically.

liõ ak-burik. lõ-tã liõ te-pè burik, paske li te-wè burik te-pigro nèg pase li. ṇu žu liõ di: "burik, mõ šè, ãn-ale fè ju ti-promnad." jo pati, jo rive bò ju dlo. liõ fè ju sèl bõ, li travese dlo-a. burik ki pa-vle rõt devã liõ šèše fè mēm bagaj ke li. li tõbe nã-dlo, kurã kõmãse trene li, dlo kõmãse ãtre nã-zorèj li. liõ ki wè sa kuri ale wete li, o-lie-burik remèsi-l, li di-l kõ-sa: "mõ-šè, pīga u žam fè mwē kõ-sa ãkò, u wè m-ap-peše pwasõ epi u vin kõtrarie-m."

The Lion and the Donkey. A long time [ago], the lion was afraid of the donkey, because he saw the donkey was a bigger man than him. One day the lion said: "Donkey, my dear chap, let's go take a little walk." They set out, [and] they came to the edge of a stream. The lion gave a single leap, [and] he crossed the stream. The donkey, who didn't want to lose face before the lion, tried to do the same thing as him. He fell into the water, the current started to pull him along, the water started to come into his ears. The lion, who saw this, hastened to go and pull him out; [but] instead of the donkey thanking him, he talked to him this way: "My dear man, don't you ever do that to me again; you saw I was fishing and then you came and pestered me."

2.   Louisiana Creole. Sentences from Morgan, 1959 (pp. 24a ff.).

j-arive kote jo papa.
mo tužu ape-buɑte.
pa-tɔm tɛ-galɔpe nɛt ã-grɛŋɛ.
t-ale rɛste kuše.
jɛ parti kuri mɛnɛ jɛ dã buɑ.

anɔ̃ dɔn pov ɛ̃ tɛl sɛ̃ sã pjɑs.

mo tɛ pɛrd tu sa mo tɛ gɛ̃.
mo mɛt muɑ sɑrše apre ti-košõ-la.

mo ti-garsõ kɔmãs travaj
   dã-klo li.
li viŋi pu-mõte ãho-la.
ɛ̃ lapɛ̃ t-ape-ãbɛte li.
ɛna ki pɛrd de plɑs, dɔt ki kul o luɛ̃.

ɛn-avɛ truaz-ã k-ɛ t-ape-dɔrmi.

alɔrs lɛ-bõ-džɛ di va rɛste sa arjɛ̃.

sa sɛ le-maladi mo trɛt.
li kup la-kɔrd kup li kup la-kɔrd.
si mo sɛ pa-rɛste si prɛ, mo sɛ kɛ́ktã
   uɑ lɛ-mun amize-jɛ.

They came home to their papa.
I've always been crippled.
Pa Tom ran straight into the barn.
You are going to remain lying down.
They went and took them into the
   woods.
Let's give poor so-and-so five hun-
   dred dollars.
I lost everything I had.
I set myself to looking for the little
   pig.
My little boy began to work in the
   field.
He managed to climb up there.
A rabbit had been vexing him.
There were some who lost their
   places, others who ran away.
There were three years that she was
   sleeping.
Then the Lord said "Let it be
   nothing."
Those are the diseases I treated.
He cuts the string.
If I didn't stay so close, I'd see the
   people having a good time some-
   times.

3.   Guadaloupe Creole. Beginning of a story, "Manzè Élodie"
("Miss Élodie"), given by Jourdain (1956a, p. 272) in Gallicizing
orthography but described by her as *une graphie très proche de la
phonétique;* phonemicized by the author on the basis of Mlle.
Jourdain's orthography.

mãzè elodi te-tini sēkãt-nèv-ã a-si-
tèt-a-i ka bitē-la-sa rive. se-pa-ãni
a-si-tèt-a-i i-te-tini jo, bjē (bjēn—?)
evidã. i-te-tini jo tu-pa-tu. mē se-
sēkãt-nèv-ã-la sa pa-te-ka-siŋifie ajē
di-tu pa-plis ki, ã-tã lõ-tã, laženès
pa-te-žãmē siŋifie-i ajē. ãfē, pu-di zòt

Miss Elodie had fifty-nine years on
her head when this thing happened.
It wasn't only on her head that she
had them, quite obviously. She had
them all over. But those fifty-nine
years, for her, meant nothing at all,
any more than youth, in far-away

la-fwãšiz verite, ajē pa-te žãmē
siṇifie-i ajē. i-te-õ-fwã vje-fi, õ-natal
vje-fi.

times, had ever meant anything to
her. In short, to tell you the frank
truth, nothing had ever meant anything to her. She was a pure old
maid, a born old maid.

4. Dominican Creole. Sentences from Taylor, 1951.

mun sot.	People [are] stupid.
nu fē.	We [are] hungry.
u pa-las sottiz.	You [are] not tired [of] stupidity.
per esit.	[The] priest [is] here.
u se-madam li.	You are his wife.
ri duvã plere deyer.	Laughter ahead, weeping behind.
parol ã-buš pa-šay.	Words in [the] mouth [are] not [a] load [*that is,* fine talk is no guarantee of deeds or intentions].
nu gade jo.	We looked at them.
jo gade nu.	They looked at us.
pa-pale sot.	Don't talk nonsense!
žordi mwē malad.	Today I [am] sick.
i-pa-ãkor malad ãpil.	He (she) [is] not yet very sick.
i-pa malad ãpil ãkor.	He (she) [is] no longer very sick.
i-ramase jo a-ter.	He picked them up off [the] ground.
mwē ba žanin sēk predjal pu-i-gãje pē ba mwē.	I gave Jeannine five "predials" [15 cents] for her [to] buy bread for me.
ba mwē i vit.	Give it to me quickly.
u ža di mwē listwer sa.	You already told me that story.
jo vini esit kote mwē.	They came here beside me.
es jo maše?	[Did] they walk? [Have] they walked?
puci u pa-vini ã-travaj ijer?	Why didn't you come to work yesterday?
mwē te-ni mal dã.	I had tooth-ache.
se-su u te-su.	It's drunk you were!
nu prã šimē par bwa, se-la solej kuše nu.	We took [the] path by [the] woods, it's there [the] sun laid us [down] [*that is,* it's there darkness overtook us].
šjē epi šat pa-ka-dakor.	Dogs and cats don't agree.
tu-le-žu kalbas kaj laivjer, jõ i-ni purete la.	Every day [a, the] calabash goes [to the] river, one day it has to remain there.

i-pa-ni mušwer poš.

piti haš ka-bat gro bwa.

troce se-pa-vole.

ler u vini, u ke-žwen mwē ka-dormi.

He hasn't got [a] pocket-handkerchief.

Little axes fell big trees.

Exchange is not robbery.

When you come, you'll find me sleeping.

III. Spanish-Based Pidgins and Creoles

1. Papiamentu. Beginning of story dictated by informant to F. B. Agard, *ca.*1949, and furnished to the author by Agard.

história di un máma ku jú. un día taba tín un máma ku su jú, i nan taba ta mašá póber. E táta taba ta piskadó, i túr día k'e bin fe lamán, e máma ta'a mand' e jú bái bende piská.

un día e jú ta'a pasa cu su bák'i piská i el a tende un hénde jam'é. óra k'el a hisa su kára na lária, el a weta ku taba ta un laréina. e laréina taba tín mašá simpatía p'e muča bendedó'i piská; el a né diés morokóto, i e dí ku n'é: "muča, pa kíko bo ta bende piská? Túr día mi ta tendé-bo ta pasa ku piská, ta grita na kája. hasí-mi un fabór di bisa bo máma ku bo táta ku mi'n ke mirá-bu na kája más ta bende piská, pa motíbu ku bo t'un buníta muča i ku mi ta gusta di kasa ku bo."

enfín ján a bái su kás i el a bisa su máma ku su táta. nan a kit'é fe ríba káya, despé ku nan a tende kíko laréina dí, i nan u'n mand'é bende piská más. Despé'i algún día laréina a manda puntr'e táta k'e máma pa kasa ku ján, i nan a keda maša ferwónder di mira kon laréina por a haṇa tántu amór pa nan jú.

Story of a mother and son. One day there were a mother and her son, and they were very poor. The father was [a] fisherman, and every day that he came up from the sea, the mother sent the boy to go and sell fish.

One day the boy was passing with his basket of fish and he heard a person call him. Now that he raised his face in the air [upward], he saw that it was a queen. The queen had a great liking for the fish-vendor boy; she took ten "morocotos," and she said to him: "Boy, why do you sell fish? Every day I hear you pass by with fish, [and] shout in the street. Do me the favor of telling your father and your mother that I don't want to see you in the street any more selling fish, because you are a handsome boy and I wish to marry you."

Finally Jan went to his house and he told his father and his mother. They took him up off the street, [and] after they heard what the queen said, they didn't send him to sell fish [any] more. After some days the queen sent to ask the father and mother for [her] to marry Jan, and they remained very much astonished at seeing how the queen could have so much love for Jan.

2. Piñaguero Panare Spanish trade jargon. Sentences quoted by Riley, 1952 (pp. 7, 8, 10). These are given in Riley's transcription, which is apparently phonemic; I have left his "y" for [j].

yo no sabyéndo ke tu disyéndo.

panáre de kučivéro vinyéndo sérka, mwí sérka, de akí, lansándo lugár de gwaniámo, matándo ómbre, kitándo muxéres, kitándo atúŋ, yo sabyéndo el.

yo kaminándo patrióta ayá, pasándo la kokwísis, vendyéndo tewá, komprándo dos kólin, parándo ayá un día, vinyéndo aká manyána. yo vendyéndo tewá, yo vendyéndo toᵖ, tu komprándo péro káro, káro, vénte día ponyéndo, tu pagándo múčo fwérte.

tu kyére pasándo mwí léhos, kwándo vinyéndo akí trayéndo kwénta, yo dándo múčo fwérte.

mapóye parándo ayá, mwí léhos, indios brávo, lansándo múčo. el vendyéndo wastáᵖ, vendyéndo mankowá, el komprándo tewá, komprándo kólin mío.

I don't know what you're talking about (I didn't understand what you said). The Cuchivero Panare came to a place very near here. They attacked the Panare group [who lived on the] Guaniamo, killed the men and abducted the women. They abducted Atung; I knew her."
I am going to take a trip to the Venezuelan trade-station on the other side of the Cocuisis river to sell baskets and to buy two machetes. I want to sell you my baskets and manioc-squeezers, but they are very, very expensive. It took a number of days to make them. You will have to pay a great deal.
You are going to leave for Caicara de Orinoco. When you get back, if you bring beads with you, I will give a great deal for them.
The Mapoiye Indians live away off to the south of here. They are a savage group. They fight a great deal. They sell us blowguns and curare and they buy our baskets and machetes.

3. Philippine Spanish contact vernacular: Chabacano. Taken down by McKaughan from an informant's dictation, and transcribed phonetically (but without indication of stress); quoted from McKaughan, 1954 (p. 207), replacing Spanish "j" by "h", but keeping "y" = [j].

si huan i su sal.
un dia el nana di huan ya manda konele kompra sal na tyangge.
kwando ta bolbe ya si huan ya pasa

John and his salt.
One day the mother of John sent him to buy salt at the market. When John was returning, he passed by a

le na un rio. Byen bonito gayót el agwa i ya pensa le baŋa antes de bolber na kasa. para hende? no roba su sal el mana hente ya pone ele el sal na rio i ya saka le un grande pyedra ke ya pone ele ensima del sal para tapa. Al akabar ya ele de baŋa i nada ya empesa le buska ke buska kon el sal pero no ay mas ele enkontra kay ya diriti ya el sal na agwa.

river. The water was very beautiful and he decided to bathe before returning home. So that people would not steal his salt, he placed the salt in the river and took a large stone with which to cover it. Upon finishing his bathing and swimming, he began to look and look for the salt, but he could not find it, for it had now dissolved in the water.

IV. Russonorsk

The following sentences are taken from the material analyzed in Broch, 1927, with slight adaptation of his phonetic transcription.

moja pɔ tvoja.	I [talk to you] in your [language].
moja tri vekkel stannọm.	I was [there] three weeks.
tvoja ŋet bra maŋ.	You [are] not [a] good man.
prinsipal pɔ laŋ.	[The] boss [is] on shore.
etta ŋe·t do·bra.	That [is] not good.
burman, zakrepi-ko trosa lita graŋ ŋemnoško.	Fisherman, tighten the hawser a little bit somewhat.
kanske den prinsipal pɔ stova.	Perhaps the boss [is] in [the] room.
ŋe snai.	I don't know.
dra·sví, gammel gọ vẹ·n pɔ moja.	Good day, my old good friend.
tvoja kọ·pọm o·rẹ́ka?	You buy nuts?
moja pra·snik.	I [have a] holiday.
moja ska si· ju· gro·t vro·s (or ly·gọm)	I must say, you [are a] big liar.
kakai tọvara kọpis-li?	What-kind wares you sell?
moja nje·t snai, moja dọmmas dragoi ra·s.	I don't know, I think another day.
stoberi motrom rusman!	Good morning, Russian!
moja tvoja pɔ va·ter kasstọm.	I [will] throw you in [the] water.
prinsipa·l pɔ ši·b?	[Is the] boss on [the] boat?
jẹ·s, pɔ skaffọm.	Yes, [he is] at eating.
jẹ·s, pɔ sli·pọm.	Yes, [he is] at sleeping.
dɛn gammel u·ri, dɛn mẹ·re bra·, dɛn pɔ moja.	The old "uri" [a kind of fish], that [is] most good, that [is] for me.
moja pɔ kristos spræk.	I speak [that is, swear] by Christ.
moja pɔ tvoja kludí.	I [will] beat you.

prinsipal pɔ kristos reisa.

værsɔgo, li·ta klæ·ga pɔ presɛntɔm.

no tvoja pɔ kastom vé̜·sit treṣka.

tvoja treṣka ko̜·po̜m pɔ dɛn dag?

kak tvoja bestíl dó·mo?

ju·pɔ morradag moja treski njem?

vil ju· pɔ moja stova pɔ morradag
skaffo̜m?

nogli ra·s pɔ ga·v ju· stanno̜m (or
spa·séro̜m)?

maŋgeli vɔga mo̜kka pɔ ɛin vɔga
paltasi·na?

kak va·ra ju· prodá·tli?

kanske tvoja vil glas· tšai?

ko̜r ju· fa·r lę·ve?

ju· spræ·k pɔ moja kanto̜·r kom.

kor ju· ikke pɔ moja mo̜kka kladí?

moja pɔ anner skip nɔkka vin drik-
kom, sɔ moja nokka lite pjan, sɔ
moja spaserom pɔ lan pɔ selskap
anner rusman, sɔ polisman grot
vret pɔ rusman, sɔ rusman pɔ
kastel slipom.

The boss has died [literally, traveled
to Christ].
Please, [a] little bread as [a] present.
Now it's up to you to throw and
weigh the cod-fish.
You buy codfish today [literally, on
this day]?
What did you do at home?
[Will] you [come] tomorrow to me,
to get codfish?
Will you eat at my room tomorrow?
How many days were you [or did you
travel] on the sea?
How many "v̌ag" of flour for one
"v̌ag" of halibut?
What wares are you selling?
Maybe you like [a] glass [of] tea?
How [does] your father live?
You said [you would] come to my
office.
Why [did] you not bring me flour?
I drank a little wine on another boat,
so I [got] a little drunk, so I went
on land in the company of other
Russians, so the policeman [was]
very angry at [the] Russians, so
[the] Russians [had to] sleep in
[the] castle [jail].

V. Chinook Jargon

This is the beginning of a myth dictated in 1930 to Jacobs by
an informant, quoted from Jacobs, 1932 (pp. 45–46, 48). In this section, an interlinear text will be given, with the Chinook Jargon words
above and the literal English meaning below each word, and at the
end a free translation will follow.

| las-mí·lait | íxt-lamyái | bi-yá-kwi'ím. | |
| They were living | one old lady | and her grandchild. | |

| úk-dənəs-lútšmən | gwá·nisim | ya-ládwa | múŋk-lagámas. |
| That little girl | always | she went | to dig camas [cat-ear roots]. |

gwá·nisim	ya-qꞏú·	kꞏíꞏlabai	kába-las-háus.
Always	she [would] come	home	to their house.

álda-ya-pꞏínəs	úk-lagamás.	álda-ya-ʼú·maʼ
Then she [would] bake	the camas.	Then she [would] give [them] to

ya-tšétš.	álda-bus-lásga-mákmak.	duma·lá-wə́xt
her grandmother.	Then they [would] eat.	Next day again (tomorrow)

ya-lá·dwa	múŋk-lagamás.	álda-bus-ya-qꞏú·ʔ
she [would] go	dig camas.	Then when she [would] come

kꞏílabai	kába-las-háus,	álda-bus-ya-ʼú·maʼ
home	to their house,	then she [would] give [them] to

úk-ya-tšə́tš.	gwá·nisim	gá·gwa-ya-múŋk.
her grandmother.	Always	thus she [would] do.

"One old lady and her grandchild were dwelling there. The little girl always used to go to dig camas [cat-ear roots]. She would always return home. Then she would bake the camas under ashes. Then she would give them to her grandmother. They then would eat. The next day she would go again to dig camas. When she reached their home, she would give them to her grandmother. That is how she always used to do."

Selected Bibliography

I N this section are listed, by author and year of publication, the works cited in the footnotes and in the references to the individual chapters (pp. 192–198), and selected other items dealing with individual pidgins or creoles, or with the problems of pidginization and creolization in general. For the most part, earlier, pre-scientific works (especially those dating from the nineteenth century) have not been included except where they were the only available discussions. For a very full bibliography of virtually all material published before *ca.*1936, see Reinecke, 1937; for French-based creoles, see Goodman, 1964.

The following abbreviations are used for frequently cited journals:

AA	*American Anthropologist.* Washington, D.C.
AnL	*Anthropological Linguistics.* Bloomington, Indiana.
AQ	*Australian Quarterly.* Sydney.
AS	*American Speech.* New York.
ASt.	*African Studies.* Johannesburg.
ESt.	*Englische Studien.*
IJAL	*International Journal of American Linguistics.* New York; later Baltimore, Maryland.
LN	*Lingua Nostra.* Florence.
PMLA	*Publications of the Modern Language Association of America.* Baltimore, Maryland; later New York.
RPh.	*Romance Philology.* Berkeley, California.
SbWien	*Sitzungsberichte der k.k. Akademie der Wissenschaften zu Wien (Philosophisch-historische Klasse).* Vienna.

StL   *Studies in Linguistics.* Washington, D.C.; later Norman, Oklahoma,
        and Buffalo, New York.
TNTL   *Tijdschrift voor Nederlandse Taal- en Letterkunde.* Leiden.
T&T   *Taal en Tongvaal.* Bosvoorde, Belgium.
WIG   *De West-Indische Gids* (later *Nieuwe West-Indische Gids*).
        's Gravenhage.
ZAA   *Zeitschrift für Anglistik und Amerikanistik.* Berlin.
ZRPh.   *Zeitschrift für romanische Philologie.* Halle, Germany; later
        Tübingen.

In this listing, the last name of the author appears first, followed
by his given name(s), the year of publication, the title of the book
or article, and the place of publication (with volume and page
numbers, in the case of a journal). If an author has more than one
item in a given year, the items are distinguished by the addition of
lower-case letters after the year. Volume numbers are given in
arabic numerals, series in roman.

ADAM, LUCIEN. 1886. *Les idiomes négro-aryen et maléo-aryen.* Paris.
ALGEO, J. T. 1960. "Korean Bamboo English," *AS* 35.117–123.
BAISSAC, CHARLES. 1880. *Étude sur le patois mauricien.* Nancy.
BAKER, SIDNEY J. n.d. [*ca.*1941]. *New Zealand slang. A dictionary of collo-
    quialisms.* Christchurch. Chap. ix: " 'Pidgin' English in New Zealand,"
    71–92.
———. 1945. *The Australian language.* Sydney and London.
BATALHA, GRACIETE NOGUEIRA. 1961. "Coincidências com o dialecto de
    Macau em dialectos espanhóis das Ilhas Filipinas," *Boletim de Fiologia*
    19.295.303.
BATESON, GREGORY. 1943. "Pidgin English and cross-cultural communica-
    tion," *Transactions of the New York Academy of Sciences* II: 6.137–141.
BERRY, JACK. 1959a. "The origins of Krio vocabulary," *Sierra Leone Studies*
    NS.3:12. (December, 1959).
———. 1959b. "Creole as a language," *West Africa* (September, 1959), 745.
———. 1960. "English loanwords and adaptations in Sierra Leone Krio,"
    Creole Language Studies 2.1–16.
BLOK, S. P. 1959. "Annotations to Mr. L. D. Turner's *Africanisms in
    the Gullah dialect,*" *Lingua* 8.306–321.
BLOOMFIELD, LEONARD. 1933. *Language.* New York.
BOS, A. 1880. "Note sur le créole que l'on parle à l'Île Maurice," *Romania*
    9.571–582.
———. 1881. Review of Baissac, 1880, in *Romania* 10.610–611.
BROCH, OLAF. 1927. "Russenorsk," *Archiv fur slavische Philologie* 41.209–
    262.

BROOMFIELD, G. W. 1930. "The development of the Swahili language," *Africa* 3.516–522.

BROUSSARD, J. F. 1942. *Louisiana Creole dialect*. Baton Rouge.

CASSIDY, FREDERIC G. 1957. "Iteration as a word-forming device in Jamaican folk speech," *AS* 32.49–53.

———. 1959. "English language studies in the Caribbean," *AS* 34.163–171.

———. 1961. *Jamaica talk: three hundred years of the English language in Jamaica*. London and New York.

CASSIDY, FREDERIC G., and LE PAGE, R. B. 1961. "Lexicographical problems of *The Dictionary of Jamaica English*," *Creole Language Studies* 2.17–36.

CHURCHILL, WILLIAM. 1911. *Beach-la-mar*. Washington, D.C. (Carnegie Institution of Washington, Publication No. 154.)

CIPL (Comité International Permanent de Linguistes). 1949 ff. *Bibliographie linguistique* [issued annually]. Utrecht-Anvers.

COELHO, F. ADOLPHO. 1881–1886. "Os dialectos românicos ou neolatinos na África, Asia e América," *Boletim da Sociedade de Geografia de Lisboa* 2.129–196 (1880–1881), 3.451–478 (1882), 6.705–755 (1886); also separately, Lisboa, 1881–1883.

COLE, DESMOND T. 1953. "Fanagalò and the Bantu languages in South Africa," *ASt.* 12.1–9.

Colloque sur le multilinguisme—Symposium on Multilingualism. Brazzaville, 1962 (CSA/CCTA Publication No. 87, 1964.)

COMHAIRE-SYLVAIN, SUZANNE and JEAN. 1955. "Survivances africaines dans le vocabulaire religieux d'Haïti," *Études Dahoméennes* 14.3–20.

COOMBE, FLORENCE. 1911. *Islands of enchantment: many-sided Melanesia*. London.

COROMINAS, JOHN. 1948. "The origin of Spanish *ferreruelo*, Ital. *ferraiuolo*, and the importance of the study of the Lingua Franca for Romance etymology," *PMLA* 63.719–726.

Creole Language Studies 2. (1961). Proceedings of the Conference on Creole Language Studies. London.

DE CAMP, DAVID. 1961. "Social and geographical factors in Jamaican dialects," *Creole Language Studies* 2.61–84.

DE JOSSELIN DE JONG, J. P. B. 1924. "Het Negerhollandsch van St. Thomas en St. Jan," *Mededelingen der koninklijke Akademie van Wetenschappen te Amsterdam (Afdeeling Letterkunde)* 57.A:3.55–71.

———. 1926. *Het huidige Negerhollandsch (Teksten en woordenlijst)*. Amsterdam. (*Verhandelingen der koninklijke Akademie van Wetenschappen te Amsterdam, Afdeeling Letterkunde, NR:26:1*.)

DIETRICH, ADOLPHE. 1891. "Les parlers créoles des Macareignes," *Romania* 20.216–277.

DITCHY, JAY K. 1932. *Les Acadiens louisianais et leur parler*. Paris.

DONGHI DE HALPERÍN, RENATA. 1925. "Contribución al estudio del italia-
nismo en la República Argentina," *Cuadernos de la Facultad de filosofía
y letras de la Universidad de Buenos Aires* 1.183–198.

DONICIE, ANTOON. 1953. "Kanttekeningen bij 'De klanken van het Neger-
Engels'," T&T 5.4–7.

———. 1954. *De Creolentaal van Suriname. Spraakkunst.* Paramaribo
(2d ed., 1959).

———. 1956. "De partikels *sa* en (*de*) *go* in de Creolentaal van Suriname,"
WIG 26.183–191.

DONICIE, ANTOON, and VOORHOEVE, JAN. *De saramakaause Woordenschat.*
Amsterdam.

DONNAN, ELIZABETH (ed.). 1930. *Documents illustrative of the history of
the slave trade to America.* Washington, D.C. (Carnegie Institution of
Washington, Publication No. 409.)

ECHTELD, JOHANNES JULIUS MARIUS. 1961. *The English words in Sranan
(Negro-English of Surinam).* Amsterdam and Groningen.

EFRON, EDITH. 1954. "French and Creole patois in Haiti," *Caribbean
Quarterly* 3.199–214.

EGEROD, SØREN. 1958. "Pidgin Portuguese A.D. 1621," *T'oung Pao* 46.111–
114.

EVANS, EILEEN M. 1938. "Notes on the phonetics of the Creole language of
Haiti," *Archiv für vergleichende Phonetik* 2.195–210.

FAINE, JULES. 1937. *Philologie créole. Études historiques et étymologiques
sur la langue créole d'Haïti* (Deuxième édition). Port-au-Prince.

———. 1939. *Le créole dans l'univers. Études comparatives des parlers
français-créoles.* Port-au-Prince.

FEIST, SIGMUND: 1932. "The origin of the Germanic languages and the
Indo-Europeanising of North Europe," *Language* 8.245–254.

FERREIRA, MANUEL. 1959. "Comentarios em torno do bilingüismo cabo-
verdiano," *Revista de Portugal (Série A: Lingua Portuguesa)* 24.226–247.

FOCARD, VOISY. 1885. *Du patois créole de l'Ile de Bourbon.* St. Denis
(Réunion).

FORTIER, ALCÉE. 1884/85. "The French dialect in Louisiana," *PMLA*
1.96–111.

———. 1891. "The Acadians of Louisiana and their dialect," *PMLA* 6.1–33.

FRENCH, A. 1953. "Pidgin English in New Guinea," *AQ* 23:4.57–60.

———. 1955. "A linguistic problem in Trust Territory," *Eastern World*
9:1.21–23.

FRIEDERICI, GEORG. "Pidgin-English in Deutsch-Neuguinea," *Koloniale
Rundschau* 1911.92–106.

FUNK, HENRY. 1950. "The French creole dialect of Martinique. Phonology
and morphology." M.A. thesis, University of Virginia.

———. 1953. "The French Creole dialect of Martinique: its historical background. Ph.D. dissertation, University of Virginia.

Göbl-Gáldi, László. 1933. "Problemi di sostrato nel creolo francese," *Revue de Linguistique Romane* 9.336–345.

———. 1934. "Esquisse de la structure grammaticale des patois français-créoles," *Zeitschrift für französische Sprache und Literatur* 58.257–295.

Goodman, Morris F. 1958. "On the phonetics of the French Creole of Trinidad," *Word* 14.208–212.

———. 1964. *A comparative study of French creole dialects.* The Hague. (Janua Linguarum, Series Practica, No. 4.)

Grant, Rena V. 1944. "The Chinook Jargon, past and present," *California Folklore Quarterly* 3.259–276.

———. 1945. "Chinook Jargon," *IJAL* 11.225–233.

Grünbaum, M. 1885. "Mischsprachen und Sprachmischungen," *Sammlung gemeinverständlicher wissenschaftlicher Vorträge* 20.613–660.

Hall, Robert A., Jr. 1936. "Linguistic theory in the Italian Renaissance," *Language* 12.96–107.

———. 1942a. "Two Melanesian Pidgin texts (with commentary)," *StL* 1:6.1–4.

———. 1942b. *Melanesian Pidgin short grammar and vocabulary.* Baltimore (2nd ed., 1944).

———. 1942c. *The Italian Questione della Lingua: an interpretative essay.* Chapel Hill.

———. 1943a. *Melanesian Pidgin English: Grammar, Texts, Vocabulary.* Baltimore.

———. 1943b. "A ritualistic sequence in Italian-English pidgin," *StL* 2.14–15.

———. 1943c. "Notes on Australian Pidgin English," *Language* 19.283–287.

———. 1943d. "The vocabulary of Melanesian Pidgin English," *AQ* 17.192–199.

———. 1944a. "Chinese Pidgin English: Grammar and Texts," *Journal of the American Oriental Society* 64.95–113.

———. 1944b. Review of Sayer, 1943, in *Language* 20.171–174.

———. 1944c. "A Melanesian culture-contact myth in Pidgin English" [with Gregory Bateson], *Journal of American Folklore* 57.255–262.

———. 1945a. "Notes on British Solomon Islands Pidgin," *Modern Language Notes* 60.315–318.

———. 1945b. "English loan-words in Micronesian languages," *Language* 21.214–219.

———. 1946. Review of Migliorini, 1946, in *Language* 22.259–261.

———. 1948a. "The linguistic structure of Taki-Taki," *Language* 24.92–116.

———. 1948b. *French—Structural Sketch.* Baltimore (Language Monograph No. 24).

———. 1949a. "Le créole haïtien et sa grammaire," *Le Nouvelliste* (Port-au-Prince), April 9, 1949.

————. 1949b. "Le créole haïtien," *Sud-Ouest* (Jacmel), April 13, 1949.

————. 1949c. "Le créole et l'orthographe française," *Le Nouvelliste,* April 21, 1949.

————. 1949d. "A la recherche d'une orthographe créole," *Le Nouvelliste,* April 27, 1949.

————. 1950a. *Leave Your Language Alone!* Ithaca, New York. Reprinted 1960 as *Linguistics and Your Language,* New York (Doubleday-Anchor Books No. A-201).

————. 1950b. "The reconstruction of Proto-Romance," *Language* 26.6–27. Reprinted in M. Joos (ed.): *Readings in Linguistics* 303–314 (Washington, D.C., 1957).

————. 1950c. "African substratum in Negro English," *AS* 25.51–54. [Review of Turner, 1949.]

————. 1950d. "Further English borrowings in Haitian Creole," *AS* 25.150–151.

————. 1950e. "Nasalization in Haitian Creole," *Modern Language Notes* 65.47–478.

————. 1950f. "The genetic relationships of Haitian Creole," *Ricerche Linguistiche* 1.194–203.

————. 1951a. "Sex-reference and grammatical gender in English," *AS* 26.170–172.

————. 1951b. Review of Hyppolite, 1950, in *RPh.* 4.326–328.

————. 1952a. "Aspect and tense in Haitian Creole," *RPh.* 5.312–316.

————. 1952b. "Pidgin English and linguistic change," *Lingua* 3.138–146.

————. 1953. *Haitian Creole: Grammar, Texts, Vocabulary.* American Anthropological Association Memoir No. 74; also issued as American Folklore Society Memoir No. 43.

————. 1954a. "Expert urges extended use of Pidgin English," *Pacific Islands Monthly* 24:10.47, 49, 50.

————. 1954b. "The status of Melanesian Pidgin," *AQ* 26:2.85–92.

————. 1954c. "Can Pidgin be used for instruction in New Guinea?" *Pacific Islands Monthly* 26:1.95, 97, 98.

————. 1954d. "The provision of literature in Neo-Melanesian," *South Pacific* 7.942–944.

————. 1954e. *Pidgin English* [unsigned]. Sydney (*Current Affairs Bulletin* 14:12).

————. 1954f. "A scientific approach to Pidgin," *Papua and New Guinea Scientific Society, Annual Report and Proceedings* (1954), 21–25.

————. 1955a. *Hands Off Pidgin English!* Sydney.

————. 1955b. "Sostrato e lingue créole," *Archivio glottologico italiano* 40.1–9.

————. 1955c. *A standard orthography and list of suggested spellings for Neo-Melanesian.* Port Moresby [mimeographed].

————. 1955d. "American Indian Pidgin English: attestations and grammatical peculiarities [with DOUGLAS LEECHMAN], AS 30.163–171.

————. 1955e. "Pidgin English in the British Solomon Islands," AQ 27:4.68–74.

————. 1956a. "Innovations in Melanesian Pidgin (Neo-Melanesian)," Oceania 26.91–109.

————. 1956b. "'Yes' and 'No' in Neo-Melanesian," Modern Language Notes 71.502–503.

————. 1956c. "How we noun-incorporate in English," AS 31.83–88.

————. 1957a. "Romance sapēre in pidgins and creoles," RPh. 10.156–157.

————. 1957b. "Introduction and comparative table of orthographies," in Mihalic, 1957.

————. 1957c. "Scopi e metodi della linguistica," Archivio Glottologico Italiano 42.57–69, 148–161.

————. 1957d. Review of Jourdain, 1956a and 1956b. Language 33.226–231.

————. 1958. "Creole languages and genetic relationships," Word 14.367–373.

————. 1959a. "Pidgin languages," Scientific American 200:2.124–134.

————. 1959b. "Colonial policy and Neo-Melanesian," AnL 1:3.22–27.

————. 1959c. "L'ortografia delle lingue pidgin e créole," Ioanni Dominici Serra ex munere laeto inferiae—Raccolta di studî in onore di G. D. Serra 205–213 (Nàpoli).

————. 1959d. "Neo-Melanesian and glottochronology," IJAL 25.265–267.

————. 1960. "Thorstein Veblen and linguistic theory," AS 35.124–130.

————. 1961a. "Pidgin," Encyclopaedia Britannica 17.905–907.

————. 1961b. "How Pidgin English has evolved," New Scientist 9.413–415.

————. 1962a. "The life-cycle of pidgin languages," Festschrift De Groot (= Lingua 11.) 151.156.

————. 1962b. "The determination of form-classes in Haitian Creole," ZRPh. 78.172–177.

————. 1964. Introductory Linguistics. Philadelphia.

HARRIS, CHARLES CLELAND. 1952. "Papiamentu phonology." Dissertation, Cornell University.

HARRISON, I. A. 1882. "The Creole patois of Louisiana," American Journal of Philology 3.285–296.

HARTT, CH. FRED. 1872. "Notes on the Lingoa Gêral or Modern Tupí of the Amazonas," Transactions of the American Philological Association 3.58–76.

HELLINGA, W. Gs. 1955. Language Problems in Surinam. Dutch as the language of the schools. Amsterdam.

HERSKOVITS, MELVILLE J. and FRANCES S. 1936. Suriname Folklore. New York. (Columbia University Contributions to Anthropology, Vol. 27.)

HESSELING, DIRK CHRISTIAAN. 1905. Het Negerhollandsch der Deense Antillen. Leiden.

————. 1933a. "Een Spaans boek over het Papiaments," *TNTL* 52.40–59.

————. 1933b. "Papiaments en Negerhollands," *TNTL* 52.265–288.

————. 1934. "Gemengde taal, mengeltaal, kreools en kreolisering," *De nieuwe taalgids* 28.310–322.

HOCKETT, CHARLES F.: 1948. "Implications of Bloomfield's Algonquian studies," *Language* 24.117–131.

————. 1958. *A course in modern linguistics.* New York.

HÖLTKER, GEORG. 1945. "Das Pidgin-Englisch als sprachliches Missionsmittel in Neuguinea," *Neue Zeitschrift für Missionswissenschaft* 1.44–63.

HORTH, AUGUSTE. 1949. *Le patois guyanais.* Cayenne.

HYPPOLITE, MICHELSON. 1950. *Les origines des variations du créole haïtien.* Port-au-Prince.

JACOBS, MELVILLE. 1932. "Notes on the structure of Chinook Jargon," *Language* 8.27–50.

JESPERSEN, OTTO. 1922. *Language: its nature and origin.* London.

JONES, E. D. 1957. "The potentialities of Krio as a literary language," *Sierra Leone Studies* 3:9.40–48.

————. 1959. "Some English fossils in Krio," *Sierra Leone Studies* NS.3.295–297.

JONES, STANLEY. 1952. "The French patois of the Seychelles," *African Affairs* 51.237–247.

JOURDAIN, ELODIE. 1954. "Le verbe en Créole martiniquais," *WIG* 35.39–70.

————. 1956a. *Du français aux parlers créoles.* Paris.

————. 1956b. *Le vocabulaire du parler créole de la Martinique.* Paris.

KAHANE, HENRY and RENÉE, and TIETZE, ANDREAS. 1958. *The Lingua Franca in the Levant. Turkish nautical terms of Italian and Greek origin.* Urbana.

KAHIN, GEORGE McT. 1952. *Nationalism and revolution in Indonesia.* Ithaca, New York.

KLEINECKE, DAVID. 1959. "An etymology for 'pidgin,'" *IJAL* 25.271–272.

KLOEKE, GERARDUS GESINUS. 1950. *Herkomst en groei van het Afrikaans.* Leiden.

KLOSS, HEINZ. 1952. *Die Entwicklung neuer germanischer Kultursprachen von 1800 bis 1950.* München.

KROEBER, ALFRED E. 1941. "Some relations of linguistics and ethnology," *Language* 17.287–291.

LANDTMAN, GUNNAR. 1918. "The Pidgin English of British New Guinea," *Neuphilologische Mitteilungen* 19.62–74.

LANE, GEORGE SHERMAN. 1935. "Notes on Louisiana French. II. Negro-French dialect," *Language* 11.5–16.

LEITE DE VASCONCELOS, JOSÉ. 1897–1899. "Dialectos crioulos portugueses de África (Contribuções para o estudo da dialectologia portuguesa," *Revista Lusitana* 5.241–261.

LENZ, RODOLFO. 1928. *El papiamentu, la lengua criolla de Curazao, la gramática más sencilla.* Santiago de Chile. (Reprinted from *Anales de la Universidad de Chile* II.4.695–768, 1021–1090 [1926] and II.5.287–327, 365–412 [1927].)

LE PAGE, ROBERT B. 1957–1958. "General outlines of English Creole dialects," *Orbis* 6.373–391, 7.54–64.

LE PAGE, ROBERT B., and DE CAMP, DAVID. 1960. *Jamaican Creole.* London (*Creole Language Studies* 1.)

LICHTVELD, LOU. 1954. "Enerlei Creools?", *WIG* 35.59–71. (Critique of Jourdain, 1954.)

LOEWE, RICHARD. 1890. "Zur Sprach- und Mundartenmischung," *Zeitschrift für Völkerpsychologie und Sprachwissenschaft* 10.261–305.

LOFTMAN, BERYL I. 1953. "Creole languages of the Caribbean area." M.A. thesis, Columbia University.

LOPES DA SILVA, BALTASAR. 1957. *O dialecto crioulo de Cabo Verde.* Lisbon.

McDAVID, RAVEN I., Jr., and VIRGINIA. 1951. "The relationship of the speech of American Negroes to the speech of American whites," *AS* 26.3–16.

McKAUGHAN, HOWARD P. 1954. "Notes on Chabacano grammar," *Journal of East Asiatic Studies* 3.205–226.

———. 1958. Review of Whinnom. 1956, in *Hispanic Review* 26.355–357.

MAIR, LUCY P. 1948. *Australia in New Guinea.* London.

MEAD, MARGARET. 1931. "Talk Boy," *Asia* 31.144–151, 191.

———. 1959. "Discussion of the Symposium papers," *AnL* 1:3.32–33.

MEDINA, JOSÉ TORIBIO. 1930. *Bibliografía de la lengua Guaraní.* Buenos Aires.

MENDONÇA, RENATO. 1935. *A influência africana no português do Brasil* (2ª edição). São Paulo.

MEO-ZILIO, GIOVANNI. 1955a. "Influenze dello spagnolo sull'italiano parlato nel Rio de la Plata," *LN* 16.16–22.

———. 1955b. "Fenomeni lessicali dell'italiano rioplatense," *LN* 16.53–55.

———. 1955c. "Contaminazioni morfologiche nel Cocoliche rioplatense," *LN* 16.112–117.

———. 1956a. "Interferenze sintattiche nel Cocoliche rioplatense," *LN* 17.54–59.

———. 1956b. "Fenomeni stilistici del Cocoliche rioplatense," *LN* 17.88–91.

MERCIER, M. 1880. "Études sur la langue créole en Louisiane," *Comptes-Rendus de l'Athénée Louisianais* 1.373–381.

MIGLIORINI, BRUNO. 1946. *Linguistica.* Florence.

MIHALIC, FRANCIS. 1957. *Pidgin English (Neo-Melanesian) Dictionary and Grammar.* Techny, Illinois.

MORGAN, RALEIGH, JR. 1959. "Structural sketch of Saint Martin Creole," *AnL* 1:8.20–24f.

————. 1960. "The lexicon of Saint Martin Creole," *AnL* 2:1.7–29.

MURPHY, JOHN J. 1943. *The book of Pidgin English*. Brisbane.

NARDO CIBELE, ANGELA. 1900. "Alcune parole usate dalla popolazione mista italiana e negra nelle 'fazende' di S. Paulo nel Brasile," *Archivio per lo studio delle tradizioni popolari* 19.18–24.

NAVARRO TOMÁS, TOMÁS. 1953. "Observaciones sobre el papiamentu," *Nueva Revista de Filología Hispánica* 7.183–189.

NEVERMANN, H. 1929. "Das melanesische Pidgin-English," *Est.* 63.252–268.

NIDA, EUGENE A. 1955. "Tribal and trade languages," *ASt.* 14.155–158.

NIMUENDAJÚ-UNKEL, CURT. 1914. "Vocabularios da Lingua Gêral do Brasil nos dialectos dos Manajé do Rio Ararandéua, Tembé do Rio Acará Pequeno e Turiwará do Rio Acará Grande, Est. do Pará," *Zeitschrift für Ethnologie* 46.615–618.

PÉE, WILLEM. 1951. "De klanken van het Neger-Engels," *T&T* 3.130–192.

PÉE, WILLEM, HELLINGA, W. Gs., and DONICIE, ANTOON. 1953a. "Voorstellen tot een nieuwe systematische spelling van het Surinaams (Neger-Engels) op linguistische grondslag," *T&T* 5.8–18.

————. 1953b. *Het Neger-Engels van Suriname: Bijdragen en Beschouwingen.* (Reprinted from Pée, 1951; Donicie, 1953; and Pée, Hellinga, and Donicie, 1953a.)

POMPILUS, PRADEL. 1961. "De quelques influences du Créole sur le français officiel d'Haïti," *Creole Language Studies* 2.91–98.

PONTOPPIDAN, E. 1881. "Einige Notizen über die Kreolensprache der dänischwestindischen Inseln," *Zeitschrift für Ethnologie* 13.130–178.

POYEN-BELLISLE, RENÉ. 1894. *Les sons et les formes du créole dans les Antilles.* Baltimore.

PRESSOIR, CHARLES-FERNAND. 1947. *Débats sur le créole et le folklore.* Port-au-Prince.

PRICK VAN WELY, F. P. E. 1912. "Das Alter des Pidgin English," *ESt.* 44.295–296.

RAY, SIDNEY E. 1926. *A comparative study of the Melanesian Island languages.* Cambridge, England.

READ, WILLIAM A. 1931. *Louisiana-French.* Baton Rouge.

REED, STEPHEN WINSOR. 1943. *The making of modern New Guinea.* New York. Appendix I: "The language adjustment: Melanesian Pidgin" 267–291.

REINECKE, JOHN E. 1937. "Marginal languages: a sociological study of creole languages and trade jargons." Ph.D. dissertation, Yale University.

————. 1938. "Trade jargons and creole dialects as marginal languages," *Social Forces* 17.107–118.

REINECKE, JOHN E., and TOKIMASA, AIKO. 1934. "The English dialect of Hawaii," *AS* 9.48–58, 122–131.

RENS, LUCIEN LEO EDWARD. 1953. *The historical and social background of Surinam Negro-English.* Amsterdam.

RÉVAH, I. S. 1963. "La question des substrats et des superstrats dans le domaine linguistique brésilien: les parlers populaires brésiliens doivent-ils être considérés comme des parlers 'créoles' ou 'semi-créoles'?" *Romania* 84.433–450.

RIBEIRO, JOAQUIM. 1939. *História da romanização da América.* Rio de Janeiro. Chapters 25–28: "Processos de romanização de elementos negroafricanos," 235–287.

RICE, FRANK (ed). 1962. *Study of the role of second languages in Asia, Africa, and Latin America.* Washington, D.C.

RILEY, CARROLL L. 1952. "Trade Spanish of the Piñaguero Panare," *StL* 10.6–11.

ROGGE, HEINZ. 1957. "Pidgin English. Eine Lingua Franca Ostasiens," *ZAA* 5.374–396.

ROSS, ALAN S. C. 1964. *The Pitcairnese Language.* London.

SAINT-QUENTIN, ALFRED DE. 1872. *Introduction à l'histoire de Cayenne, comprenant une grammaire créole.* Antibes.

SAMARIN, WILLIAM J. 1955. "Sango, an African lingua franca," *Word* 11.254–267.

———. 1962. "Lingua francas, with special reference to Africa," in Rice (ed.), 1962, 54–64.

SAPIR, EDWARD. 1921. *Language.* New York. (Reprinted 1955, Harvest Books No. HB-7.)

SAYER, EDGAR SHEAPPARD. 1943. *Pidgin English* (2nd ed.; mimeographed). Toronto.

SCHEBESTA, J., and MEISER, L. n.d. *Dictionary of "Bisinis-English" (Pidgin-English).* unpaged. [Alexishafen].

SCHNEIDER, GILBERT D. 1960. *Cameroons Creole dictionary* (mimeographed). Bamenda.

SCHÖNFELDER, KARL-HEINZ. 1956. *Probleme der Völker- und Sprachmischung.* Halle.

———. 1958. "Pidgin English," *ZAA* 5.374–396. (Critique of Rogge, 1957.)

SCHUCHARDT, HUGO. 1881. Review of Coelho, 1881, and of Baissac, 1880. *ZRPh.* 5.580.

———. 1882a. "Kreolische Studien. I. Über das Negerportugiesische von S. Thomé," *SbWien* 101.889–917.

———. 1882b. "Kreolische Studien. II. Über das Indoportugiesische von Cochim," *SbWien* 102.799–816.

———. 1882c. "Sur le créole de la Réunion," *Romania* 11.589–593.

———. 1883a. "Kreolische Studien. III. Über das Indoportugiesische von Diu," *SbWien* 103.3–17.

———. 1883b. "Kreolische Studien. IV. Über das Malaiospanische der Philippinen," *SbWien* 105.111–150.

———. 1883c. "Kreolische Studien. V. Über das Melaneso-Englische," *SbWien* 105.131–161.

———. 1883d. "Kreolische Studien. VI. Über das Indoportugiesische von

Mangalore," *SbWien* 105.882–904.

―――. 1884. *Dem Herrn Franz von Miklosich zum 20. Nov. 1883. Slawo-deutsches und Slawo-italienisches.* Graz.

―――. 1888a. "Beiträge zur Kenntnis des kreolischen Romanisch. I. Allgemeineres über das Negerportugiesische," *ZRPh.* 12.242–254.

―――. 1888b. "Beiträge zur Kenntnis des kreolischen Romanisch. II. Zum Negerportugiesischen Senegambiens," *ZRPh.* 12.301–312.

―――. 1888c. "Beiträge zur Kenntnis des kreolischen Romanisch. III. Zum Negerportugiesischen der Kapverden," *ZRPh.* 12.312–322.

―――. 1888d. "Kreolische Studien. VII. Über das Negerportugiesische von Annobom," *SbWien* 116.193–226.

―――. 1888e. "Kreolische Studien. VIII. Über das Annamito-französische," *SbWien* 116.227–234.

―――. 1888f. "Beiträge zur Kenntnis des englischen Kreolisch. I.," *ESt.* 12.470–474.

―――. 1889a. "Beiträge zur Kenntnis des kreolischen Romanisch. IV. Zum Negerportugiesischen der Ilha do Principe," *ZRPh.* 13.463–475.

―――. 1889b. "Beiträge zur Kenntnis des kreolischen Romanisch. V. Allgemeineres über das Indoportugiesische (Asioportugiesische)," *ZRPh.* 13.476–516.

―――. 1889c. "Beiträge zur Kenntnis des kreolischen Romanisch. VI. Zum Indoportugiesischen von Mahé und Cannanore," *ZRPh.* 13.516–524.

―――. 1889d. "Beiträge zur Kenntnis des englischen Kreolisch. II. Melaneso-Englisches," *ESt.* 13.158–162.

―――. 1890. "Kreolische Studien. IX. Über das Malaioportugiesische von Batavia und Tugu," *SbWien* 122.1–256.

―――. 1891. "Beiträge zur Kenntnis des englischen Kreolisch. III. Das Indo-Englische," *ESt.* 15.286–305.

―――. 1909. "Die Lingua Franca," *ZRPh.* 33.441–461.

―――. 1914a. "Zum Negerholländischen von S. Thomas," *TNTL* 33.123–135.

―――. 1914b. *Die Sprache der Saramakkaneger in Surinam.* Amsterdam. (Verhandelingen der koninklijke Akademie van Wetenschappen te Amsterdam NR.16:4.)

Silva-Fuenzalida, Ismael. 1952. "Papiamentu morphology." Dissertation, Northwestern University.

Silva Neto, Serafim de. 1938. "O crioulo de Surinam," *Miscelânea de estudos em honra de Saïd Ali.* Rio de Janeiro. Reprinted in *Cultura* (Rio de Janeiro, 1949), 2.57–70 and in Silva Neto, *Lingua, Cultura e Civilização* (1960), 127–153. (On Portuguese vocabulary elements in Sranan.)

―――. 1949. "Falares crioulos," *Brasilia* 5.

Simons, R. D. 1941. *Het Neger-Engelsch: Spraakkunst en Taaleigen.* Paramaribo.

————. 1954-1955. "Het partikel *sa* in het Surinams," *WIG* 35.166-170.

SIMONS, R. D., and VOORHOEVE, J. 1955/56. "Ontlening van Nederlandse samenstellingen in het Surinaams," *WIG* 36.61-64.

SMITH, WILLIAM C. 1933. "Pidgin English in Hawaii," *AS* 8.15-19.

SOMMERFELT, ALF. 1958. "Sur le rôle du substrat dans l'évolution d'une langue créole," *Omagiu lui Iorgu Iordan* 815-817 (Bucureşti).

STEWART, WILLIAM A. 1962. "Creole languages in the Caribbean," in Rice (ed.), 1962, 34-53.

SWADESH, MORRIS. 1948. "Sociologic notes on obsolescent languages," *IJAL* 14.226-235.

SYLVAIN, SUZANNE. 1936. *Le créole haïtien: morphologie et syntaxe.* Port-au-Prince and Wetteren.

TABER, CHARLES. 1964. "French loan-words in Sango: a statistical study of incidence." M.A. thesis, Hartford Seminary Foundation.

TAGLIAVINI, CARLO. 1931. "Créole, Lingue," *Enciclopedia Italiana* 11.833-835.

————. 1932. "Franca, Lingua," *Enciclopedia Italiana* 15.837.

TAYLOR, DOUGLAS McR. 1945. "Certain Carib morphological influences on Creole," *IJAL* 11.140-155.

————. 1947. "Phonemes of Caribbean Creole," *Word* 2.173-179.

————. 1951. "Structural outline of Caribbean Creole," *Word* 7.43-59.

————. 1952. "A note on the phoneme /r/ in Dominica Creole," *Word* 8.224-226.

————. 1953. Review of Hall, 1953, in *Word* 9.292-296 and 10.91-92 (1954).

————. 1955a. "Phonic interference in Dominican Creole," *Word* 11.45-52.

————. 1955b. Review of Voorhoeve, 1953a, in *Word* 11.168-174.

————. 1956. "Language contacts in the West Indies," *Word* 12.399-414.

————. 1957. Review of Jourdain, 1956a-b, *Word* 13.357-368.

————. 1959. "On function versus form in 'non-traditional' languages," *Word* 15.485-499.

————. 1960. "Language shift or changing relationships," *IJAL* 26.155-161.

————. 1961a. "Some Dominican-Creole descendants of the French definite article," *Creole Language Studies* 2.85-90.

————. 1961b. "New languages for old in the West Indies," *Comparative Studies in Sociology and History* 3.277-288.

————. 1963. "The origin of West Indian creole languages: evidence from grammatical categories," *AA* 65.800-814.

TENÓRIO D'ALBUQUERQUE, MIGUEL. 1929. "Apontamentos para a Grammática Ava'Nee," *Revista do Museo Paulista* 16.329-488.

THOMAS, T. 1869. *The theory and practice of Creole grammar.* Port-of-Spain.

THOMPSON, ROBERT WALLACE. 1961a. "A note on some possible affinities between the Creole dialects of the Old World and those of the New," *Creole Language Studies* 2.107-113.

————. 1961b. Review of Lopes da Silva, 1957, in *Creole Language Studies* 2.129–130.

TURIALT, J. 1874. *Etude sur le langage créole de la Martinique.* Brest.

TURNER, G. W. 1960. "Written Pidgin English," *Te Reo* 3.54–64.

TURNER, LORENZO DOW. 1949. *Africanisms in the Gullah dialect.* Chicago.

————. 1964. *An anthology of Krio folklore and literature* (mimeographed). Chicago.

URRUTY, JEAN. 1950–1951. "Le patois créole de l'Île Maurice," *Revue Guadeloupéenne* 31., 32.

VALKHOFF, MARIUS. 1960. "Contributions to the study of Creole," *ASt.* 19.77–87, 113–125, 230–244.

————. 1964. "Notes socio-linguistiques sur le parler créole de la Réunion," *RPh.* 17.723–735.

VAN WIJK, H. L. A. 1958. "Orígenes y evolución del papiamento," *Neophilologus* 42.169–182.

VEBLEN, THORSTEIN. 1899. *The theory of the leisure class.* New York.

VÉRIN, PIERRE. 1958. "The rivalry of Creole and English in the West Indies," *WIG* 38.163–167.

VOORHOEVE, JAN. 1953a. "De studie van het Surinaams," *WIG* 33.175–182.

————. 1953b. *Voorstudies tot een beschrijving van het Sranan-Tongo, Negerengels van Suriname.* Amsterdam.

————. 1955–1956. Review of Hellinga, 1955, in *WIG* 36.197–199.

————. 1957a. "Missionary linguistics in Surinam," *The Bible Translator* 8.179–190.

————. 1957b. "The verbal system of Sranan," *Lingua* 6.374–396.

————. 1957c. "Spellingsmoeilijkheiden in het Sranan," *T&T* 9.147–158.

————. 1958. "Structureel onderzoek van het Sranan. IV. De bouw van de substantiefgroep," *WIG* 37.205–211.

————. 1959. "An orthography for Saramaccan," *Word* 15.436–445.

————. 1961a. "Spelling difficulties in Sranan," *The Bible Translator* 12.

————. 1961b. "Linguistic experiments in syntactic analysis," *Creole Language Studies* 2.37–60.

————. 1961c. "A project for the study of Creole language history in Surinam," *Creole Language Studies* 2.99–106.

————. 1961d. "Le ton et la grammaire dans le Saramaccan," *Word* 17.146–163.

————. 1962. *Sranan syntax.* Amsterdam.

WAGNER, MAX LEOPOLD. 1920. "Amerikanish-Spanisch und Vulgärlatein," *ZRPh.* 40.286–312, 385–404.

WARD, IDA CAROLINE. 1952. *An introduction to the Yoruba language.* Cambridge, England.

WATTMAN, FRANCINE HARRIET. 1953. "Papiamentu morphology and syntax." Thesis, Cornell University.

WEBSTER, GRANT. 1960. "Korean Bamboo English once more," *AS* 35.261–265.

WEDGWOOD, CAMILLA. 1953. "The problem of 'Pidgin' in the Trust Territory of New Guinea," in *The use of vernacular languages in education* 103–115 (Paris, UNESCO). Reprinted in *South Pacific* 7.782–789 (1954).

WEINREICH, URIEL. 1958. "On the compatibility of genetic relationship and convergent development," *Word* 14.374–379.

WELMERS, WILLIAM E. 1946. *A descriptive grammar of Fanti.* Baltimore, Maryland.

YULE, HENRY, and BURNELL, ARTHUR COKE. 1886. *Hobson-Jobson: being a glossary of Anglo-Indian colloquial words and phrases, and of kindred terms.* . . . London.

ZUMTHOR, PAUL. 1953. "Le français créole de Haïti," *Levende Talen* 1953.6–16.

———. 1957. Review of Hall, 1953, in *ZRPh.* 73.515–517.

Phonetic Symbols

L ETTERS in a phonetic or phonemic transcription are always used consistently, the same letter always stands for the same sound (in a phonetic transcription) or for the same phoneme of a particular language (in a phonemic transcription). In phonetic transcriptions, it is normally the custom to follow the usage of the IPA (International Phonetic Alphabet/Association) and to enclose the transcriptions in square brackets: [ ]. Phonemic transcriptions vary rather more extensively according to the preferences of the transcriber and the phonemic system of the language; they are normally enclosed in slant lines: / /. In the main body of our text, pidgin and creole languages are normally cited in phonemic transcription; in the sample texts given in Appendix A, all the texts are in phonemic transcription except the Gullah material (p. 207), which is in a phonetic transcription adapted from IPA.

The meanings of the individual letters are as follows:

a   low-central vowel, approximately that of Italian or French *a* or of *a* in most Americans' pronunciation of *father.*

ɑ   low-back central vowel, approximately like the *â* of French *âme* "spirit".

æ   low-front vowel, as in English *hat.*

b   voiced bilabial stop, as in English *boob.*

c   voiceless palatal stop, approximately /t/ followed by a *y*-like release.

č   voiceless palatal assibilate, approximately /t/ followed by /š/, as in English *church.*

d   voiced dental or alveolar (gum-ridge) stop, as in English *did.*

e   mid-front unrounded vowel, as in French *été* "summer" or (without the final *y*-like glide) English *bay* or *hate.*

e   an especially close [e].

ə   mid-central vowel, as in the final vowel sound of English *sofa*.

ɛ, è   mid-front unrounded open vowel, as in English *bed*.

f   voiceless labio-dental fricative, as in English *fief*.

ɟ   voiced palatal stop, approximately /d/ followed by a *y*-like release.

g   always stands for voiced velar stop, like the g of *get;* never stands for "soft" sound of *gem*.

ǧ   voiced palatal assibilate, approximately /d/ followed by /ž/, as in English *gem*.

h   voiceless aspirate, as in English *hit*.

i   high-front unrounded tense vowel, as in French *ici* "here" or (without the final *y*-like glide) English *eat*.

I   high-front unrounded lax vowel, as in English *hit*.

j   high-front unrounded semi-consonant, like the *y* of English *young*.

k   voiceless velar stop, as in English *kick*.

l   voiced dental lateral, as in English *lee*.

ł   voiceless dental lateral, as in Welsh *Llewellyn*.

m   voiced bilabial nasal, as in English *mom*.

n   voiced dental or alveolar (gum-ridge) nasal, as in English *Nan*.

ɲ, ṇ   voiced palatal nasal, like the *gn* of French *baigner* "to bathe" or the *ñ* of Spanish *bañar* "to bathe".

ŋ   voiced velar nasal, like the *ng* of English *sing*.

o   mid-back rounded vowel, like the *o* of German *rot* "red" or (without the *w*-like glide) of English *boat*.

ǫ   an especially close [o].

ɔ, ò   mid-back-rounded open vowel, like the *aw* of English *awful*.

œ   mid-front-rounded open vowel, like the *eu* of French *heure* "hour".

ø   mid-front-rounded vowel, like the *eu* of French *feu* "fire".

p   voiceless bilabial stop, as in English *pip*.

r   voiced dental flap or trill, as in Spanish *hora* "hour"; or voiced retroflex consonant, as in English *red*.

s   voiceless dental sibilant, as in English *Sis*.

š   voiceless palatal sibilant, as in English *shirt*.

t   voiceless dental or alveolar (gum-ridge) stop, as in English *tot*.

u   high-back-rounded tense vowel, as in French *bout* "end" or (without concluding *w*-like glide) in English *boo*.

ʊ   high-back-rounded lax vowel, as in English *put*.

v   voiced labio-dental fricative, as in English *valve*.

ʌ   mid-central vowel, as in English *but*.

w   high-back-rounded semi-consonant, as in English *wow*.

x   voiceless velar fricative, as in the *ch* of Scottish *loch* or German *Bach* "brook".

y   high-front-rounded vowel, as in French *du* "of the".

z   voiced dental sibilant, as in English *zoom.*

ž   voiced palatal sibilant, as in the consonant occurring between the two vowels in English *azure, pleasure.*

˜   over a vowel letter indicates nasalization, as in French /bõ/ *bon* "good".

!   after a consonant letter indicates "emphatic" pronunciation—that is, with greater muscular tension and sharper release than usual.

ʔ   glottal stop or "catch in the breath."

·   (raised dot) indicates extra length of the vowel sound represented by the preceding letter.

´   (acute accent) indicates stress on the syllable of the vowel over whose symbol it is written.

ˆ   (circumflex accent) following a vowel letter indicates tongue-raising or tenseness of the vowel-sound.

Index